Capitalism, Pedagogy, and the Politics of Being

Also Available from Bloomsbury

Critical Human Rights, Citizenship, and Democracy Education,
Michalinos Zembylas and André Keet
Education, Equality and Justice in the New Normal, *Inny Accioly
and Donaldo Macedo*
Education, Individualization and Neoliberalism, *Valerie Visanich*
Pedagogy of Resistance, *Henry A. Giroux*
Politics and Pedagogy in the "Post-Truth" Era, *Derek R. Ford*
Transnational Feminist Politics, Education, and Social Justice, *edited by
Silvia Edling and Sheila Macrine*
Transnational Perspectives on Democracy, Citizenship, Human Rights and
Peace Education, *Mary Drinkwater, Fazal Rizvi and Karen Edge*

Capitalism, Pedagogy, and the Politics of Being

Noah De Lissovoy

BLOOMSBURY ACADEMIC

LONDON • NEW YORK • OXFORD • NEW DELHI • SYDNEY

BLOOMSBURY ACADEMIC
Bloomsbury Publishing Plc
50 Bedford Square, London, WC1B 3DP, UK
1385 Broadway, New York, NY 10018, USA
29 Earlsfort Terrace, Dublin 2, Ireland

BLOOMSBURY, BLOOMSBURY ACADEMIC and the Diana logo are trademarks
of Bloomsbury Publishing Plc

First published in Great Britain 2022
This paperback edition published 2023

Cover design: Charlotte James
Cover image © Vince Cavataio/Getty Images

A catalogue record for this book is available from the British Library.

A catalog record for this book is available from the Library of Congress.

ISBN: HB: 978-1-3501-5745-3
PB: 070-1-3502-2515-2
ePDF: 978-1-3501-5746-0
eBook: 978-1-3501-5747-7

Typeset by Deanta Global Publishing Services, Chennai, India

Contents

Acknowledgments

I want to acknowledge everyone for surviving and struggling through crisis, dislocation, and repression. These have been tough years. I am grateful for the love and solidarity of family, friends, and colleagues.

Thanks to my immediate family, Arcelia, Caleb, and Lali, for your light and love every day. Thanks also to my parents, Sue and Pete, and my brother, Sandy, for everything.

Scholarship is always a collective project; our individual contributions come out of conversations that nurture them. So many comrades and colleagues have helped me, through their work, the discussions that we have had, and their friendship, to come to the understandings I offer in this book. I am grateful to Luis Urrieta, Alex Means, Anthony Brown, Keffrelyn Brown, Juan Carrillo, Olmo Fregoso Bailón, Graham Slater, Wayne Au, Ken Saltman, Sandy Grande, Dan Heiman, Jennifer Keys Adair, Fikile Nxumalo, Claudia Cervantes-Soon, Ramón Martínez, Sepehr Vakil, Greg Bourassa, Kevin Lam, Richard Kahn, Cinthia Salinas, José García, Jeannette Alarcón, Clayton Pierce, Blanca Caldas Chumbes, David Hursh, Tyson Lewis, Derek Ford, Sheila Macrine, Molly Wiebe, and Frank Margonis, among others. Thanks as well, for their generous support, to Peter McLaren, Angela Valenzuela, Antonia Darder, Bill Schubert, Ming Fang He, and Wayne Ross.

I also want to extend thanks to the brilliant students I work with in the Cultural Studies in Education Program and the Department of Curriculum and Instruction, including Courtney Cook, Alex Armonda, Adam Martinez, Celine Vallejo, Nathaly Batista-Morales, Pablo Montes, Judith Landeros, Beth Link, and all the students in the program and beyond.

I am deeply grateful for the steadfast support of my editor at Bloomsbury, Mark Richardson, as well as to Evangeline Stanford. Your constant enthusiasm has meant so much throughout my work on this project.

Finally, I am grateful for permission to revise the following essays for this volume: "Value and Violation: Toward a Decolonial Analytic of Capital" (*Radical Philosophy Review* 21(2), 2018), "The Violence of Compassion: Education Reform, Race, and Neoliberalism's Elite Rationale" (in K. Saltman

& A. Means, Eds., *Handbook of Global Educational Reform*, Wiley-Blackwell, 2019), "Pedagogy of the Anxious: Rethinking Critical Pedagogy in the Context of Neoliberal Autonomy and Responsibilization" (*Journal of Education Policy 33*(2), 2018), and "Against Reconciliation: Constituent Power, Ethics, and the Meaning of Democratic Education" (*Power and Education 10*(2), 2018).

Introduction

I first learned about the tradition of radical education known as critical pedagogy when I was a teacher in Los Angeles in the late 1990s and early 2000s. This approach, which was also a way of seeing the world, was a revelation to me. Based on an investigation of and challenge to the oppressive "limit-situations" (Freire, 1996) confronting communities, critical pedagogy gave me a framework for understanding the conditions that my students experienced as well as a context in which to think about the purpose of education. It also gave me a network in which to struggle alongside like-minded comrades. The critical roots of this tradition were connected to political and philosophical orientations that I was already somewhat familiar with—Marxism in particular—and bringing all of these tools together, it was possible to begin to understand the history unfolding around me. This was a period of labor militancy in Southern California as well as a moment of important working-class movements in contexts of immigration, education, and urban space—movements which immediately opened onto a global horizon of struggles against the depredations of neoliberal globalization (NAFTA and its aftermath in particular). Neoliberalism was gathering steam in education too, as high-stakes standardized testing and scripted curricula proliferated in the schools. Recognizing that reality was not an indifferent sedimentation of events but rather the expression of basic class struggles, that schooling was a crucially contested site within this broad landscape, and that teaching itself—as *pedagogy*—was already an enacted ethics and politics (in one direction or another) gave me a new and transformative perspective on myself, my students, and the city.

At the same time, for anyone with a progressive or radical outlook in Los Angeles in that moment, it was clear that struggles around resources, work, and capitalism itself could not be separated from questions of race and culture. Racism organized every moment of life in the city, as well as its overall structure and topography. This racial logic was enforced by the Los Angeles Police Department, whose terrorism against Black people and other communities of color was an everyday reality. Anti-immigrant initiatives at the statewide level were motivated by a deep hostility to Latinx and Indigenous peoples. In education, overcrowding and hypersegregation disproportionately impacted Black and Brown students, and underfunding of inner-city schools laid the foundation for the school-to-prison pipeline. I was learning that what we had to contend with were not separate structures but rather a flexible and encompassing system of what Robinson (2000) calls *racial capitalism*. This was a period of difficult interrogations of my own privileges and perspectives as a white person as well as efforts to put into practice my own race-traitorism on the ground (in union activism and the movement against police brutality) that was clear about the force and extent of white supremacy. My initial intuition about the racial order of capitalism (and capitalism as a racial order), for which Los Angeles provided daily evidence, has stayed with me ever since and has provided an intellectual and affective foundation for my thinking.

Since that time, a long period of relentless austerity, the weakening of organized labor, and a set of economic crises that capitalist societies have experienced (the Great Recession above all) have confirmed the need for a critical understanding of capitalism. Likewise, North America's opportunistic racism, expressed in the so-called global War on Terror, continuous state violence against Black people, Indigenous people, and other people of color, as well as in the attack on public education, indicates the need for an analysis that thinks capitalism and racism together, and that is able to respond to the ongoing dispossessions of settler colonialism and the ongoing enforcement of global relationships of domination and dependency between the North and the South. Over this period, an understanding of the imbrication of capitalism, racism, and cultural oppression has been developed by a number of intellectual projects, including critical race studies, Black feminism, and critical pedagogy itself, among others. Of particular importance for this volume, the Latin American traditions of decolonial theory and philosophy of liberation (e.g., Dussel, 1985; Quijano, 2008) have described a condition of coloniality, coincident with modernity, that fuses diverse registers of social life in a process of domination of the Global South as well as Indigenous and marginalized communities globally. This scholarship provides a framework for understanding the persistence of colonial relationships (beyond the moment of the "postcolonial") as well as the depth to which coloniality reaches—showing its construction of fundamental epistemological and ontological possibilities in addition to structures of exploitation and cultural oppression that characterize colonialism proper. Together with the work of thinkers in critical Indigenous studies (e.g., Coulthard, 2014; Grande, 2004) who have exposed the settler-colonial determination of North American society in even its most "progressive" expressions, decolonial theory reveals a *foundation to the foundation* of familiar forms of oppression in capitalist society. The notion of coloniality that emerges out of this work provides an intellectual and political context in which to understand the confluence of conditions that I observed as a teacher as well as a starting point from which to transform our standpoint on the world—beyond the Western epistemological frame that underwrites, at least in part, critical theory itself—and reconceptualize our responsibilities to it, as these are conditioned by our own different geopolitical and biographical locations.

Furthermore, from my teaching days up to the present, capitalism in its neoliberal form (which emphasizes individualism, deregulation, and market-based competition) has been on the march, and has progressively absorbed more and more of experience and social possibility. Assaults on economies, classrooms, and working people have accelerated in the name of market-oriented efficiency, and the concentration of resources in the wealthiest percentiles of the population has reached astounding levels (Piketty, 2014). While critical pedagogy allows us a shattering view into the process of hegemony and the rule of elites in schooling, critiques of neoliberalism have exposed the way that capitalism seeks, beyond the imperative of social reproduction, to assimilate and control imagination and understanding at the most fundamental level. Austerity and responsibilization generally, and the impoverished and punitive pedagogies of neoliberal education in particular, crucially shape subjectivity, habitus, and relationships. In this context, theorists have been led to an investigation of the politics of being in capitalism, and neoliberalism's particular innovations in this regard (Dean, 2009).

In the present, it appears that neoliberalism may have reached an inflection point, as the consensus that supports it is newly interrogated—though it is certainly not unraveling, especially at the level of the basic senses of self that are available to us. This moment is a crucial opportunity to look both within and below its logic, in order to glimpse the fundamental determinants of capitalism itself. The critical and Marxist traditions are indispensable in this regard, since they are able to see past the appearances that we usually take for the final word on history to the hidden drama that produces it. But these traditions need to be pushed toward a more sensitive consideration of the phenomenology of capitalism and the way that it is implicated as much in the ineffable domains (or background conditions, as Fraser and Jaeggi, 2018, put it) of self, spirit, and relationships as it is in the visible architecture of politics and economics. The crucial point for me is that we need to understand capitalism as crucially working at the level of being—not as a kind of prerequisite to familiar forms of exploitation, but rather as the expression of an underlying assimilative drive. In fact, the organization in capitalism of ways of being is itself, I argue, a kind of special moment of accumulation.

The history I have just traced seems potentially to be ruptured in the most recent period by the exceptional circumstances of resurgent authoritarianism and global pandemic on the one hand, and unprecedented uprisings against racism and sexism on the other hand. The catastrophes of the Trump administration and Covid-19 have profoundly impacted schools and other educational spaces, and deeply hurt young people; at the same time, the collective community-based responses in some cases have opened up surprising possibilities for rethinking teaching and curriculum. These events have taught us, among other things, that fascism is not so distant a possibility, that the material and symbolic infrastructure of the US state is more frayed than we had imagined, that the school is not and cannot be thought of as the sole locus of learning, and that broad multiracial coalitions are possible against anti-Blackness and colonialism as they are expressed in the state and civil society. But as wrenching or surprising as many of these events have been, I think they also confirm continuities within the history of capitalism as much as they represent interruptions—namely, the fact of capitalism as fundamentally a system of organized violence, and on the other hand the fact of persistent resistance to this system. I consider this recent history along the way in this volume and how it should provoke a pedagogy and politics that are creative, organized, and solidaristic with movements built from the ground up.

In this historical and scholarly context, I aim to integrate insights toward the outlining of a complex system. In particular, this volume seeks to articulate a decolonial analysis of the basic logic of capitalism, an inquiry that foregrounds questions about the nature of social domination, value (in economic and ethical terms), violence, and emancipation. The situation of education shows, I argue, that we cannot make sense of these processes without understanding them as epistemological and ontological problems. Likewise, we need to analyze accelerating concentrations of wealth, shifting forms of racism, and the decay of democratic possibility in the present with reference to basic modes of subjection and subjectivization in capitalism. In this book, I describe phenomenologies of assimilation, concentration, and violence, traced by power and capital, which constitute both a contemporary repertoire of domination and a landscape confronted by liberatory praxis. On the other hand, and in support of this praxis, this book seeks to identify key generative themes from which critical pedagogy might start, central registers in which it might operate, and essential commitments that might define it. This has to be a revolutionary project, I believe, but the meaning of this term cannot be taken for granted, given the depth at which power works and given the limits normally placed on the concept of revolution. I argue in this volume that critical pedagogy has to transgress the epistemological coordinates that have established the meaning of radical change, and that it has to engage a political-existential project of *destitution* (of capital's clotted archive) as much as of *construction* (of another ethics and sociality). I also argue that it needs to seize the opportunities that the cataclysmic current moment makes at least provisionally available—to imagine new selves, new schools, and new solidarities.

The thesis that emerges in the course of my analyses is that capitalism is deeply flexible and mutable, and yet that it is always rooted, across its shifting periods, in a variable process of assault that realizes a material and immaterial surplus. This surplus is economic, but also symbolic, psychic, and ontological, and the system that is built on its accumulation is coincident with Western modernity and the forms of reason and relationship that belong to it. For educators, this means that we confront this system at once in our working conditions, curricula, teaching practices, governing policies, and institutions—as well as in the underlying grammar of our teaching identities and in the symptoms of our spiritual illnesses. For students, capitalism as process is even more encompassing, setting the terms of their own experience as well as of the imaginations of those with power over them. At the same time, I argue in this book that capitalism, as always *capitalism-coloniality*, has a complex *sided-ness* that it disavows. That is, there is an outside, or two overlapping outsides, with which capital is in relation and upon which it depends: the "internal" outside of the global working classes, who are the immediate source of legitimation, and the "external" outside of the marginalized and colonized—whom Dussel (1985) understands as an *exteriority*, as they oppose themselves to domination even as they are refused and oppressed. This means that there are standpoints on capitalism that it cannot own or control. Considering these points, I argue that critical pedagogy needs to be as flexible as capitalism itself, that it needs to investigate the obscure injuries that make up the texture of reality for students, and that it needs to be attentive to the differences in location, in the deepest sense, that condition radical teaching projects.

In this regard, it is important to acknowledge the ways that my own bio-geo-graphical location influences this project. However much I have learned and experienced, my ideas are articulated, in the first instance, out of a lived background of gendered whiteness and Northern-ness. My analysis is filtered first of all through the instincts and syntax given by that background, even as I challenge them close up as well as in the themes that I develop. The complement here is my long history of engagement with, and study of, revolutionary and antiracist theory/movements/teaching alongside people of color and other white people. This means that there is perhaps an internal struggle, at the level of my own writing, between the contradictory impulses of whitestream closure and un-settling refusal. I suppose that this contest can never be quite decided, and I think that its tensions are necessarily baked in as affordances and foreclosures in my arguments. What is important is not this drama itself, but the upshot— that is, that there are crucial limits to my arguments and perspectives, and that others, differently situated, will need to fill them out and also to correct them where they are mistaken.

This book is organized into three parts. Part I sets out a sociological and philosophical framework for understanding capitalism, which I approach as a set of fields or drives as much as a set of structures. In Chapter 1, I describe the monstrous centripetal force of capital in the context of what Piketty (2014) describes as a twenty-first century "new patrimonial capitalism," and argue that this force systematically organizes moral discourses in education even as schools and universities are nominally opposed to the current moment's devastating inequities. In this moment, accumulation in capitalism is characterized at once by processes of clotting and stagnation as well as by an eruptive violence that ties the present to capitalism's origins. Chapter 2 considers this violence more closely, making use of the tools of decolonial theory to analyze three central figures in the Marxian critique of capital: enclosure, valorization, and real subsumption. My analysis exposes an architecture of injury that comprehends the structure of value and that organizes subjectivity. Furthermore, capitalism's progressive absorption of externalities can be understood as an extended violation working beyond the dialectic, crucially through the process of coloniality. This analysis makes visible the crucial continuity between colonialism, coloniality, and capitalism, and argues that it is important for us to investigate this nexus if we want to understand the contemporary clotting of capital described in the first chapter.

Part II focuses the argument developed earlier, considering in particular how processes of race and racism are central to education in capitalism. This section of the book also addresses the context of neoliberalism, showing both how it is fundamentally a racial project and how it is connected to a historical process of material and immaterial *violation*. Chapter 3 describes the commitment to elite reason that underpins the philosophy of neoliberalism in school reform and argues that this rationale is at the same time and inseparably a logic of racial domination and abjection, as the policy experiments of philanthropists and "reformers" in schools work to pathologize communities of color even as they exalt white elites. Chapter 4 grounds neoliberalism's racial logic in the long history of what I call, rearticulating Marcuse (1955), *surplus-assault*—a process that begins with the original colonial encounters in the Americas, as contemporary accounts reveal. Reckoning with this historic and present-day process means that educators have to confront the injuries that schooling enacts at the level of being itself, and that they should center, in solidarity with social movements, a struggle against white supremacy. Chapter 5 develops these insights into a more systematic project for critical pedagogy, describing how Mignolo's (2011) notion of "pluriversality" can be a starting point for drawing from diverse epistemological standpoints to frame a set of specific generative themes for teachers, articulated at the global level, that respond to shared challenges across communities. I show how these themes express a new approach to curriculum and efforts to link it to student experience.

Part III turns to the themes of emancipatory praxis and pedagogy in the context of the conditions investigated in the first parts of the book. The frame of *practice* is important here, since it emphasizes the processual character of teaching and resistance and suggests that a break from the accumulative drive at the center of capitalist culture and education has to be concretely enacted. Chapter 6 explores how central principles in Paulo Freire's work need to be rethought in the context of neoliberalism's encompassing condition of anxiety. This chapter argues that we need to break from the oppressive compulsions (which differ from the paralysis of the oppressed emphasized by Freire) that tie educators to rituals of accountability and students to the logic of competition. While this chapter reconsiders critical pedagogy in the context of neoliberalism, Chapter 7 reconsiders progressive education in the context of emancipatory politics. This chapter shows that a critical conception of democracy in teaching that starts from decolonial and Marxian foundations (Dussel and Negri in particular) can share progressivism's emphasis on relationality but that it must also center an open and revolutionary imagination. This means, even as we pursue collaboration in classrooms and movements, refusing simple impulses toward reconciliation. Chapter 8 begins from the moment of upheaval produced by the pandemic and recent uprisings for racial justice to offer new approaches to notions of value, canon, and experience in curriculum and teaching. This chapter, in its experimental proposals, serves as a conclusion to the book's investigations, exploring the possibilities that contemporary crises produce as well as the way that they allow us to newly glimpse, at the deepest level, the contests that define capitalist society.

I have written this book as part of a lifelong project, initiated even prior to the experiences described at the beginning of this Introduction, to understand the society around me and the suffering that it continuously produces. This long project stems from an instinct that understanding offers a kind of healing. At the same time, while understanding may not *only* be valuable as a foundation for struggle against domination, it is not worthwhile if this struggle is not in some way advanced by it, and so I hope that what I offer here can be put to good use by scholars, teachers, and activists, and that, with extrapolations and corrections, it can be woven into future efforts oriented toward liberation in education and beyond.

Part I

The Field of Capital

1

Education and the Clotting of Capital

The current moment is characterized by extreme inequalities of wealth and income that recall those of the Gilded Age. In addition to these disparities, many are experiencing a tremendous degree of absolute suffering, as real wages remain stagnant in historical terms and employment becomes increasingly precarious. These conditions are exacerbated by the economic dislocation caused by the Covid-19 pandemic and other crises. In this context, there is a renewed interest in radically redistributive and even socialist alternatives to the current system. The work of economist Thomas Piketty, and particularly his ambitious volume, *Capital in the Twenty-First Century* (which I focus on here), is an important intervention in this moment. In this work, Piketty aims to describe and account for long-term trends in patterns of accumulation, and especially to contextualize the contemporary concentration of capital and associated social inequality globally. While there are problems in his account, as I will note, Piketty's work is helpful for making sense of the current juncture in the economy. Furthermore, understanding the tendencies that he describes is important for capturing the broader phenomenology of contemporary capitalism. In particular, his account evokes a crucial *centripetalism* of wealth, power, and prestige that characterizes the present; this tendency collaborates with a set of complementary *centrifugal* and fragmenting effects associated with neoliberalism.

In this first chapter, which opens my broad investigation in this book, building from Piketty's account, I argue that we can conceptualize contemporary capitalism, in which the ratio of capital stock to national income is soaring, in terms of a kind of *monstrous* accumulation, understood in a *technical sense*— that is, as overwhelming, assimilative, rupturing, and powerfully versatile. Furthermore, I describe how these characteristics show up as field effects, systematically refracting discourse and action across social domains, including in alternative and progressive spheres of praxis. Education is an essential area in which the centripetalism of capitalism and the distortions it produces are visible, as the moral frame of schools and universities is oriented in terms of what I call a *service to the center*, with the effect of protecting and amplifying the power of the powerful. This centripetal logic, working across society, means that capitalism—even in its more social-democratic manifestations—is unable to outrun its own atavistic violence, as can be seen in contemporary irruptions of authoritarianism and aggressive white supremacy. In this context, and against Piketty (who ultimately advocates regulatory and tax reform), I argue that we need to confront and dismantle not merely the scandalous concentrations of wealth and power that characterize contemporary capitalism but rather the very logic of accumulation that produces them. In education and beyond, this means collective action from the bottom up rather than isolated efforts from individual teachers or public intellectuals. The great virtue of Piketty's work is to center our attention on the process of accumulation; however, rather than seeking to tame this principle, we need to imagine and struggle for a kind of life organized beyond it.

The Concentration of Capital

Piketty's basic argument in *Capital in the Twenty-First Century* is that there is a historical tendency (which can be observed over centuries) for the rate of return on capital to exceed the rate of demographic and economic growth, leading in the long run to "powerful and destabilizing effects on the structure and dynamics of social inequality" (2014, p. 77). As the ratio between the capital stock and national income increases, the share of income going to capital (as opposed to labor) increases and so too does the wealth and power of the owner class. This has led in the present to extreme disparities in resources, and indeed potentially to a return to a regime of patrimonial capitalism in which inherited capital is the decisive factor in determining income disparities. Piketty argues that we tend to assume rates of overall growth for capitalist societies that are inaccurate over the long term, as well as unsustainable in terms of the population increases and transformations in technology they presuppose. In this context, the average *rate of return* on capital will always be greater than the *rate of growth* of the economy over the long run; combined with higher rates of saving, this leads to a rapid increase in the capital stock. Furthermore, in this context, "it is almost inevitable that inherited wealth will dominate wealth amassed from a lifetime's labor by a wide margin" (2014, p. 26). This is true even taking into account a relative decline in the rate of return as capital becomes more concentrated as well as the structural changes that make "human capital" (the labor of educated workers, in Piketty's terms) central to the structure of the economy. In these theses, Piketty challenges apologists for capitalism's stark inequities as well as the sunny predictions of shared prosperity from economists of all stripes.

Piketty paints a picture of a system slowly overcome by its own secular tendencies. However, he does not center a theory of crisis, and the logic of contradiction that is central to Marxism (at the levels of the theory of capital as well as of class struggle) is absent from his account, as Harvey (2014) points out. Thus, the fundamental trend that he describes (the long-term concentration of capital) is in his account the effect of a *historical tendency* rather than an effect of the *inner logic* of capitalism as a system. In Marxism, by contrast, crises of overaccumulation are not mere tendencies but rather necessary expressions of capitalism's organization as a system of exploitation of the unique commodity labor-power—the ultimate source of surplus value and the contradictory subject-object at the center of the crucible of class struggle. Nevertheless, if we attend particularly to Piketty's description of the historical data he has compiled, we can find in his account a useful illumination of aspects of the phenomenology of capitalism that are sometimes under-emphasized in Marxist accounts; studying these aspects can help us to gain a deeper understanding of contemporary social and economic crises.

Interestingly, in contrast to the historical dynamism emphasized by mainstream economists in their accounts of capitalism, in Piketty's analysis, a basic tendency toward concentration, immobility, and regression is prominent. In his historical narrative as well as in his descriptive statistics, he vividly describes a persistent *clotting* of wealth and power in the upper percentiles of the population of Western capitalist countries:

> The most striking fact is no doubt that in all these societies, half of the population own virtually nothing: the poorest 50 percent invariably own less than 10 percent of national wealth, and generally less than 5 percent. In France, according to the latest available data (for 2010-2011), the richest 10 percent command 62 percent of total wealth, while the poorest 50 percent own only 4 percent. In the United States, the most recent survey by the Federal Reserve, which covers the same years, indicates that the top decile own 72 percent of America's wealth, while the bottom half claim just 2 percent. (2014, p. 257)

Neoliberal privatization is an important contributor to the current consolidation of wealth in capitalist societies, Piketty argues, but by and large the extreme inequalities of the current era are the expression, in his analysis, of a much longer-term tendency for the relative stock of capital to rise. In this regard, Piketty no doubt underestimates the aggressiveness of the class offensive against workers and the public sphere that defines the neoliberal agenda; on the other hand, he points usefully to key moments of capital in the present that we should not overlook: *capital as agent of stagnation, suffocation, and historical sickness.* Piketty's account of accumulation does not exactly contradict that of Marx; rather, his outlook is in some ways grimmer, since he suggests that the social nightmare Marx described is an epochal one that may continue indefinitely. Indeed, Piketty suggests that "there is no natural force that inevitably reduces the importance of capital and of income flowing from ownership of capital over the course of history" (2014, p. 234).

In the present, this appears to be a social as much as an economic proposition. Thus, the spread of the Covid-19 pandemic illuminates the contours of the broken sociality of capitalism. The pandemic captures those who are most vulnerable and feeds off of the absence of solidarity that defines present disparities. In battling this pandemic, we are battling capitalism itself, which is mirrored in the rise and fall of the curve of infection, and which had already infected with its own pathogens all of the terrains that were most hospitable to the virus: illness, old age, racism, and obligatory consumption. Piketty does not offer us a theory of class, but he does usefully describe the congealing of value and power in an elite that stares down the deciles of the wealth and income distribution at a decimated population, a process the pandemic so vividly exposes and one that Streeck (2016) describes as "oligarchic redistribution." Is not this elite's unceasing accumulation and command of resources the real "super spreader" event, the deadly emanations of which diffuse across society and drain it of vigor and hope?

In this regard, what appears as an exceptional current crisis is actually tied to a deep history. While Piketty argues that both long-term and medium-term trends are important, the thrust of his argument is that key twentieth-century events (especially the response to the World Wars) and policies (e.g., progressive tax rates and wage supports) that mitigated economic inequality have not been able to resist the organic long-term tendency toward the concentration of wealth. While Piketty perhaps understates the impact of conflict and disruption in shaping history (as Lordon, 2015, notes), it is also true that there are crucial historical continuities that are tied to the underlying constitution of capitalism as structural framework for modernity. His emphasis on repetitive movements in the history of accumulation—the vagaries of policy and politics have not challenged the basic tendency to concentration—is suggestive. Crucially,

Piketty's "Second Fundamental Law of Capitalism" states that the national capital/income ratio rises in proportion to the ratio of savings to growth:

> This formula . . . reflects an obvious but important point: a country that saves a lot and grows slowly will over the long run accumulate an enormous stock of capital (relative to its income), which can in turn have a significant effect on the social structure and distribution of wealth. (2014, p. 166)

With a return of rates of population and economic growth to historical norms since the 1970s (after the rapid growth of the post-war period), the relative proportion of capital to income naturally increased—a development that Piketty frames as an exit from a unique period of equalization in the last century. What is important in this historical consistency is not the economic formula but rather the picture of accumulation that it sketches. Accumulation from this perspective is something larger than the project of a class; it is a defining condition of modernity, organizing basic social structures, relationships, and possibilities.

Theorists of coloniality including Aníbal Quijano (2008) and Enrique Dussel (1998) have likewise sought to highlight an underlying process of domination that is *continuous with* modernity. For these theorists, this process will not be overcome through modernity's own progress but rather in breaking from it and grounding society in what has been constructed up to now as *exteriority*: the knowledge and standpoint of the colonized and oppressed. Paraphrasing Piketty, we might say that there is no force, within domination's own logic, that eventually interrupts it; that is, there is a basic contingency to domination that is unredeemed by any hidden dialectic. Thus, from a decolonial perspective, we might understand capital as the effect of a systematization of violence that defines modernity, which produces at the same time the hallowed culture and sciences of the West. Piketty's account is hardly decolonial (the non-Western world is notably marginalized in his account), but his work does evoke the simple and obstinate epochal determination that is expressed in the capital system: to collect, concentrate, and control the planet's resources and possibilities. If capital is domination, then Piketty's bird's-eye view of economic history helps us to see the tendency toward the consolidation of domination over decades and centuries.

Piketty ultimately proposes forms of regulation and taxation that would mitigate this tendency, but his own analysis reveals the intractable centripetal force of wealth. He argues that its concentration, and the inequalities that result, are not the effect of specific policies but rather of a long-term discrepancy between the rate of return and the rate of growth. It seems clear, even from his own account, that the only answer to disparities and immiseration is the dissolution of this social and economic system. Indeed, Piketty shows that the destitution of the rentier class in Europe beginning after the First World War was the decisive event that allowed for a more egalitarian society to take shape in the mid-twentieth century—not any tendency toward equality inherent in capitalism itself. He underlines this point: "Herein lies a fundamental lesson about the historical dynamics of the distribution of wealth, no doubt the most important lesson the twentieth century has to teach" (2014, p. 274). In a society organized on the basis of private property, this shift in the twentieth century could only happen through a traumatic collapse of the system and its accumulated stock of value. Nevertheless, the slow recovery of capitalism and the eventual emergence, in the late twentieth century, of a new rentier class show that it is only through a decisive repudiation of this system that we can hope to shatter not just the disparities that define modernity but also the rule of capital itself as a form of value and a form of life.

Education: Service to the Center

There has been much discussion of the *centrifugal* forces acting on education systems in the present. For instance, the proliferation of charter operators has fragmented the public K–12 system in the United States (Saltman, 2007). In addition, the increased stress that accompanies testing regimes, along with stagnant salaries, has led to churn in school staffing (Ryan et al., 2017). The complex effects of white flight and gentrification have destabilized school demographics. Likewise, the casualization of teaching work in colleges and universities has brought this sector into the gig economy for the majority of instructors (McNaughtan, García, & Nehls, 2017), and the unstable financial position of many institutions has made higher education almost as chaotic as the K–12 sector. However, these processes of fragmentation have an obverse, and it is important to attend to this other side of the process of neoliberal educational restructuring. Starting from my analysis of Piketty's argument, we can note a complementary *centripetal* dynamic that works through education in the present, and that is expressed in a set of trends characterizing the motion of the economy more broadly: hyper-accumulation, concentration, and stagnation. I argue that these trends, which describe the movement of capital itself over the long term, can also usefully illuminate the contemporary material and symbolic restructuring of education at both the school and post-secondary levels.

The Higher Education "Community"

In higher education, the centripetal tendency toward concentration and consolidation is evident first of all in the dramatic differentiation between the most elite private universities and all other institutions. The power and prestige of the former are driven by endowment growth, which provides these universities with resources that dwarf those available to second-tier institutions and others. The top 1 percent of institutions now hold over half of the total endowed wealth in US higher education (Meyer & Zhou, 2017). This is a direct expression of the tendency toward capital concentration discussed in the first section of this chapter, as Piketty himself describes; however, in the education context, it is important to note that this financial concentration supports and coincides with a consolidation of symbolic capital. Meyer and Zhou (2017) call this the "Harvard-Yale-Stanford-Princeton" complex, as super-elite institutions are able to monopolize the top faculty, students, and research projects. The hyper-accumulation of capital and prestige at the center of the higher education sector corresponds to an intensification of competition for admission to the top tier. Even highly privileged students and families are forced into an intense scramble for the academic distinctions and extracurricular experiences that will open the college doors for the lucky few (Weis & Cipollone, 2013).

Furthermore, as institutions with smaller endowments strain to compete in the facilities and experiences they can offer and in the faculty they can recruit, tuition is forced up. The growth in student debt, and in the number of large borrowers in particular (Looney & Yanelis, 2018), points in effect to a kind of gravitational pull of the accumulated capital at the center of the system, as ever-greater disparities seem to be accompanied by ever-greater discipline for ordinary families. This centripetal force can be seen likewise in the spectacular salaries paid to the presidents and provosts of prominent universities. Importantly, these salaries are themselves part of the symbolic economy that ranks institutions in the mind of the consumer, and so it is not surprising that there is a race to the top in regard to compensation as well (Binkley, 2020). All of these are distortive effects that weaken the higher education sector as a whole and that are ultimately unsustainable. Ironically, however, in the individual instance, the inflation of wealth and privilege at the center (i.e., in the most elite institutions and in the topmost administrators) functions as a signifier, for the public at large, of the university's health and virtue.

At the same time that they are characterized by enormous excesses and disparities, universities in the current moment seek with special vigor to project a sense of "community" and concern—particularly as this community faces unprecedented crises and hardship. New initiatives on diversity, dialogue, and inclusion proliferate, and "communications" takes on a special urgency as staff, students, and faculty confront financial instability and the ravages of the pandemic. The distance between the cheerful propositions of higher education administration and the harsh reality of academic labor is longstanding (Bousquet, 2003). More recently, a neoliberal multiculturalism has predominated within the moral economy of universities, as they promote diversity initiatives that often seem to function more to trap faculty and students of color in the eddies of committee work than to effect real change. In this process, "diversity pride becomes a technology for reproducing whiteness" (Ahmed, 2012, p. 151). Social justice in this context becomes a mandatory marketing exercise.

But beyond the doublespeak of institutional forms of social justice, Piketty's analysis of the centripetal force organizing power and capital can help us to understand the moral discourse of the university in a larger frame. If the concentration of capital is an organic and secular tendency, and if the re-emergence of a profoundly unequal "patrimonial capitalism" in the present represents a return to the historical norm of capitalism's organization rather than an aberration, then we can see how the moral contradictions of educational institutions may stem from the basic premise of the virtue of accumulation rather than from simple bad faith. Starting from this premise, the opulence of elite universities (in terms of endowments, executive salaries, and research facilities) is not, in the minds of administrators, in contradiction to the good works that their institutions initiate (in terms of student support, diversity efforts, and partnerships with local communities). Rather, opulence and outreach are both taken to indicate exceptionality, and the university that can display them thereby proves its excellence. As I will show in Chapter 3, the doctrine of neoliberalism rests on a philosophical exaltation of the elite (exemplified in the writings of F. A. Hayek). But even the good feelings that surround social justice projects in higher education (many of which would be anathema to Hayek) are connected to a faith in the brand of the university and its power and prestige. Doesn't the increasing concentration of power (and compensation) in the offices of the president, vice-president, and deans produce an aura that sanctifies their initiatives in advance, and that glows in the rhetoric of community and concern that surrounds all of their efforts?

This logic is particularly clear in the case of university responses to the Covid-19 pandemic. The fall of 2020 saw a surge of infection across the United States; higher education was among the most important sites of transmission, with approximately 400,000 college and university-based cases by December 2020 ("Tracking the Coronavirus at U.S. Colleges and Universities," 2020). Nevertheless, to project a sense of normalcy and to hold on to tuition dollars, higher education institutions in many cases asked faculty to stay in the classroom or to switch to "hybrid" classes that included at least some in-person component. The callousness of this response was often clothed in the language of caring and mutual aid in a time of crisis. While no doubt in some cases quite cynical, we can also understand these decisions in the context of a system in which the prioritizing of the institution's bottom line is felt as a fundamental moral act. From this perspective, as it shepherds us through a difficult moment, the university proves its devotion to community precisely in its insistence on anxious assemblages of students and instructors showing up in the socially distanced lecture hall. *Solidarity, flexibility, consideration*: these have been the watchwords of the university in pandemic-induced crisis. But in the gravitational pull exerted by the concentration of wealth and power at the center, such expressions come in practice to refer to a yielding up, by the actual members of the "community," of their safety and security.

Schools in the Field of Capital

We can see this process of material and symbolic consolidation in the schools as well. The justified focus of critics on processes of privatization and fragmentation of the public school system in the neoliberal era should not blind us to ongoing race and class disparities *within* traditional public education or to new forms of concentration of power and prestige in schooling. De facto segregation persists more than fifty years after the nominal desegregation of schools, and even as the demographic base of students becomes more diverse, this segregation corresponds to dramatic inequities in resources: "Stark gaps are apparent across all of the nation's largest metro areas, both in the urban centers and in outer suburban rings, where non-White students are much more likely to attend schools with high concentrations of poor students" (Mordechay & Orfield, 2017, p. 197). Just as funding is concentrated in white communities, so too is prestige attached to districts and schools serving the more affluent. This can be seen not only in familiar between-district disparities but also in the celebrated boutique magnet programs that emerge as islands of "excellence" within underfunded and struggling urban districts. Consolidation and concentration create a vertical organization of power that works across the system and creates centers of power at multiple levels. This results in a contradictory situation in which school principals, for instance, are sometimes granted novel forms of authority over budgets and curriculum and at other times subjected to restrictive audits and oversight (Cleary, 2017).

Just as in higher education, in K–12 schools we can see how the field created by the concentration of financial and symbolic capital systematically refracts the moral frame within which policy and practice are articulated. The most vivid instances of this are in cases in which interventions originally aimed at supporting marginalized students are translated, over time, into additional supports for the privileged. Piketty's analysis of the persistent tendency for the relative proportion of national capital stock to rise can help us to understand, with regard to a broader social field that includes immaterial as well as material forms of capital, consolidation and retrenchment not as the effect of cynical calculation but rather as the effect of a systematic institutional gradient—an inexorable *sucking in* by power of the range of social projects that circulate in its midst. For instance, Cervantes-Soon et al. (2017) show how the goals of two-way immersion dual language instruction have shifted over time from affirming and supporting the knowledge and learning of students whose first language is not English to mainly serving as curricular "enrichment" for monolingual English speakers, in which the linguistic resources of non-dominant students are exploited to serve the interests of more privileged and white students. In this context, teachers who remain faithful to the original purpose of dual language instruction must be deliberate about taking on a critical stance and pressing against the pedagogical and ideological centering of white families' interests (Heiman & Yanes, 2018).

For those who are working against processes of domination and exploitation in education, the appropriation of equity discourses and practices is deeply demoralizing and confusing (Ahmed, 2012). However, for the managers of the system, their efforts are not sinister or dissonant; they are simply undertaking reform *within the grammar that secures the intelligibility of the system*. This is perhaps different from an ideological disposition in favor of neutrality or technocracy, though this is also important; rather, administrators' commitment to education and students necessarily takes the form of a constant referral to, and solicitude for, institutional power/reason—or what we might call a *service to the center.* To understand even equity initiatives in these same terms is not contradictory for them, then, but coherent. While acting on this basis means operating according to an ethics of domination against the interests of those who are oppressed and marginalized (Dussel, 1985), from the perspective of those at the center, there is no other way of acting that can be called ethical. Is not ethics, in capitalist society, underwritten by the imperative of accumulation—of wealth and privilege, certainly, but also of the *good feeling* that surrounds collective efforts toward "achievement"? After all, the institution is the framework for educational work, and thus for the goodness that we understand education to mean. If the community of the school is actually ragged, exhausted, and bitter, it is not the fault of the local managers or the distant elites around whom the system turns, it is suggested, but rather of community members themselves.

The central shortcoming of Piketty's analysis is that he is not able to offer a theory of capital, only to describe its variations (Harvey, 2014). By contrast, Marx shows that capital is in fact the congealed surplus value produced by the working class. Capital's miraculous agency and aura ironically "belong," on a Marxist analysis, to the workers who are exploited by it. Likewise, we can see that the moral force of the consolidated centers of power in the school system—from the offices of the school principal to the Secretary of Education and political elites, as well as the obscure forces exerted by philanthropists—is ultimately derived from the collective dedication of teachers and students. Children, in their continuous application and submission—that is, in their willingness to be schooled—are the ultimate producers of the moral surplus attached to the education system that is appropriated by managers, a system that in its totality ultimately depends on the fundamental biopower of students (Bourassa, 2019). Furthermore, from the perspective of educational elites, students are the ideal constituents since they are disqualified at the outset from having a say in the organization of schools, even as their value is the moral premise of the system. In this way, both the material and the symbolic capital of schools flows toward the center of the system, elevating the donors and officials who preside over education, and leaving teachers and students as the mute referents of the processes these elites command.

Accumulation as ("Subjective" and "Objective") Violence

Ultimately, the content of the secular tendency of progressive capital concentration, described by Piketty, is violence, as the clotting of capital produces continuous suffering for the majority as a basic condition of everyday life. This condition is consolidated in norms and institutions. Likewise, Slavoj Žižek (2008b) argues that outbreaks of spectacular, "subjective" violence (e.g., terrorist attacks) tend to blind us to the more important "objective" violence (of the system), which is the heart of capitalism: "Subjective violence is experienced as such against the background of a non-violent zero level. . . . However, objective violence is precisely the violence inherent to this 'normal' state of things" (Žižek, 2008b, p. 2). Thus, outraged by spectacular human rights abuses, we overlook the true evil—namely, the liberal philanthropists whose initiatives stanch society's bleeding just enough to allow their class to continue to exploit and accumulate. Žižek's account is incisive, but do we not see a kind of convergence of subjective/spectacular and objective/structural violence in the present? For instance, the suffering caused by the Covid-19 pandemic is an effect of capitalism's ravaging of the environment (which creates the conditions for the circulation of viruses and their traversal of the animal-human boundary) and a clear expression of its persistent inequalities (since poor people are more likely to have complications or die from infection). To that extent, the pandemic represents a form of structural violence, or at least follows the social contours of this violence in the distribution of its effects. At the same time, the pandemic also clearly represents a form of spectacular "subjective" violence in the horrors it visits upon individuals and families, and in the terrifying images of strained intensive care units, hazmat-suited first responders, and mobile morgues that have proliferated with its spread. This convergence of the subjective and the objective is evident in society's two-sided response: The pandemic provokes a frenzied search for an immediate technological cure at the same time as it prompts a call for more robust systems of public health.

In the political register, we can see this convergence of the "subjective" and "objective" violence of capitalist accumulation in the global rise of racist authoritarianism, of which the Trump administration was the leading edge. Trump's spectacular assaults on vulnerable communities and his xenophobic America-first orientation signaled to some a break with a genteel globalism; certainly, his administration excited the liberal reflexive outrage that Žižek associates with the fixation on "subjective" violence. And yet, the Trump administration's racism was continuous with an aggressive defense of the decades-long class war waged by capitalist elites. The administration's judicial appointments, signature tax cuts, and rollback of environmental, labor, and educational regulations—many of which occurred under the liberal radar— faithfully served the corporate elite, even if in a different idiom from that employed by the technocratic "liberal communists" indicted by Žižek. What was distinctive about Trump was not his supposed break from globalism but rather the convergence of neoliberalism and proto-fascism in his policies. Indeed, it may be that the Republican Party's unswerving allegiance to the administration (even through the January 6, 2021, storming of the Capitol) may stem from an intuition that Trumpist authoritarianism *is the very form* that a defense of the neoliberal project (and of the new patrimonial capitalism corresponding to it described by Piketty) must take in the context of capitalism's own deepening contradictions as well as proliferating global crises.

Piketty's account of the effects of the increasing inequality associated with this new patrimonial capitalism may appear merely quantitative: As the concentration of capital slowly rises, inequality becomes increasingly unbearable. But the quantitative is never *merely* quantitative; as conditions grow wretched for the majority, as disparities become obscene, and as the earth itself floods and burns, an elite commitment to the very *principle of quantity*—that is, the principle of continued and uninterrupted capital accumulation and the concomitant rise of the relative stock of capital—assumes monstrous dimensions. While we can imagine a social-democratic strategy to ease tensions toward a more sustainable trajectory for capitalism (the more liberal wing of the Democratic Party no doubt represents this perspective), Piketty documents the exceptionality of compromise on the part of the capitalist class, and more importantly the inexorability of the process of concentration, given the return in the twenty-first century to a historic regime of slow growth: "With a capital/income ratio of seven to eight years and a rate of return on capital of 4-5 percent, capital's share of global income could amount to 30 or 40 percent, a level close to that observed in the eighteenth and nineteenth centuries, and it might rise even higher" (2014, p. 233). In this context, and in a world literally set on fire by capitalism, defenders of the prerogative of uninterrupted accumulation are forced to rediscover and rouse the authoritarianism that is always waiting patiently to be awakened at the center of the system.

In John Carpenter's classic 1982 film, *The Thing*, an extraterrestrial monster terrorizes a group of scientists at an arctic research base, infecting and taking over their bodies one by one. The monster is defined by the ability to assimilate and reshape organic material into a multitude of forms and even to combine elements of bodies (eyes, limbs, viscera) into horrifying assemblages which erupt suddenly from those who are infected—sowing panic among the residents of the base. On a first read, it is clear that the monster is an allegory for the deep paranoia lurking behind the cheery façade of the Reagan-era United States and its conservative retrenchment: the monster's eruptions materialize a collective inner alienation (see Jones, 2020). But from the perspective of the twenty-first century, we can perhaps understand the monster as a figure for capitalist accumulation itself. Assimilating all available bodies, breaking through the normal unpredictably, and producing awful new formal combinations, the monster dramatizes the increasing absorption of social life and subjectivity into the circuits of capital and the devastation caused by capitalism's proliferating excesses and attacks. In *The Thing*, the terror is in the inability of bodies to contain the roiling accumulation of biological possibilities set loose by the alien infection. Likewise, the implacable concentration of wealth and power in capitalist society (jump-started at the time of the film's production by Reagan's supply-side economic policies) is ultimately uncontrollable and persistently catastrophic, seeping through—and collecting—multiple layers of private and public life only to convulse them with its horrifying shocks and excrescences. The ravages of the Great Recession, the devastation of public education, and the naked commodification of repression in the prison system are only a few examples of the forms of violence—"subjective" and "objective"—that capitalism invents and visits upon society as an expression of, and in fidelity to, the principle of unceasing concentration of wealth.

That we cannot read the monstrousness of capitalism in purely psychoanalytic terms—even according to the symbolic logic of Žižek's Lacanian analysis in which ideological fantasy defers an inevitable confrontation with the impossible Real (of capital)—is demonstrated by the way that capitalism is marked by history and culture. In Carpenter's film, the monster has a repertoire of shapes, copied from the existing biological forms it has assimilated. Likewise, the concentration of capital in the twenty-first century outlined by Piketty is shaped by histories of oppression, which it draws on continuously. Above all, as can be seen in official politics and in the organization of everyday life, capitalism is fundamentally organized by racial violence (Robinson, 2000). The prominence of Confederate symbols on the Right shows the durability not just of racism but of the organized political project of white supremacy; the persistence of this project, however, is inseparable from the material and ideological logic of capitalism, which combines the drive for racial repression and supremacy with the imperative of accumulation. Capitalism's flexibility is connected to its age-old determination as a racial project, which gives it an unlimited stock of sites and strategies for domination. In this regard, Piketty's broad historical analysis, which traces the long-term pooling and capture of wealth and power dating from capitalism's beginnings, resonates with the work of theorists of global racism (Mills, 1997; Quijano, 2008), who describe an *epochal* project of colonial and capitalist imposition that coincides with modernity itself.

What is important here is that the eruptions of the present are absolutely connected to this history. Pundits point out that the racism and authoritarianism of the contemporary Republican Party have roots in the party's policies and rhetoric over decades (e.g., Krugman, 2021). However, this analysis misses the deeper continuity, which is the dependence of capitalism from its origins on racial domination. This racism is fundamental, persistent, and continuously renewed both at the base and by elites in the US political system. In *returning to itself* in its defense of uninterrupted accumulation and the prerogatives of the owners of wealth even in the face of evidence of the global unsustainability of these trends (as Piketty describes), twenty-first-century capitalism also returns to itself as white supremacy (Davis, 2005). It is not surprising that the crises produced by the accelerating disparities analyzed by Piketty, which he describes as expressions of the continued rise in the ratio of national income from capital to income from labor, are fused with crises produced by the continuous assertion of white racial rule—in the halls of power and on the streets. (In this regard, it is instructive that even as they condemn right-wing militias, Democratic Party elites—notwithstanding vague calls for "reform"—are united with the Right in their defense of the police.) If the rulers double down on repression in the face of world-historical economic, political, and public health crises in the present, is that not an expression of the fact that capitalism is itself already and always a *doubling down*—an implacable multiplying, from its origins to the present moment, of opportunities for exploitation and domination, even at the cost of the system's own survival?

Ultimately, we need to turn to a consideration of the *epistemological* organization of capitalism (Lukács, 1971), if we want to understand why the powerful persist in their addiction to Piketty's Second Law (which describes the progressive concentration of capital stock)—a course that is eventually suicidal for the system as a whole. That the proliferation of conspiracy theories (the QAnon phenomenon is the best example) and the collapse of faith in science are tolerated by elites is not only a cynical political strategy but also an extreme expression of the distorted understanding of society that has always characterized bourgeois thought. After all, capitalism has always been an "alternative facts" system, since the *central fact* of modernity—the process of exploitation—has always been obscured and denied by its leaders and intellectuals. The fantasies of the conspiracy theorists are outlandish, but so too are the absurd fictions of the system: for instance, that the opulence of the powerful is somehow identified with the happiness of the exploited; that the United States has lived a history of splendor and munificence; or that the despoliation of the earth by capital is to be celebrated and forever accommodated.

Conclusion: Beyond the Surplus of Command

In the face of the return of the system of patrimonial capitalism that he documents, Piketty recommends, as the centerpiece of a progressive economic policy agenda, the establishment of a global tax on capital. Along with raising needed revenue and providing a means of mapping international and national distributions of wealth, this would most importantly serve as a check on the rising ratio of capital stock to national income: "The goal is first to stop the indefinite increase of inequality of wealth, and second to impose effective regulation on the financial and banking system in order to avoid crises" (2014, p. 518). However, given the implacable force of capital concentration over the long run and the forms of social power that correspond to it—that Piketty demonstrates as his central argument in *Capital in the Twenty-First Century*—it appears that his policy prescriptions are inadequate even within the terms of his own argument. In addition, the more fundamental problem with Piketty's proposals is that he fails to attend to the way that the process of class struggle determines the historical trends he describes. This does not detract from the compelling implications of the story he tells of long-term processes of accumulation, as I have described in this chapter, but it does mean his prescriptions do not confront the full or proper target. More specifically, if his suggestions are utopian (as he acknowledges), this is not because of short-sightedness on the part of capitalists with regard to policy but rather because of the commitments of neoliberalism as a class project. Another way to say this is that a truly radical economic reconstruction (toward which his proposals gesture) is indeed not realistic—*within the framework of the capitalist system.*

It is helpful to contrast Piketty's "fundamental laws of capitalism" (which describe the rising concentration and share of income from capital) with Marx's (1867/1976) own General Law of Capitalist Accumulation, which describes the increasing immiseration of the population that accompanies accumulation and the reservoir of surplus workers it produces. For Marx, the changing organic composition of capital that comes with industrial development (as constant capital, or means of production, increases in comparison to variable capital, which corresponds to labor) means that even as increasing accumulation of capital in the first instance leads to greater demand for workers (as industry expands), the technical changes in production simultaneously reduce the need for labor in proportion to machinery:

> Since the demand for labour is determined not by the extent of the total capital but by its variable constituent alone, that demand falls progressively with the growth of the total capital, instead of rising in proportion to it, as was previously assumed. It falls relatively to the magnitude of the total capital, and at an accelerated rate, as this magnitude increases. With the growth of the total capital, its variable constituent, the labour incorporated in it, does admittedly increase, but in a constantly diminishing proportion. (p. 781)

The complex process of incorporation and repulsion of labor that comes with increasing accumulation thus gives rise to "a relatively redundant working population, i.e. a population which is superfluous to capital's average requirements for its own valorization" (Marx, 1867/1976, p. 782). This population includes cast-off and underemployed workers as well as true paupers. This surplus population or "industrial reserve army" is essential to capitalist accumulation, providing a constant source of labor and a downward pressure on wages. In the present we see this systematic asymmetry between capital and labor, which underlies the superficial dynamics of supply and demand, in attacks on unions and the growth of the gig economy. The advantages for employers that result are not just strategic but rather necessary conditions for accumulation; capitalists have a vested and fundamental interest in inequality.

Marx's analysis shows how capital, like John Carpenter's monster, assimilates and assaults at once, taking over human beings and then undoing them in its regular upsurges, as, with increasing accumulation, the "greater attraction of workers by capital is accompanied by their greater repulsion" (1867/1976, p. 783). The violence of capital is not incidental but rather necessary to its survival and multiplication. This is not ultimately a monster that can be tamed, as Piketty's proposals would suggest. As Cuban revolutionary José Martí (1891/2002) put it, writing of the struggle against colonial oppression in Latin America, "The tiger, frightened away by the flash of gunfire, creeps back in the night to find his prey" (p. 292). The persistence of predatory accumulation across eras, as documented by Piketty himself, means that the struggle has to take aim at the monster itself and not merely at the terror it sows. Is it not a form of respect for capital's formidableness to understand its systematic and inalterable determination as accumulation of violence? In this regard, socialism takes capitalism much more seriously than do its bourgeois apologists, who in being embedded in it are unable to make out its proper outlines or even to consider it—as a total social system—an object worthy of much attention.

Contemporary education is afflicted by the same myopia. Twisted between the rhetoric of *humanitas* and the reality of extreme competition within the prestige economy, the university is incapable of understanding the logic that is unraveling it. The opulence of its glittering heights (the most elite private universities) is in stark contrast to the struggles of its base (no-frills working-class colleges)—and yet, administrators up and down the system seem to have nothing more at their disposal in the face of educational crisis than a familiar earnestness and a familiar set of "working groups." In the public schools, the situation is worse. Struggling, under attack, and unsure about whom they serve, schools grasp at the grifts of foundations, privatizers, and even their own state education officials. The tremendous dedication, courage, and expertise of the teachers hold together this threadbare enterprise, but the teachers are abused by the system itself, as the crisis of Covid-era instruction showed so clearly. In fact, it is capital which is tearing apart the education system, as it saturates the lifeworld of students and as its accumulating pools of value remake the geography of cities, the relationships between disciplines, and the occupation of teaching at all levels (Means, 2018; Peck, Theodore & Brenner, 2009). In a system in which the "health" of institutional power (and the endowment in the case of higher education) is valued more than the health of students, staff, and instructors, the answer cannot be to adjust the funding formulas. Rather, we need a radical reconstruction of education, a reconstruction that undoes and abolishes the value system at its base.

Among critical scholars, we urge each other toward public intellectualism and a willingness to stand up and call out (e.g., Giroux, 2015). That is fine as far as it goes, but capitalism has learned to live comfortably with such complaints. Just as the university assimilates the social justice initiatives of those within it who seek to make change, flattening these efforts and converting them into bright advertisements for the institution, capitalist culture broadly knows how to press critical academics into a restricted celebrity circuit on the margins, and even to sell touched-up versions of their ideas to the (liberal) masses—as can be seen, for instance, in the brisk, if brief, market for literature on white allyship that materialized during the uprisings following the murder of George Floyd. Scholars ought to speak out, but more importantly they ought to work in comradeship with working-class organizations, movements, and struggles. Within educational institutions, this means initiatives driven by and based on the interests of students, workers, and teachers together, rather than projects packaged by administrators—even when they are conceived by a working group made up of the most well-intentioned faculty. In society generally, this means struggles that can recognize their adversary at the center of the system—the unrepentant and implacable accumulative drive that is capital, as both particle (wealth) and wave (power)—and resolve to expose and destroy it.

In conclusion, we need to break with the tyranny of the long sloping graphs of accumulation that dot Piketty's account of the history of capitalism. This must be a material, ontological, and epistemological shift that includes but goes beyond an undoing of neoliberal hegemony. As Piketty's analysis suggests, capital is not a political dispensation but rather an epoch. To depart from it is to depart from meaning, value, and personhood as we have known them. *Capital in the Twenty-First Century* shows—in spite of its own policy prescriptions—that while progressives seek to pull as much of society as possible back and away from the abyss, capital remains nevertheless a black hole in the technical sense: a region whose gravity is so strong that nothing appears to escape from it, and which grows as it absorbs and accretes surrounding matter. We can see this effect in the multitude of ways in which this system assimilates and rearticulates discourses that would seem antithetical to it ("social justice" above all) and then decorates its horizon with them as with so many trophies.

We often imagine potential alternative social relationships in terms of greater fairness or efficiency or sustainability. However, the central question that we should take up in struggling for a society beyond capitalism is: "What would it look like to live in a world not defined and organized by accumulation?" And thus: "What would it look like to live in a world in which the center does not absorb and control all value and meaning?" "What would it mean not to be bent and twisted in life and labor by the rulers' ever-concentrating surplus of command?" We are not in a position now to answer these questions, but, against common sense, we ought to determine to seriously consider them in education and elsewhere. The upward-sloping curve of accumulation, however constant, "rational," and familiar, is ultimately *impossible* in the most fundamental sense. Against this history, we should ask, "What would it look like to imagine, learn, and live beyond the laws of capital?"

2

Toward a Decolonial Analytic of Capital

In *Reading Capital*, Louis Althusser (2009) argues that Marx's signal contribution was to introduce a new *problematic* into political economy, and in this way to initiate a paradigmatic break in the science of theory. The notion of labor-power, Althusser argues, shifted not only the meaning of the labor theory of value that Marx inherited from the classical political economists but also the entire standpoint and process of analysis, revealing the obscure source of profit and the essential antagonism between bourgeois and proletarian. In the process, Marx initiated a true critical science against the ideological-theoretical work of his predecessors. In turn, Althusser attempts to read Marx against the grain to surface an absent conceptual structure on which the latter's discourse depended—that is, historical materialism itself, which surpasses the mystifications of the bourgeois ideologists and Hegel's dialectic. Althusser ultimately argues that theoretical discourses work from their own internal criteria of validity, and that these criteria remain necessarily invisible to their practitioners. That is, they are organized by characteristic problematics which are given by history and which inescapably determine the possibilities of thought as a concrete field. This does not mean simply that historical events and interests impinge on theoretical work; rather, it means that the field of theory, rather than being arbitrary or indeterminate, has a determinate ideological structure on the exclusive basis of which its productions are possible.

I believe that this fundamental historical-ideological determination of theory, described by Althusser, conditions the epistemological crisis that Marxism confronts in the present. Theorists have argued that the revolutionary standpoint on society that Marxist theory has articulated has remained at least partly internal to a Western and Eurocentric history of knowledge. The claim to a unique validity of interpretation in Marxism is itself the clear inheritance of this history, a claim that disavows the possibility of epistemological diversity, or what Walter Mignolo (2011) calls "pluriversality." Philosophy of science and cultural studies have argued for, in the words of de Sousa Santos (2007), an "ecology of knowledges," for the value of diversity in knowledge projects, and also for the necessity of a specific repudiation of the West's claim to epistemological exceptionalism. Certainly these arguments pose very particular challenges to Marxism, to the extent that this tradition is in this regard both partly outside the history of Western thought (as the most systematic critique of mainstream bourgeois philosophy) as well as inside (in its development and rearticulation of key projects in the Western tradition).

Following Althusser (2009), however, it is important to investigate this epistemological crisis not only with regard to the *structure of knowledge* but also with regard to the *objects of knowledge*. For Althusser, the central categories of value, use-value, and surplus-value mark an epistemological break from the classical political economists, the implications of which are not fully registered even by Marx himself. Thus, Marx's new philosophy is working on objects that are themselves absolutely new, even if they appear at first to resemble categories in earlier accounts. These discoveries inaugurate a new system, Althusser argues, which breaks with classical economics in spite of first appearances, and which can ultimately only be understood on its own terms. This new system decisively abandons the idealist and humanist dialectic of the early Marx, which is concerned with labor as a moment of bondage and alienation. Likewise, I argue here that considering central categories in Marxist thought from the standpoint of decolonial theory can allow us to deepen the analysis of the epochal determination of capital as both stagnation and eruption that I described in the previous chapter, providing a conceptual foundation for my account in that chapter of the violence of accumulation.

Just as the decolonial turn calls into question the structure of Western knowledge projects themselves, so too does it suggest an investigation of the meaning of the central objects, categories, and processes of these projects—and it is this investigation that I undertake in this chapter in relation to Marxism. My question here is whether it is possible to *apply a decolonial analysis even to the central categories of Marxism*, rather than pointing away from them to other categories and principles belonging to other knowledge traditions. Another way to ask the question is the following: Is it possible to understand capitalism not from the perspective of its internal dialectical antagonist (the undifferentiated working class) but rather from the perspective of that which is radically outside, from the perspective of those whom it violates and erases, from the perspective of what Mignolo (2011) calls the "colonial wound"? This would mean reading Marx against Marx, in part, in order to surface not only the absent questions (as Althusser aims to do) but also the crucial exclusions and aporias. Capital has a relationship both to an internal and incorporated Other and to an external Other, an Other that it disavows. A decolonial reading allows us to surface and comprehend this latter relationship. While the primary purpose of this reading is to rethink key philosophical pillars in Marxist theory on the basis of conceptual tools provided by critiques of coloniality, this chapter also seeks to contribute to decolonial theory by extending the reach of this scholarly conversation and pressing it toward a more pointed confrontation with Marxism.

I aim in this investigation to go beyond a consideration of capitalism as a racial and cultural system—a line of investigation that is already well established (see Gilmore, 2007; Goldberg, 2009; Kelley, 2002; Robinson, 2000). Rather, building from the decolonial emphasis on the centrality of processes of annexation and injury in Western modernity, I interrogate the structure of the philosophical concept of capital, and consider how we might differently understand the meaning of the fundamental categories of accumulation and value. There is a tension that is inherent in this project between, on the one hand, the imperative to reconceptualize capitalism *as a whole* from the vantage point of the "periphery" and, on the other hand, the necessity of centering the *specific difference* of coloniality and the colonial context. In this investigation, I begin from the latter imperative in order to respond to the former. Thus, I first consider key tendencies in anticolonial and decolonial thought, with special reference to the work of Frantz Fanon (1963, 1967a, 1967b); then, pressing these tendencies toward a confrontation with Marxian conceptions of three central moments in (or figures for) capital accumulation, my analysis of these figures exposes an architecture of imposition that underpins the structure of value. The body of the chapter shows that this architecture organizes moments not only of enclosure but also of production. Furthermore, capitalism's progressive subsumption of externalities can be understood as an extended violation working beyond the dialectic, crucially through the logic of racism, which is nevertheless survived by those it would erase. This analysis makes visible the continuity between colonialism, coloniality, and capitalism, without reducing capitalism to a simple expression of either of the former terms, and suggests important rearticulations, outlined in my conclusion, of possibilities for emancipation in the present.

Framework: From the Margins to the Center

The work of Frantz Fanon systematically exposes the exploitation and expropriation intrinsic to colonialism, which produces the misery of the colony and the wealth of the West: "Confronting this world, the European nations sprawl, ostentatiously opulent. . . . The well-being and the progress of Europe have been built up with the sweat and the dead bodies of Negroes, Arabs, Indians, and the yellow races" (1963, p. 96). This material plunder is accompanied by a psychic and existential offensive, a violent rewriting of the identity of the colonized: "At times this Manicheism goes to its logical conclusion and dehumanizes the native, or to speak plainly, it turns him into an animal" (p. 42). Importantly, this dehumanization reflects the logic of colonialism as essentially as does the economic crime. Dehumanization and exploitation are effects in two different registers of the same underlying assault.

Within this broad context, Fanon describes the strange dialectic of the colonial encounter, which is marked by subterranean circuits of disgust on the one hand and dread on the other hand. While the structure of the colony initially appears to be settled and objective, Fanon reveals it to be the effect of an obsession on the part of the colonizer with the dangers and pathologies of the colonized. Even in the therapeutic context, the basic imperative to care for and cure is undermined by the European doctor's dehumanization of the African patient. Fanon (1967b) describes the attitude of the doctor confronted by North African patients who suffer from no visible lesion, but rather from a "multisegmented insecurity" deriving from the colonial context itself; for the doctor, "When you come down to it, the North African is a simulator, a liar, a malingerer, a sluggard, a thief" (p. 7). This conclusion is repeated across encounters, and in this way each intimacy between colonizer and colonized, and indeed the infrastructure of everyday life, is governed by violation.

In analyses that would at first seem to echo Fanon, critical theorists have connected objectification and reification in capitalism with a pathological and sadistic orientation. Thus, Fromm (1964) argues that a functionalist orientation that reduces knowledge to an isolated content and human consciousness to a receiving object is related to a "necrophily" that can understand relationship only in terms of possession. In this way, capitalism's accumulative drive is at the same time an orientation against life, since it seeks to immobilize and control in the interest of power. This is a crucial starting point. But Fanon's account of the colonial encounter should push us to inquire into the logic of *injury* that underwrites both capitalism's visible social violence and its reduction of being and doing to a set of objects to be controlled and possessed. The dynamics of the colonial situation harden the diffuse necrophily of Fromm into an aggressively racist *necropolitics* (Mbembe, 2001).

I argue that Fanon's critique is not limited to the colonial encounter proper, but rather grasps basic tendencies of capitalism more broadly. On the one hand, this is simply to argue that colonialism and coloniality live in the heart of capitalism as essential contradictions. But in addition, I believe that moments of capital that are taken as standing apart from processes of racial and cultural domination can themselves be more powerfully analyzed from the standpoint of decolonial critique. In familiar forms of capitalist culture, including the specialized work of philosophy and science, we can uncover both an ethnocentric orientation and an epistemology of invasion. As Lukács (1971) describes, Western philosophy is caught in antinomies that can be traced back, at the level of the concept, to a bourgeois class standpoint. But Lukács does not confront the violation that works through philosophy's claims to exceptionalism, the rigid forms of its exposition, and its substantive justification for European domination. The impasses of philosophy, and the logic of reification that characterizes them, are not just an ideological effect, but a will to violence.

The contemporary blossoming of decolonial theory supplements Fanon's analysis through a focused interrogation of Western humanism (Smith, 1999; Wynter, 2003), a development of the analysis of the multidimensionality of colonial dynamics (or "coloniality of power") (Quijano, 2008), and a tracing backward of the exclusions described by Fanon to the level of understanding, knowledge, and theory (Byrd, 2011; Mignolo, 2011). This work makes visible the violence that constructs the intelligibility of the West and renders its Others as less than human and captured in an ontological exteriority with no legible claim on the consolidated centers of power and agency. These accounts reveal that capitalism itself is a crucial moment of coloniality, dependent on as well as reproducing the condition of colonial partition. They show that the history of capitalism, from its origins to the present, moves from the "outside" in, as the plunder of the colonies allows for the development of metropolitan capitalism, and as the discursive framework of race supports global projects of empire building. However, the distinction between *colonialism* (a concrete and historical social formation) and *coloniality* (an ontological, epistemological, and cultural logic) is significant here. My argument is not that capitalism can be reduced to a form of colonialism but rather that the process of imposition that coloniality depends on, and that colonialism visibly exemplifies, works fundamentally to organize capitalism as well. To this extent, the theoretical tools that decolonial critique makes available can crucially deepen our understanding of capitalism.

Decolonial theory has focused attention on what capitalism and colonialism (and their ideologists) have ignored, erased, and overlooked, and how these erasures and occupations are fundamental to the meaning of Western modernity.

In this chapter, I extend this interrogation to what has *not* been ignored—that is, to the central objects and categories against which the exterior has been contrasted. Of course, Marxism as a critical project has shared in the work of exposing the dominative architecture of Western culture and thought. But pressing forward the project of decentering the center (or what Chakrabarty, 2000, calls "provincializing Europe"), I explore how analyses of annexation and violation that decolonial theory has proposed can work as conceptual starting points for rethinking even Marxism's critical categories for understanding the world, and in this way open up a path toward a decolonial analytic of capitalism itself in its innermost determinations. I do not suggest that this investigation uncovers a new universal essence, which works across diverse experiences in the same way. Instead, I argue that a decolonial analytic can expose crucial determinations of capital that are not otherwise visible, and that unevenly affect different communities.

In this analysis, I consider three central moments of capital: enclosure, valorization, and (real) subsumption. These have been taken by theorists as crucial historical markers in the development of the capitalist system and alternatively as central aspects of its ongoing metabolism. Thus, Marx (1867/1976) argues that enclosure is the key historical condition for the extended valorization of capital, which in turn leads to a progressive subsumption of use values by exchange value. At the same time, these moments can be thought of as key *figures* for capital—ways of sketching its essential shape and tendency. In rethinking these figures, I engage in each case with a theorist in the Marxist tradition who has been important in explicating the process in question (in the case of valorization, this is Marx himself). Beyond Marx, I have started from Marxian theorists who have themselves been interested in a creative reimagination of political economy, so that in interrogating their theses I can more closely indicate the distinct rethinking that a decolonial analysis produces. Across these cases, I explore how the logic of capital in its fundamental determinations, *viewed in a different light, shows up differently*, and how thinking from the standpoint of the colonial encounter can reframe the taken-for-granted senses in Marxism of accumulation and value.

Enclosure and Imposition

Massimo De Angelis (2007) argues that we need to understand capitalism, from its origin to the present, in terms of the separation of producers from the means of production. He describes so-called primitive accumulation (the initial seizure of wealth that allows for the development of capitalist production) and enclosure (the appropriation of collectively held lands and resources) not as part of a prehistory to capitalism but rather as the persistent condition of accumulation. In this way, we can see that moments of direct expropriation are continuous with the "normal" process of exploitation in wage labor:

> Within Marx's theoretical and critical framework therefore, the divorcing embedded in the definition of primitive accumulation can be understood not only as the origin of capital vis-à-vis precapitalist social relations, but also as a reassertion of capital's priorities vis-à-vis those social forces that run against this *separation*. . . . If we conceive social contestation as a continuous element of capitalist relations of production, capital must continuously engage in strategies of primitive accumulation to recreate the 'basis' of accumulation itself. (p. 140)

In every case, what is essential is the assimilation of the material world, subjectivity, and social life within the value practices of capital, and the refusal of any outside. Economic production is in this way linked to social production and we must understand both ultimately in ethical terms, as reproducing market-based values and forms of relationship. From De Angelis' (2007) perspective, capitalism is an ethical, social, and biopolitical process of enclosure, against which we must struggle on the basis of different values, remembering and reconstituting the outside on which capitalism depends and which it seeks perpetually to capture and subsume. Enclosures, then, "define a strategic terrain among social forces with conflicting value practices" (p. 140). De Angelis, along with other open Marxists, challenges an account of class struggle that understands it as internal to capitalism's law of value and which ignores ongoing struggles for alternative forms of measure and meaning.

These insights are indispensable and open up a set of strategies for struggles around the common(s) based on emergent "values of *the outside*" (De Angelis, 2007, p. 32). However, while De Angelis' account challenges conventional readings of production and class, primitive accumulation and enclosure in his account nevertheless still remain a means to the end of the universalization of capitalism's law of value. Incorporation is capitalism's goal here, and the market works as the organizer of a basic governmentality to which all must submit. What partly disappears in his account is the process of extended violence and occupation that is associated with enclosure, and which we can see as itself the expression and fulfillment of capitalism's fundamental drive. It is not incidental that capital comes into the world "dripping from head to toe, from every pore, with blood and dirt" (Marx, 1867/1976, p. 926), through global violence intimately linked to European enclosures in which, as Federici (2004) notes, "even before the Reformation, more than two thousand rural communities were destroyed" (p. 70). Certainly these annexations articulate a system of value practices which come to be normalized as an economy, but can we not see this economy as the shadow or echo of the fundamental event of imposition? As Maldonado-Torres (2007) points out, occupation involves not simply a plunder of resources but also an assault on being, and its historical energy comes from this assault. In the daily moments of production in the capitalist workplace, the surplus that is captured is as much the immaterial surplus of the worker's abjection (which at the same time exalts the capital that organizes it) as it is a purely "economic" appropriation. This is not only the case in authoritarian workplaces; indeed, this determination lurks behind management's contemporary effort to reimagine work in capitalism as collaborative, creative, and autonomous (Boltanski & Chiapello, 2005).

The point is not that archaic relationships of domination continue to work through capitalism. On the contrary, the logic of occupation and imposition that I emphasize here is a capitalist and modern one, since it has the systematicity that this mode of production innovates, and since it produces a surplus value. However, we have to conceptualize that value more complexly. If one important insight in the work of De Angelis is that capitalism is a system of values in an ethical sense (i.e., that "economic" value is identified with a larger ethical sense of value and the struggles around it), then it is also the case that occupation, in ethical terms, also expresses a systematic logic, its own proper "economy," which yields a spiritual surplus to the settler and to the capitalist, while producing a corresponding denigration of Indigenous ways of being, knowing, and governing (Alfred, 2009). Not only does exploitation depend on a process of expropriation and coercion which allows the capital system to be set in motion (whether this is thought of as a past event or an ongoing process of "accumulation by dispossession," as David Harvey, 2003, puts it); furthermore, exploitation, surplus value, and capital itself can be seen as the effects of a continuous series of assaults, and as an *index* of imposition—that is, as a series of propositions whose meaning is given by a grammar of violation. Thus, the pathologization of the colonized described by Fanon (1963) reveals a spiritual logic, which even as it acts in a unique way and with special force within the colonial encounter, at the same time works variously across contexts of accumulation. In this way, both colonialism and capitalism, even as they differ, might be thought of as processes of multiplication and organization of an original injury.

Scholars of settler colonialism likewise point to a "logic of elimination" that ties present dispossessions to past ones, marking "invasion [as] a structure rather than an event" (Wolfe, 2006, p. 388). This analysis points beyond the value struggles highlighted by De Angelis to an eliminatory project linked to the taking of land as well as to the assimilation of Indigenous people. As Goodyear-Ka'ōpua (2019) shows in the case of the experiences of the peoples of Oceania, annexation of territory, physical violence, and epistemological substitution (of settler-colonial knowledges of control for Indigenous knowledges of positionality and directionality) collaborate to secure settler hegemony and spacio-temporality. The notions of injury and violation that I propose in this chapter and elsewhere in this volume likewise suggest a project of imposition that links the plunder of land and resources to sociocultural marginalization and assimilation, within a recognition of annexation as central to the history and logic of capital. It should be noted that the notion of *coloniality* may risk at times de-emphasizing the materiality of colonization which is at the center of critiques of settler colonialism proper; in applying the insights of Quijano and Dussel, this is a problem that must be attended to. On the other hand, the flexibility of the Latin American coloniality thesis allows for its application to diverse experiences of colonialism, as well as for an account of the global metabolism of Western modernity. The notion of violation that I develop here aims to contribute to a description of that metabolism.

Contemporary economic predations mark key moments in that process and repeat in their own way the plunder undertaken by Europe on a global scale in the early modern period. The destabilization that privatization occasions echoes the disruptions of societies by colonialism. Of course, these are two moments in a *continuous* history of dispossession (Smith, 1999). The terror sown against Latin American communities by twenty-first-century extractive industries should recall the brutality of the gold and silver fever of the colonial period vividly described by Galeano (1973), in which "of every ten [Indians] who went up into the freezing wilderness" of Potosí's silver mines, "seven never returned" (p. 39). Beyond material dispossession, its invasion of body, being, and spirit exposes capitalism as an extended celebration of destruction. Its relentless enclosure of knowledge, culture, and even organic life forms expresses this dramatically. This enclosure occupies the time of life and evicts other possibilities, even where the degree of violence is nothing like that of the early colonial period. For instance, the overwhelming of public education in the present by rigidly scripted curricula governed by standardized assessment and punitive "accountability" frameworks is as much an ontological invasion (of the being of students, teachers, and learning) as it is an ideological offensive.

Capitalism, from this perspective, is not just the unfolding drama of a set of already constituted antagonists, but rather the installation of a more basic imaginary, an imaginary that depends for its initial coherence and continued preservation on an occupation of being and knowing. From this perspective, imperialist expansion, enclosures of the commons, and the establishment of the global capitalist market enroll communities and individuals into a new universe organized on the basis of an architecture of assault. The genocide of Indigenous communities in the Americas inaugurated not just a new form of rule but also a new spiritual and ontological grammar, whose forms and phrases are invasions and erasures. Just like the rapid sequence of images produces a film's narrative, in the same way the meaning and development of Western modernity can be seen as the effect of a series of innumerable local impositions. So too, up to the present, the forms of social, economic, and psychic life that we inhabit are the effect of annexation.[1] Capital, from this perspective, is not a derivative of this annexation but above all the annexation itself, of which the surplus of production and social life is an index.

Value, Valorization, and Violation

Beyond the moment of enclosure, how might we see the logic of imposition described earlier working through capitalist production more broadly? Answering this question involves consideration of the process of valorization. The heart of Marx's analysis in *Capital* (1867/1976) is his account of the production of surplus value through the commodity labor-power, the use-value of which is in fact the creation "not only of value, but of more value than it has itself" (p. 301). In other words, in the process of valorization, which "is nothing but the continuation of the [creation of value] beyond a definite point" (p. 302), labor-power generates more value than that which is required to produce it. This analysis lays out the consistent inconsistency of capitalism, which remains true in the process of exploitation to the law of value even as it fleeces the workers, in a deeper sense, through appropriation of the surplus that their labor has created.

What makes this account so revelatory is the way that Marx's unraveling of the mystery of surplus value shifts conceptual registers, exposing an obscure link between the concrete subjectivity of the worker and the abstract and objective logic of capital itself. Capitalism's systematicity is impersonal, without malice, and yet the drama of Marx's account turns on the invisible moment of the worker's violation—which takes place not in mere labor, but rather precisely in the extraction of an excess—the production of a surplus. The capital relation is a relation between classes, between objective antagonists within a historical dialectic, but this relation depends on and refers to a subjective imposition:

> When we leave the sphere of simple circulation or the exchange of commodities, which provides the "free-trader *vulgaris*" with his concepts and the standard by which he judges the society of capital and wage-labour, a certain change takes place, or so it appears, in the physiognomy of our *dramatis personae*. He who was previously the money-owner now strides out in front as a capitalist; the possessor of labour-power follows as his worker. The one smirks self-importantly and is intent on business; the other is timid and holds back, like someone who has brought his own hide to market and now has nothing else to expect but—a tanning. (Marx, 1867/1976, p. 280)

These two registers—the objective and the subjective—do not run parallel but rather intersect obscurely. The smirk of the capitalist is not merely inward and particular but rather reveals a systematic determination of the class: it indicates a structure of assault which, as such, must be registered at the limit by a subjectivity, the subjectivity of the worker. Indeed, the complex structured totality of capitalism that Althusser (2009) names as the object of the new philosophy invented by Marx cannot rid itself of its obscene underground—that is, a systematic and impersonal pleasure in injury.

As Marx (1867/1976) explains, the labor process, viewed qualitatively, is the production of specific articles and use-values. However, "if it is viewed as a value-creating process the same labour process appears only quantitatively" (p. 302), that is, as a certain quantity of socially necessary labor time. In this traumatic split between the qualitative and the quantitative we find the condition of estrangement that is the focus of the early Marx's (1964) humanist critique of capitalism, since the species-being of the worker is alienated in the ruthless grip of abstraction. But this trauma is different from the violation that I described earlier, which belongs to the specific category of surplus value. In the latter case, what counts is the "specific use-value which [labor-power] possesses of being a source not only of value, but of more value than it has itself" (p. 301), a use value on which the capitalist unconsciously depends. Labor-power's *excessiveness* is the hidden source of capital, and of capital's complex structuration, and it is the *intimacy* of the capitalist's relationship to this excessiveness that is the effective scandal.

This relationship is different from the colonial one explicated by Fanon (1963), which is based on vilification of the native and on continuous coercion. And yet the dialectic between separation and intimacy that Fanon describes, in which colonizer and colonized are constructed as belonging to two different species and yet dream obsessively of each other, contains crucial lessons for understanding the relation of exploitation in capitalism more generally. For the colonizer, the native population is "the depository of maleficent powers" (p. 41), and yet colonial society depends upon this population absolutely, and "as soon as the native begins to pull on his moorings, and to cause anxiety to the settler, he is handed over to well-meaning souls who in cultural congresses point out to him the specificity and wealth of Western values" (p. 43). Here there is always an excessive element that threatens to get out of control, and around whose terrifying agency the infrastructure of colonial society, both material and ideological, is constructed. Can we not extrapolate from Fanon, and understand capital's historical antagonist not simply as an objective and consolidated (working) class but rather as an unpredictable agency which threatens at every moment to exceed itself and undo the coherence of society?

This terrifying agency, captured and controlled, is also the effective principle of valorization. Capital is not the indifferent accumulation of value, but rather the specific accumulation of surplus value. And surplus value is not simply *more value*, but is rather an impossible surpassing of its own limit (as embodied in labor-power)—an obscene operation on the subject staged by capitalist production. Surplus value is not simply the indifferent output of labor-power set down to work but depends rather on the scandalous union of the capitalist and the worker—it is the effect of a violation. These are the actual stakes of the shift in paradigm that Althusser aims to explicate in Marx, a shift that leaves behind a crude political economy of calculation and a detached naturalization of the conditions of capitalist production. Surplus value is the effect and registration of imposition, hidden in the form of the commodity and in the complex articulations of capitalist society.

This is not to suggest an equivalence between diverse forms of domination and accumulation, such as slavery, *encomienda*, and wage labor, but it does mean foregrounding the colonial architecture that structures each of these historical experiences. Rather than seeing forms of exploitation outside of wage labor as peripheral derivatives or preliminaries, this analysis would see these forms as primary, and the wage-labor relation as a rearticulation of their basic themes. This means conceptualizing social totality from a decolonial standpoint that finds in the "center" a crucial reflection of the experience of the "margins" (see Dussel, 1998; Quijano, 2008).

Real Subsumption and Ontological Terrorism

The third figure for capital that I want to consider is that of real subsumption—the moment of absolute expansion in which all use-value is drawn into exchange value and capital becomes coextensive with social life. In this moment, according to Antonio Negri (2003), work becomes the time of life, as capital determines social being. At this point, the law of value that underlies the process of valorization is exceeded, as time ceases to function as measure. In this moment, the long arc of the process of enclosure that is discussed earlier is complete. In the historical stage of real subsumption, subjectivity becomes a crucial site of struggle, since the creative possibilities of imagination and identity—in addition to the material spaces of production—are increasingly occupied by capital:

> We will start from the analysis of *collective time* as determined by the displacement marked by real subsumption, identifying on the one hand the *capitalist analytic* of the subsumption of labour by capital, and on the other, its specific antagonism—that is—social work, the *social worker* and the crisis of the social analytic of capital. (Negri, 2003, p. 44)

We can see this process in capitalism's annexation of moments and meanings that were previously at least partly external or antagonistic to it. On the side of the worker, we can observe the ways that the labor process increasingly absorbs affective and communicative capacities (for example in the service industries). On the side of the system, we can point to the invention of instruments that enable the commodification and securitization of more and more dimensions of the material world and social life. Thus, the complex derivatives whose collapse was implicated in the 2008 recession were themselves refinements of the fictitious capital that has allowed for the expansion of the credit system in late capitalism, as Harvey (2006) describes. The very distance of these instruments from the real assets to which they refer only enhances their allure.

For Negri (2003), in the moment of real subsumption, struggle needs to work outside of the familiar dialectic and produce new temporalities and subjectivities that refuse capital's time of life: "It is here that *antagonism* erupts. The time of cooperation constitutes itself as a subject against capital" (p. 59). Negri's account moves away from familiar Marxist notions of crisis stemming from capitalism's internal dynamics, and instead emphasizes the historical agency of that which is outside the time of capital, a reframing that is shared by decolonial critiques. However, Negri overlooks the fact that the alterity of the colonized is not *innovated* in the context of a global struggle against "social capital," but has always been present—at once disavowed by the colonizer (registered only as blankness) while also constituted as the express target of colonial violence. As Enrique Dussel (1985) describes, the Being of the West is consolidated and consecrated on the basis of the destruction of that which is Other to it, the non-Being of the colonized: "Beyond the horizon of Being, the other is the barbarian" (p. 45). Even as capital assimilates social being and potentiality, seeking to institute itself as synonymous with totality, it has to prove this dominion through a persistent violence against an inassimilable exteriority. This necessity remains up to the present. It is no accident that the period of neoliberalism's expansion was also the period of a sequence of neocolonial interventions. For instance, we can understand the Reagan administration's adventures in Central America, which are usually analyzed in terms of a Cold War struggle over spheres of influence, in terms of the renewed assertion of an ontological order, in which the exteriority of the Indigenous and colonized was registered in campaigns of genocide.

From a decolonial perspective, capital is not only a logic of assimilation (of the outside) and an *overcoming* of distance but also a logic of exaltation (of empire) and *maximization* of distance.[2] From this perspective, the spectacular abstractions of finance capital derive their aura from the height at which they look down on the real economy and the actors within it. The *spiritualism* of capitalism's magnificent abstractions, and of its high priests and priestesses, is produced out of the gap that separates them from ordinary existence. The vicissitudes and catastrophes (including of the market itself) that ordinary people must confront and survive proves this gap. The commanders of the economy are exalted through the contrary abjectness of the masses and their proximity to the real, to the margins of value. The masses are forced to live a continuous devastation, a devastation which concentrates at its center the blessed circle that belongs to the elect.

Starting from Fanon, Maldonado-Torres (2008) argues that in the colonial situation we need to reframe the existential problematic to account for the way in which the colonized are exiled from Being. As Fanon (1967a) described, unable even to occupy the place of the oppressed in Hegel's dialectic of master and bondsman, Black people are constituted by whites as the substrate of colonialism's material and symbolic economy. Bringing this account into dialogue with Negri's (2003) analysis, in which capitalism increasingly works to capture being and subjectivity, we can point to a process of *ontological terror*. The history of colonialism shows that at its boundaries capital is murder. But the consolidated forms at its interior also violently separate subjects from that in them which would remain outside of capital's time of life. Supplementing Negri, it is important to note that the total time of contemporary capitalism, which he describes as escaping its determination as measure and becoming continuous command, appears only through a disavowal of exteriority (Dussel, 1985)—an exteriority which persists, even if it is violated and refused—both at the edges and in the core of capital.

The structure of racism in the capitalist "core" is instructive in this regard. Racism in the United States reveals the colonial character of capitalism, since this racism (as mass incarceration, segmentation of labor, and ideology) is essential to the meaning and function of the system. And yet, the long history of struggle by communities of color has built and preserved a time of life (in community, culture, and resistance) beyond capital's commandments (Kelley, 1993). This horizon of struggle is an outrage to the system, since it proves the limits of the latter, and since in challenging the supremacy of the principle of violation it challenges capitalism at its heart, and so proposes a revolutionary horizon. This history demonstrates both the relentless annexation of being and time by capital that Negri describes as well as its ultimate failure to completely subsume what Vizenor (1994) has called Indigenous *survivance*. Indeed, the process of settler colonialism anticipates capitalism's ontological annexation, even if Negri does not acknowledge this. In this context, Indigenous survivance and resurgence mark the limits of subsumption and articulate a form of autonomy working beyond Western notions of sovereignty (Alfred, 2009), at the limit perhaps even transcending the dominative topography of interior and exterior that Dussel critiques.

Extrapolating from this perspective, and as a corrective to Negri, we might say that the triumph of capitalism in the present is not exactly to absorb the full human and social being of the worker (in real subsumption), and to convert this potentiality immediately into surplus value but rather to split the worker off absolutely from that in her which cannot be comprehended by capital's dialectic. This is different from saying that *labor-power* can never be fully controlled by capital, since even if this is true, labor-power as a category already belongs to the dialectic of capitalist production. Rather, a decolonial perspective remembers the irreducible difference in subjects (from the sameness of coloniality), by which they are connected to histories beyond that of domination (see Alcoff, 2006, and Urrieta, 2017). While different people are positioned differently in this regard, this *beyond* of domination has nevertheless persisted through the history of the expansion and "universalization" of capitalism. Rather than imagining a *flight* from empire, as some would have us do, I believe that we should learn from those communities that have managed, even as they have been caught in this system, to *remember* their inextirpable autonomy.[3]

Conclusion

The analytic I have outlined exposes capital as a process of continuous injury. It understands the production of surplus value in terms of a process of violation, and points beyond the assimilation of the subject's affective and imaginative potential to the terror that forces subjectivity into forms that can be commanded by capital, even as capital seeks to destroy any outside or alterity. This architecture of assault, grounded in coloniality proper, nevertheless also exceeds it. In other words, this account locates coloniality at the center of capitalism's history and logic, while also seeing coloniality as the key to understanding the diverse forms and expressions of capitalism. As I have described, from this standpoint, capital's key moments and figures need to be reinvestigated and rethought. In concluding, I want to briefly consider the implications of this argument for imagining possibilities for resistance in the present. Understanding capitalism and the processes of enclosure, valorization, and subsumption it comprises in terms of a process of annexation—on the basis of the conceptual tools of decoloniality— has important implications for the effort to contest it.

From this perspective, capitalism in the present can be seen as an occupation of space and subjectivity, an occupation which simultaneously takes the form of a substitution of the market for the social and the form of an exclusion of communities and individuals from the space of society altogether. Racism is a privileged mode in this dual process. Thus, recent decades have seen on the one hand increasing privatization of public institutions like schools, and on the other hand the carceralization of these same institutions—a literal expression of this latter tendency being the hypertrophy of the prison system (Gilmore, 2007). Both of these developments have depended on a pathologization of communities of color, while also progressively extending their effects to society as a whole. In short, we cannot separate the complex effects of contemporary capitalism from the underlying principle of violation that it innovates, or what

Wynter (2003), starting from Fanon, describes as the particular "sociogeny" prescribed by Western modernity.

Furthermore, the transition in the present to a right-wing antiglobalism can be contextualized within the frame I have outlined. Critics have wondered if we witnessed in the Trump administration a transition away from neoliberalism toward a more statist, nationalist, and authoritarian form of governance in the United States and globally (see West, 2016). And yet the anti-trade and populist rhetoric of both the US administration and neo-fascist currents in Europe coincided with an even more aggressive push for deregulation, market models for public policy (for instance in education), and upward transfers of wealth ("tax reform"). We can partly unravel these tensions from the perspective of a decolonial analytic of capital. If we understand the process of accumulation as at once a process of violation, whose meaning lives in the first instance in the twisted intimacy of the relationship between colonizer and colonized, then it is not surprising that the breathless dispossessions that characterize the pursuit of surplus value in the present are matched by a resurgent right-wing populism and a diffusion of racist violence. It is not simply that this racism, solicited by elites even as it is embraced by disaffected whites, works as decoy and division; rather, like shocks in the economic sphere, it aims at the particular spiritual surplus that derives from a humiliation of the outside and Other.

What does my reconsideration in this chapter of these three underlying figures of capital imply for contemporary emancipatory struggles, and what might emancipation itself mean in this context? An important starting point for a response to these questions is the conclusion of *The Wretched of the Earth*, in which Fanon calls for a final departure from European humanism. Mignolo (2011) has echoed and updated this call in his argument for a cultural and epistemological "delinking" from coloniality, and Coulthard (2014) argues that Indigenous peoples should look beyond the politics of recognition offered by the settler-colonial state. These calls share with certain Marxian theorists a rethinking of the process of emancipation outside of the familiar dialectic of revolution. Thus, Hardt and Negri (2004) argue for an *exodus* from Empire that would create unprecedented subjectivities and social relationships, and De Angelis (2007) argues for the collective creation of new value practices outside the logic of enclosure. And yet an important difference is that the decolonial outside pointed to by Fanon, Mignolo, and Coulthard is not indeterminate and abstract, as it tends to be for these Marxian theorists of the common, but rather starts from existing marginalized understandings and traditions. Likewise, Dussel's (1985) "analectic," which he contrasts with the dialectic of Western philosophy, starts not from any empty exteriority but rather from the specific and populated exteriority of the oppressed and colonized.

These decolonial theories of emancipation grow out of the territorialized and historically specific experience of invasion. In this context, resistance means first of all confronting and repudiating colonial violence, and envisioning and enacting other ways of being, a process that is also a recalling of marginalized traditions (Cusicanqui, 2012; Smith, 1999). If, as I have argued, we should understand capitalism as repeating and innovating a logic of violation across moments of social production, then the struggle for emancipation from capital in the present has to confront diverse expressions of this logic, especially the instance of racism, that give capital its coherence and enact its imperative to accumulation as injury. The notion of coloniality names a process that works across registers of politics, knowledge, psyche, and being, and an understanding of capital that centers this notion has to imagine a struggle that likewise works across all of these registers. Fanon's oeuvre originally proposed this conceptual juxtaposition of material and immaterial violence, and in the present we need to follow through on his analysis.

Althusser (2009) discovered in Marx a paradigmatic shift away from the mystifications of the bourgeois political economists and toward a new philosophy; his own rearticulation of Marxism refused the expressivism of the early Marx in favor of an emphasis on complexity and asymmetry. In the next step that I have proposed in this chapter, the point is not to finally dislodge the centrality in capitalism of the "last instance" of the economy that Althusser famously preserved, but rather to recognize in the economy a principle of injury that is shared and continuous across each moment of capitalism's complex structured whole. Capitalism both emerges from and ceaselessly reinvents the moment of invasion—from the order of the economy to the organization of the subject. If capital is invasion, then resistance is refusal, healing, and resurgence (Simpson, 2017). Imposition is prodigious, but it is so against a persistent outside. In this context, to resist imposition is to recall a different kind of making, and to make a different kind of being.

Notes

1   Critical perspectives and movements that do not confront this determination of modernity risk being trapped in a settler-colonialist dialectics of recognition; see Coulthard (2014), and Grande (2013).

2 See Dussel (1985); Dussel grounds his discussion of oppression and liberation in the first instance in a phenomenological dialectic of proximity and distance.
3 See Smith (1999) for a description of "celebrating survival" and "remembering" as crucial Indigenous research projects.

Part II

Race, Repression, and Critical Pedagogy

3

Race, Reform, and Neoliberalism's Elite Rationale

The epochal logic of accumulation that I sketched out in the first part of this book appears in the current period in a particular form: the philosophical doctrine and economic program of neoliberalism. Generally emphasizing individualism, deregulation, and privatization, neoliberalism is hostile to the public sphere and insists on the inevitability of capitalism. Neoliberals argue that relationships are most rationally arranged when brought under the rubric of the capitalist market, and that social life should be organized on the basis of competition and efficiency. At the same time, the specific tonality and presentation of neoliberal doctrine have shifted over the last several decades. In the present, neoliberal reform in education and beyond is often presented as an expression of care for the less fortunate, rather than simply a way to increase efficiency or improve results. This neoliberal "compassion" is expressed both in foundation-driven philanthropic efforts and in official government initiatives (as well as in the considerable gray area in between). The reorganization of public education through choice and accountability systems and the expansion of the influence of the private sector are increasingly framed in the United States and globally in the language of human and civil rights.

Evidence shows that the claims of improvement made by neoliberal reformers are often dubious, and that their efforts are self-serving, aiming as they do at increasing the potential for profit and influence for business. However, even as critical scholars have debunked the rhetoric of reformers, not enough attention has been paid to the philosophical and ideological structure of contemporary neoliberal care. A consideration of this structure, I argue, suggests that underneath the effort to rethink society in market terms is a basic commitment to the notion of the virtue of elites and elite perspectives. Forms of inequality that shore up elite privilege are covertly valorized even within educational reforms and reform discourse that ostensibly aim at decreasing gaps in opportunity. At the same time, I argue that the elite rationale that governs neoliberal philanthropy and policy draws on, and is inflected by, a long history of racist paternalism toward communities of color. Neoliberal care in this context works to refuse and erase the agency of the students and communities it ostensibly targets. In short, a complex symbolic economy works through contemporary reform, rearticulating tendencies I have described in the previous chapters; I believe that a deeper understanding of this economy and its foundational commitments can help us to formulate more useful responses and alternatives.

This chapter begins with an investigation of the philosophical roots of neoliberalism's elite rationale through a consideration of the philosopher F. A. Hayek's (1960/2011) defense of social privilege and inequality. As I describe, Hayek considered inequality to be an indispensable engine of civilizational advance. Reading Hayek critically, I aim to uncover elements that persist in the philosophical structure of contemporary reform. The next section explores the racial organization of white gestures of empathy toward people of color, via the work of Saidiya Hartman (1997) and related race-critical scholarship. I then apply this compound framework to an analysis of key instances of contemporary educational reform. I show that we can make sense of the contradiction between the putative focus on improving educational conditions and the process of antidemocratic appropriation that reforms actually enact with reference to Hayek's argument that privilege bestows on elites the right and duty to *experiment* with social conditions; this operates as a central rationale within contemporary neoliberalism's "good works." At the same time, Hartman's framework for analyzing the structure of racism within liberal projects of racial solidarity allows us to understand the aura of contemporary reforms for white elites. I argue that these efforts assume the abjectness of communities of color, and that the circulation of representations of Black and Brown beneficiaries serves ultimately to exalt elites themselves. I conclude by considering the implications of my analysis for understanding the stubborn persistence of neoliberalism's elite rationale and for efforts to challenge it.

F. A. Hayek and the Defense of Privilege

The philosophical roots of neoliberalism include a defense of elite reason that continues to work through reform in the present, often below the surface of public debate. The central assumption that concerns me here is the notion that the advancement of some, against others, constitutes progress for the whole of society, and can thus be presented as both desirable and ethical. Starting from a faith in the virtue of competition, the "compassion" that motivates neoliberal philanthropic and policy initiatives ultimately envisions the access of all to a field of high-risk opportunity, in which the opportunity to succeed must always be simultaneously the opportunity to fail. Examining the original defense of this vision—which I consider here in the work of F. A. Hayek—allows us to surface founding commitments of what became the neoliberal program at a time when they were idiosyncratic rather than dominant. Hayek was a transitional figure between the older liberal tradition in politics and economics and the later fully fledged neoliberalism of disciples like Milton Friedman. His work was a decisive influence on the architects of neoliberal policies globally, but precisely the germinal character of his arguments—articulated against the prevailing social-democratic regime of the time—exposes key determinants of neoliberal theory and practice that are often obscured in the present.

For Hayek (2011), inequality is both the result (and proof) of a free society and the condition of civilizational and material progress. Given basic differences in capacity between individuals, a society that grants to all the freedom to develop and be rewarded for their skills will necessarily be unequal in terms of outcomes. Indeed, equality of outcomes in terms of wealth and status from this perspective can only indicate the pernicious interference of the state. More importantly, inequality acts as the essential condition of progress (for both individuals and the collective), since the privileges of wealth and education allow for experimentation and innovation by elites (with regard to technology and lifestyle) which can then diffuse to the rest of society once these innovations are perfected and made affordable. Thus, this position grounds trickle-down economics in a larger argument about the mechanism of accelerating technological and cultural advance. Hayek argues that this advance "seems in a large measure to be the result of this inequality and to be impossible without it. Progress at such a fast rate cannot proceed on a uniform front but must take place in echelon fashion, with some far ahead of the rest" (p. 96). In fact, according to Hayek there is no degree of inequality that should in principle be considered unacceptable, since the gain of some has to be reckoned as the gain of all.

Hayek's defense of privilege is aggressive, going so far as to oppose the argument that social rewards should correspond to individual merit (understood as a measurement of effort). Instead, what matters is the product or performance: "What determines our responsibility is the advantage we derive from what others offer us, not their merit in providing it" (p. 161).

For this reason, not only should the terrain of necessarily unequal individual capacities not be tampered with; in addition, unequal conditions (in terms of inherited wealth, family status, and education) cannot be objected to, since they provide the necessary foundation for even greater advance (pp. 152–5). Hayek's argument here has two moments: the first is that a "better elite" is an index of the level of society as a whole; the second is that the elevation of this elite above the mass works as the ground for innovation, and is therefore the condition for the material and cultural development of all. Hayek argues, paradoxically, that society benefits most when we renounce the idea of social responsibility. Hayek thus repudiates the progressive tradition in education and beyond in one fell swoop. Not only can there be no social responsibility in fact, but only responsibility to those who concern us; in addition, the refusal of a "general altruism" actually benefits everyone, since it makes possible the accumulation, by some, of material and symbolic capital that is the foundation for the advancement of all.

If progress takes place for Hayek as a result of the uncontrolled experiments that the accumulation of capital and privilege allow, and not through any grand social designs which would interfere with the freedom of elites, the corollary of this principle is that actually existing institutions and norms in capitalist society represent the sedimentation of previous collective experience and experimentation, and so we should submit to them, "whether or not we can see that anything important depends on their being observed in the particular instance" (p. 128). Hayek contrasts this submission to the norm to coercion by the state, which he points to as the unacceptable alternative means for achieving social cohesion. In this way, *obedience*—not to a despot, but rather to custom and convention—works as an essential moderating principle supplying consistency of social conditions. For Hayek, the most important moral principle that we must obey is the principle of individual freedom—which he defines not as a right of access but rather in negative terms as a lack of coercion (p. 57). In submitting to this formal rather than substantive definition of liberty, it follows that we must obey those rules and institutions that in practice organize very unequal conditions, for different groups, for the exercise of freedom. This argument is echoed in contemporary neoliberal denunciations of state "monopolies" in education and in calls for submission to the overarching principle of competition.

The principles of inequality and obedience explicated here set the stage for a defense of the market and entrepreneurialism. The submission that Hayek demands in moral terms becomes in fact submission to the market, and to its pricing of our capacities and potentials. Likewise, the form itself of the market can be seen in Hayek as setting the terms for his perspectives on politics and morality. But I want to highlight the way that these principles also cohere as a pedagogy that supports a set of material and immaterial privileges and that justifies an aggressive elitism that operates not just as a class instinct but as a philosophical formation. From Hayek's perspective, not only are (even brutal) disparities in conditions for different groups productive for society as a whole, but by the same token, the moral authority of elites is thereby justified.

In spite of transformations in the ideological structure and field of neoliberalism in the present, I argue that this elitism persists as a kind of philosophical and moral kernel. Of course, the most striking difference between the discourse of contemporary neoliberals and Hayek's own language is that neoliberal reform in the present more often than not presents itself in the form of disinterested philanthropy, or in the language of civil rights. (The rhetoric that surrounded the No Child Left Behind Act is an exemplary case.) In short, neoliberalism in the present putatively aims to remedy precisely those inequalities that it has not only contributed decisively to producing but *upon which it continues to depend at the level of its philosophical rationale.* This discursive shift has occurred at the same time as neoliberalism has moved from the margins to the center of public policy and government. The cruelty of Hayek's apology for inequality and exploitation has been transformed, in the age of mature neoliberalism, into an extended "objective violence" (Žižek, 2008b) in which the ravaging of the mass becomes the very premise of economic and social production. In this context, neoliberalism's current moral discourse, framed in terms of compassion, rights, and even equality, works as a kind of obscene supplement to the violence that neoliberal reform in fact everywhere produces.

Neoliberalism's Racial Fantasies and the Whiteness of Empathy

Freire (1996) described the invidious effects of a "false generosity" on the part of the oppressors that immobilizes and pathologizes the oppressed even as it softens the hard edges of domination. False generosity defuses resistance and reroutes it into a psychology of self-blame. This concept remains useful in making sense of the structure of contemporary neoliberal "compassion." Nevertheless, in two respects it seems less than adequate in relation to a contemporary education policy context that is deeply inflected by race. First, rather than working to ameliorate the effects of the injuries that capitalism produces, neoliberalism's good works are very often the form itself that this injury takes. This can be seen clearly in the field of education, in which damaging reforms often arrive in the first place by way of elite philanthropic efforts. Second, rather than seeking only to colonize the minds of those it injures, these initiatives arguably seek to efface the very presence and agency of the communities of color that are disproportionately affected by reform. Thus, officials and foundation representatives often conceptualize and plan school reform projects in closed-door meetings and implement them without a considered effort to consult with community members or even to convince them of the necessity of reform (Dixson, Buras, & Jeffers, 2015; Hursh, 2015). In this regard, the familiar critical analysis needs to be more finely tuned. Specifically, in order to grasp the logic at work in neoliberal reform, I believe that we have to consider more closely the dimension of racism, a dimension that is symptomatically excluded from neoliberalism's own discourse.

Racism structures the political economy of neoliberal education reform writ large, as scholars have pointed out (Lipman, 2011; Stovall, 2015), but I argue that it also organizes the structure of neoliberal ideology and desire: in this structure, understandings of who needs to be reformed and who is competent to organize reform are deeply racially coded. In this regard, neoliberalism harnesses and also rearticulates dynamics of whiteness that have motivated capitalism from the beginning. Race-critical work on processes of identification and subjection is very helpful here. In particular, Saidiya Hartman (1997) shows that racism in the context of slavery determined expressions of white protest as much as it did the institution itself. Her close analysis exposes the way that whiteness organized expressions of disgust at the cruelty of slavery, in such a way that whites' very expressions of empathy performed an erasure of Black being and agency. Considering the flights of imagination in which white observers sought to empathize with the suffering of Black people, Hartman points out that this empathic identification was "as much due to [their] good intentions . . . as to the fungibility of the captive body" (1997, p. 19). Describing the way that revulsion against the cruelty of slavery worked via whites' imaginary substitution of themselves as the targets of terror, Hartman points out how, at the same time, "by virtue of this substitution the object of identification [Black people] threaten[ed] to disappear" (1997, p. 19). This racial logic and anti-Blackness, central to the history of capitalism, is a key register of neoliberal projects of control and subjection, including in education (Dumas & ross, 2016).

Neoliberal generosity arguably depends upon precisely this effacement of its object, such that the white elite reoccupies the center of symbolic investment in the very moment of supposed extension toward the Other. For instance, urban "redevelopment" projects emphasize the cultural history and identity of neighborhoods; this history then works as a marketing tool to entice affluent whites to move in (Lipman, 2011). In education, accountability is presented as a means of exposing the inadequacies in the schooling that is offered to students of color; however, the resulting metrics celebrate the performance of the privileged. Rather than appearing as actors and agents in their own histories, communities of color show up in the narrative of neoliberal reform as the backdrop or occasion for initiatives that are supposed to help them. We can see in this way how a colonial "necropolitics" (Mbembe, 2003) underwrites neoliberalism, such that the lives of people of color constitute a field of experimentation for white social engineers, even as their experiments are couched in terms of uplift and empowerment. Recalling Hayek's apology for privilege, neoliberal reform imagines white reason as the seat of virtue, and its mere attention to the lives of the "disadvantaged" as proof of magnanimity.

The speculative alchemy of neoliberalism launders appropriation and dispossession into the highest virtues. Thus, as people of color disappear from historic urban communities and schools, they reappear spectrally on the homepages of philanthropic foundations, universities, and hip urban entertainment establishments. In this logic of symbolic invasion, "there [is] no relation to blackness outside the terms of this use of, entitlement to, and occupation of the captive body" (Hartman, 1997, p. 25). In the "compassion" of neoliberal reform, a coldblooded responsibilization of the marginalized is sutured to the potent fantasies of the white philanthropic imagination. Forced into these fantasies by elites' pet policy initiatives, Brown and Black children serve as the raw material in a process of "accumulation by dispossession" (Harvey, 2003) that proceeds symbolically as much as materially. Thus, as communities and their schools are appropriated, whites capture both material educational resources and credit for rescuing historic urban neighborhoods from decay.

If neoliberal generosity in education ultimately points back to Hayek's cherished principles of inequality and obedience, a race-critical perspective allows us to see how racial fantasies work as the indispensable setting for these ideological commitments. Recent neoliberal educational policy initiatives have been deeply racial projects, imagined from the outset in relation to presumed gaps between whites and people of color (see for instance Leonardo's [2007] analysis of No Child Left Behind). To this extent, the symbolic economy that has historically characterized projects of elite white assistance to people of color is at work in these contemporary initiatives as well. Furthermore, far from softening the rough edges of neoliberalism's tough love, the framing of neoliberal education reform in terms of a commitment to racial progress has only served to sharpen its cruelties and ironies. This neoliberal care, expressed in choice, charter, and redevelopment initiatives, repeats on an expanded policy terrain the eliminative logic of a white empathy that has always sought to occupy the experiences and identities of Black people (Hartman, 1997). In the sections that follow, I consider how the violence of neoliberal compassion, whose rough outlines I have outlined up to this point, is expressed in specific instances of educational reform in the United States and globally.

Epistemology of Elitism: Social Engineering and the New Educational Philanthropy

Neoliberalism has reoriented philanthropy in society and education in business terms. The new venture philanthropy seeks to measure the effects of its contributions in terms of a return on investment and to produce a series of specific policy changes beyond merely contributing to the public good (Ball, 2012). While there is no doubt an important role played by cold calculation in neoliberal philanthropic projects in education, we also need to consider the force of basic ideological commitments at the heart of neoliberalism's elite rationale. Recent experiences of neoliberal education reform show that the market logic expressed in philanthropic initiatives cannot be separated from a deep Hayekian faith in the virtue of the elites who command and benefit from it. This faith justifies a sense of care as imposition and appropriation, in which those who are thought to know best take responsibility for organizing society as a whole.

In the United States, elites have taken advantage of crisis conditions to reorganize school systems in urban areas across the country, including New Orleans, Chicago, and Newark, among others. Wealthy individuals and their foundations have been major contributors to these projects, which have been framed not simply in terms of improvement or redevelopment but also as projects of compassion. This "conscious capitalism" converts the arrogance of imposition into a virtue. The reforms it has led to have resulted in the displacement of communities and the deterioration of already difficult educational conditions (Buras, 2011; Lipman, 2011). For elites, however, these results prove their power to make change and to upend the barriers to a process of social experimentation that is inherently desirable. A political option in favor of business models of organization is at work here, but these experiments in social engineering—even where they are framed as efforts at "closing gaps" in opportunity—cannot be fully explained without recognizing the grounding of these efforts in an (un)conscious belief, defended and illuminated by Hayek, in the *positive virtue of inequality itself*.

Recent educational reforms in Newark, New Jersey, set in motion by the foundation of Facebook founder, Mark Zuckerberg, exemplify these dynamics. What stands out in this case is the framing of the difficult conditions in the Newark schools as a crucial opportunity for investment and experimentation by wealthy philanthropists. As Russakoff (2015) has narrated in detail, Newark mayor Cory Booker and New Jersey governor Chris Christie worked secretly with Zuckerberg in 2010 to plan a series of dramatic changes to the school system in Newark, which was at the time under the control of the state board of education as a result of a record of poor performance. This triad was convinced that progress for the schools could only come through a business-model restructuring (involving removal of seniority protections for teachers, implementation of performance-based pay systems, and expansion of the charter school sector), and that this restructuring process in Newark could serve as a laboratory for reforms to be generalized to the nation as a whole. It is clear from this history that the undemocratic nature of this process, in which community members did not have a voice, was not conceived of as a problem, but rather as *the crucial condition for reform*. An imposition of the market model as the inner logic for organizing teaching and learning was at the heart of this experiment, but this imposition at the same time expressed a more fundamental faith in the wisdom of elites.

In fact, the actual disaster produced by the Newark reforms neither halted the political ascension of the protagonists involved nor dampened the resolve of neoliberal reformers in other school systems (Russakoff, 2015). The restructuring of the Newark schools failed to achieve even the narrowly framed goals of the reformers themselves, at the same time that they destabilized and alienated the community. Similar efforts, with similar results, have taken place across the country as elites and wealthy donors have moved aggressively to influence policy at both the local and national levels (Reckhow & Tompkins-Strange, 2015). The evidence of these failed projects reveals the paternalism of neoliberal compassion, as the power of these initiatives is greatest where democracy and community voice have been most marginalized (Stovall, 2015).

It is important to note that "conscious capitalism" in education has been touted not only as a more determined effort to improve school conditions against a status quo supported by bureaucrats and teacher unions but also as a crucial form of *social engineering* that seeks to innovate in local contexts in order to refine "transformational" (i.e., business-oriented) reform models. In the same way, as I have described, Hayek argues that the wealthy enjoy both the privilege and the responsibility to experiment in the economic and social spheres. The inequalities that shore up this privilege cannot be condemned, he argues, because they make possible social innovation that ultimately benefits all: "A large part of the expenditure of the rich . . . thus serves to defray the cost of the experimentation with the new things that, as a result, can later be made available to the poor" (2011, p. 97). The moral charge of this elite "burden" can be felt in the statements of neoliberal reformers, who frame the exercise of their power to remake conditions on the ground for regular people as a kind of categorical imperative. Thus, according to the Eli and Edythe Broad Foundation, "That's why we start each day by asking ourselves: How can we help our partners and grantees create better conditions in America's public schools to prepare all students for a productive life?"—a commitment that the foundation understands, of course, in the context of "entrepreneurship for the public good" (Broad Foundation, 2016). While the virtues of this exercise of power may often be difficult to see (especially for those who suffer from them), Hayek tells us that we must nevertheless all hold on tight and give ourselves over to this ride, however rough. Obedience to the market, and to its lucky commanders, is a basic ideological commitment, which cannot be challenged by any unhappy consequences. If experiments often fail, with negative effects for many (Hayek, 2011, p. 81), this cannot be allowed to stand in the way of the freedom of the privileged to remake reality.

This elite prerogative to experiment and innovate, a kind of common sense for neoliberal reformers, casts the public at large—whom reforms are nominally intended to serve—as either obstacles or mute targets. For instance, in the case of Newark, Zuckerberg's top priority was reorganizing the system of teacher compensation on a competitive business model. He wanted to replace a pay system for teachers based on years of service with one based on student performance (as measured by test scores), and to make it easier to remove teachers with the lowest evaluations. This restructured contract would then serve as a model for compensating teachers across the country (Davis, 2014). While the reformers ultimately did not succeed in removing seniority rights for teachers in Newark, they did manage to tie raises to a new merit-based evaluation system. Importantly, teachers were framed as adversaries in this process, and their objections were considered irrelevant. In this epistemology of elitism, teachers, students, and community members became the *objects* of knowledge and action, the *subjects* of which looked down on them from the air-conditioned upper floors of power and policy.

Recalling Hayek's argument allows us to make sense of the arrogance that works through contemporary educational reform and philanthropy. His defense of privilege is echoed in the tacit claim by elite reformers to a unique access to the truth. Russakoff (2015) reports that Christopher Cerf, the Christie-appointed New Jersey education commissioner, commented, in reference to the Newark reforms, that "change has casualties. You can't make real change through least-common-denominator, consensus solutions. One reason school reform has failed is the tremendous emphasis on consensus" (p. 77). While neoliberal reforms putatively aim to combat the inequalities that plague public schooling and society, the imagined authority of reformers is grounded in a sense of their own superior understanding, a superiority that is seemingly supported in fact by these same disparities of wealth and access. In this way, within the political unconscious of neoliberal philanthropy, inequality is ultimately the essential condition of social advance.[1] And as Hayek would have it, for ordinary people the proper response is not to question decisions, the virtue of which they are not in a position to judge, but rather to obey, trusting their fates to those who must know better than they do.

Race, Neoliberal Care, and Global Education Reform

The "good works" of contemporary neoliberal education reform are grounded in a deep sense of the virtue of elite privilege, as I have described. But they are also organized through particular economies of racism (Brown & De Lissovoy, 2011). On the one hand, race works as a system that neoliberalism exploits to effect its reorganization of society; on the other hand, the logic of racial imposition itself determines the meaning and experience of neoliberalism—especially in the form of the neoliberal care that is projected by philanthropic initiatives. In this way, neoliberalism can be seen as perfecting historical processes of violation that have always organized capitalist society (De Lissovoy, 2013a). In the case of contemporary education reform, both in the United States and globally, elites at once rationalize their interventions in terms of a challenge to race-based inequalities while also refusing to consider the racial politics that actually frame reform projects. In both contexts, the enactment of neoliberal reform proceeds on the basis of a process of a substitution in which white elites appropriate the spaces of action and decision-making that belong to communities of color, refusing the latter's agency. At the same time, the aura of virtue that surrounds these initiatives works through a rescue fantasy in relation to a racialized and abject Other, a fantasy that has roots in the long history of white imagination of Black suffering (Hartman, 1997).

In the United States, the case that perhaps best illustrates these dynamics is that of New Orleans. After Katrina, the epochal flood of 2005 that devastated the city, white reformers moved aggressively to reorganize the school system, seizing the opportunity of the crisis created by the flood to close historic schools, convert the public system to a network of charter schools, and to replace the majority African American teaching force with a new group of young (mainly white) recruits. This process was put in motion by a network of think tanks, foundations, businesspeople, and politicians set on reorganizing the schools on the basis of neoliberal principles of choice and flexibility and in accordance with the interests of the white middle class (Buras, 2011). In the process, established rules and procedures for school reorganization, termination of teachers, and communication with the public were violated and/or rewritten. Black teachers, parents, and students were not meaningfully consulted and their objections were ignored or overruled (Dixson, Buras, & Jeffers, 2015). Importantly, at the same time, these reforms were framed as an act of care for the community, ostensibly rescuing students from a failing and inefficient public school system, improving the teaching force, streamlining governance, and inviting generous contributions from wealthy foundations.

As Dixson et al. (2015) describe, white elite projects for reform in New Orleans went forward without regard to the history of the schools they aimed to reorganize, without consideration of longstanding work by teachers in these schools to support African American students, and without serious engagement with student and community groups that formed to protect their schools against closure. In this regard, the New Orleans case resembles restructuring that has taken place in many other US cities, such as Chicago, which has seen the gutting of the public school system, as historic schools serving communities of color have been replaced by turnaround and charter schools under cover of a market-based discourse that frames choice as the route to improvement—over the objections of the communities actually affected by this restructuring (Lipman, 2011), and without attention to the actual experiences of students and teachers in the city (Means, 2013). In these cases of urban educational reform, not only are space and resources taken within the school system and through the process of neighborhood gentrification that accompanies it, but also the framing of reform as an act of care—often via the appropriation of civil rights and equity discourses (Scott, 2009)—serves at the symbolic level to substitute a white elite agency and understanding for the actual desires and perspectives of people of color.

This act of substitution depends on an underlying refusal of humanity to people of color, and on a "constancy of Black subjection" (Hartman, 1997, p. 171) from the past to the present. If the denial of humanity to Black people has always conditioned white subjectivity (Wilderson, 2010), and not least in education (Brown, 2013), this relationship is visible in the lack of hesitation with which elites remake the lives of Black communities. In addition, it is important to see that the logic of neoliberal care, as expressed in educational reform projects, involves not only the annexation of resources but also, in a second moment, an exaltation of the white agent of reform. For instance, a crucial moment in the narrative of Newark's ill-fated reform effort was the spectacular celebration—delivered in 2010 to a mass audience via *The Oprah Winfrey Show*—of Mark Zuckerberg's $100-million gift to underwrite the restructuring of the city's schools. As Russakoff (2015) reports, the studio audience gave Zuckerberg a standing ovation. Here the elite privilege lauded by Hayek comes together with the specific symbolic structure of white paternalism. As Hartman describes, within a "selective acknowledgment of [Black] sentience that only reinforces the tethers of subjection" (1997, p. 35), whites produce both the material reality of subjection and a fantasy of Black acquiescence that sustains domination. This process of symbolic substitution permits the racist and undemocratic roll-out of reform, as in Newark, New Orleans, and Chicago, since in place of the community's actual response whiteness can only see the imaginary reflection of its own triumphalism.

Philanthropy and neoliberal educational reform at the global level are likewise crucially framed in the context of a specific racial politics and project. International financial institutions for decades have structured economic support to the Global South in such a way as to discourage self-determination and self-sufficiency on the part of recipient nations, continuing a colonial legacy that reproduces a relationship of dependency on the West (Petras &Veltmeyer, 2002). However, in the present, wealthy private and corporate foundations are responsible for an increasing share of support, as they participate in a broad international shift in education policy from government to public-private governance (Rizvi & Lingard, 2010). This support is framed in terms of developing senses of civil society in target societies that foreground entrepreneurialism and market orientations (Vogel, 2006)—that is, in a decidedly neoliberal frame. At the same time that such projects promote a market-based discourse for development, they also importantly work to burnish the images of wealthy funders and foundations. Both aspects of this ideological work are inflected by and accomplished within a racial frame. The excitement that surrounds philanthropic efforts in this context, which Ball describes as being driven by "a particular mix of caring and calculation" (2012, p. 70), often serves to distract attention from the actual effects of education reform (Srivastava and Oh, 2010). As in the United States, in the international arena elites find permission, in their own wealth and privilege, for projects designed from afar and premised on the presumed incapacity of regular people to understand their own conditions and needs. The insistence on the abjectness of poor populations outside the West works at once as an invitation for intervention and as the occasion for an aggrandizement of white elite reformers.

One player that has emerged as increasingly important in this arena is the Clinton Foundation, founded by former president Bill Clinton after he left office in 2001, which is involved in a diverse range of projects around the globe. The foundation has raised hundreds of millions of dollars for projects related to health, education, and agriculture (Clinton Foundation, 2016b). In education, it has been involved in global literacy projects, leadership development, youth mentoring, and other initiatives. This global work is organized in an entrepreneurial frame, oriented around notions of "empowerment," "change," and "commitment," and starting from such basic principles as: "There is always a way to be faster, leaner, and better" (Clinton Foundation, 2016a). An example of this orientation in the educational arena is the foundation's Banking on Education initiative, which provides loans through Opportunity International (a microfinance organization) to entrepreneurs to open private schools in poor regions of the world, tying philanthropy to so-called social enterprise (Ball, 2012). As the Clinton Foundation (and its signature Clinton Global Initiative program) has rapidly expanded, it has been pointed out that Bill and Hillary Clinton have personally benefited from generous speaking fees (totaling many millions of dollars)—even as they are invited to address audiences on the foundation's charitable work (Farenthold, Hamburger, & Helderman, 2015).

The Clinton Foundation has a strong focus on work in Africa and Latin America. Its website prominently features images of the smiling Clintons next to Brown and Black faces from all over the world. Cheerful beneficiaries of the foundation's good work from Haiti, Peru, Kenya, El Salvador, and elsewhere appear in its many photos and videos. However, this imagery and the accompanying narratives do less to educate us about the social context of communities than to advertise the achievements of the foundation and the Clintons themselves. Much of the glow that emanates from these carefully produced materials depends precisely on the racial "optics" that operate barely below the surface: The *brightness* (whiteness) of global philanthropy's good work is magnified here precisely by the Blackness of the global communities that are its beneficiaries. The thrill of assistance that is felt in such initiatives is proportional to the presumed abjectness of the recipients of aid—an abjectness that is crucially signified by race. There is a double circuit of excitement that works through these new global projects of generosity: on the one hand, the same promise of hard *results* and *return* that one finds in investment fund prospectuses, and on the other hand, the enjoyment of a transaction with the distant and destitute, a transaction that promises to redeem the sin of privilege while at the same time reinforcing whiteness' global position of mastery.

This dynamic is reproduced across the literature and online presences of wealthy foundations. Thus, Goldman Sachs introduced its 10,000 Women educational initiative, which provided training in management and funding to aspiring businesswomen around the world, with the smiling faces and heartwarming stories of recipients from Nigeria, Kenya, and India, and the observation that "Entrepreneurship is all about perseverance, about believing enough to withstand anything and everything that comes your way" (Goldman Sachs, 2016). In the life narratives of the beneficiaries, Goldman Sachs' initiative is figured as the singular turning point. Extrapolating from Hartman (1997), we ought to look past the surface of such carefully crafted communications to observe the way that "these scenes of enjoyment provide an opportunity for white self-reflection" (p. 34) while working to transform struggle "into a conspicuous, and apparently convincing, display of contentment" (p. 35). Furthermore, in such contemporary displays elites seek audaciously to symbolically appropriate the resilience itself of communities who are injured by the very global systems of exploitation and marginalization that these elites command.

In this way, neoliberal gestures of care and aid, as much as systems of domination, serve to exalt the powerful and insist on the incapacity of the marginalized. Likewise, the celebration of the good deeds that neoliberal reform and philanthropy accomplish covertly affirms Hayek's apology for global inequality: "There can be little doubt that the prospect of the poorer, 'undeveloped' countries reaching the present level of the West is very much better than it would have been, had the West not pulled so far ahead" (2011, p. 100). This "so far ahead" is a judgment not only on material conditions but also on racial and civilizational progress. This judgment reappears in the present in the discursive presentation of the Global South as culturally paralyzed and perpetually waiting on aid. The smiling faces that look out from the brochures and websites of global philanthropic foundations indicate an ideological system in which Black and Brown people can only be imagined as forever grateful to be rescued from the inescapable "death-in-life" that whiteness understands as defining existence outside of the West (Mbembe, 2003).

Conclusion

I have argued in this chapter that the emphasis on privatization and marketization in neoliberal education reform is connected to a basic commitment to privilege. Privilege, in the deep structure of the neoliberal ethos, is identified with virtue. In Hayek (2011), this is an explicit philosophical position; in contemporary neoliberalism, it works generally as a covert premise of reform. In neoliberalism, the elites who possess and command privilege, in both its material and symbolic forms, are understood to have a natural authority or epistemic advantage in questions of public policy. The virtue of this authority, when it is expressed in the philanthropic work of wealthy foundations, is amplified even further. The initiatives of such foundations, even as they ultimately pursue the interests of business rather than ordinary people, acquire a powerful aura in the media and in official narratives—an aura that serves to exalt these foundations and the elite individuals who run them. This is perhaps especially the case in education, in which the targets for reform are young people, whose vulnerability constitutes the perfect backdrop for the spectacular initiatives of neoliberal compassion.

In fact, neoliberal educational reform disregards and injures local communities. The specific structure of this injury, I have argued, has to be understood in terms of racial politics—and in particular through a consideration of the historic erasure of the subjectivity and agency of Black people by white elites (Hartman, 1997; Wilderson, 2010). This foundational anti-Blackness works in the neoliberal era as a crucial condition for reform, giving it its specific shape and character in both the United States and global contexts. Privatization, charterization, and marketization in education start from assumptions about the incapacity of students, parents, and communities of color (Dixson et al., 2015). Furthermore, as I have described, the racial gradient of the landscape of neoliberal care, in which white foundations, agencies, and individuals explicitly target communities of color, operates as the essential platform of reform narratives.

My analysis of the ideological structure of neoliberal faith in elite reform explains why a supposedly "results-oriented" system is unfazed by its own persistent failures. Even as neoliberal efforts in education fail to improve school conditions, opportunities, and even narrowly measured student achievement (De Lissovoy, Means, & Saltman, 2014), policymakers and philanthropists are unshaken in their commitment to competitive market models of teaching and learning. Even as challenges rise up from the grassroots, as students and parents protest against school closures, test-based accountability, and attacks on teachers, though elites may recalibrate their messaging they do not abandon their faith in their own incontrovertible good sense. The champions of disastrous reform efforts generally move forward along their political trajectories untainted by a reckoning with the destruction they have caused. Similar patterns are visible outside of education: as the Black Lives Matter movement in the United States has aggressively pressed a reckoning with racist police violence to the center of the public conversation, (neo)liberal elite politicians have maneuvered to place themselves next to the parents of those who have been killed while still refusing any fundamental rethinking of policies around law enforcement and criminal justice. In education and beyond, as the neoliberal vision increasingly diverges from reality, the glossiness of new initiatives in entrepreneurship, new public-private partnerships, and new journalistic and academic discourses that repackage familiar assumptions serves to distract attention from the deterioration of conditions on the ground and the increasing anger of communities.

My analysis suggests that neoliberalism's elite rationale needs to be interrupted rather than just interrogated, and that the violence of its putative compassion needs to be denounced. We should encourage and support the many ongoing efforts by community members, activists, and scholars to do just that. In addition, the argument I have elaborated here suggests that the symbolic economy of neoliberal reform is just as important to attend to as the material one. The material disruption and degradation of public schooling that contemporary reform produces are premised on a set understandings, discourses, and images that works powerfully to demonstrate, in the public mind, the superiority of the standpoint of the elite. In this system, the principles of acquiescence to inequality and submission to whiteness are unspoken touchstones—if it is a scandal to speak them out loud, they nevertheless silently secure the validity of the rationality of neoliberal care. Against this system's condescension, we need true community control of education; against its market fantasies, we need a process of engagement in schools that starts from the actual needs of people. And in all of these efforts we need to think from the bottom up, against elite reason, even if that sounds like impudence and unreason to those whose unreflective intuition currently rules the day.

Note

1   It is important to note that while there are important signs now, in the first months of the Biden administration, of provisional departures from the austerity politics of preceding administrations, so far the neoliberal consensus that governs education policy and curriculum (and the philosophical framework underwriting it), the roots of which run very deep as I describe, has not been interrupted.

4

Repression, Violation, and Education

The power (and scandal) of critical theory is its indictment of what is good and true—its discovery of a domination that is the content of the norm and the normal. Critical theory traces histories of violence in the laws, technological innovations, and cultural forms that modernity celebrates. In this regard, it extrapolates from Marx's uncovering of the process of exploitation that constitutes the kernel of capitalist production and development. On the other hand, critical theory points to a collective guilt and repressive drive that precede capitalism itself, but which are systematized and massified in the context of industrialization. Critical theory crucially exposes the hidden determinations of social structures and experiences. In its refusal of what is sanctified as right and reasonable—in fact as reason itself—critical theory opens up indispensable vectors of investigation and intellectual struggle. At the same time, I believe that in this effort, it often overlooks the determinative force of drives and processes, within the context of colonialism, that are *oriented toward the exterior* rather than the interior of modernity, and which inaugurate the latter as a logic of imposition. In this chapter, I consider how central starting points in critical theory can be rethought in this regard, and I explore the implications of this rethinking for education. Having described the racial logic of contemporary school reform in the last chapter, here I circle back to contextualize race and repression in my broader consideration of coloniality (opened in Chapter 2), the implications of which reach beyond policy to pedagogy itself.

For this investigation, Herbert Marcuse's work is especially interesting as an exemplar of critical theory, focusing as it does on the concrete and contemporary cultural and political expressions of domination, and on the ongoing contest between forces of repression and forces of liberation. In this regard, Marcuse shares critical pedagogy's interest in methodologies of emancipation as well as the latter's focus on culture, identity, and understanding as terrains of struggle. Marcuse's work illuminates the psychic, material, aesthetic, political, discursive, and philosophical dimensions of alienation and repression in contemporary society. Particularly relevant for my investigation in this chapter is Marcuse's investigation of the connections between psychic/libidinal structures of repression and political/economic ones. He explores the curious identification between the level of the individual (ontogeny) and the level of the "genus" or social collective (phylogeny) with regard to experiences of injury, guilt, and rage—an identification that is central to the notion of *violation* that I elaborate later in this chapter. In his arguments, Marcuse presses against received boundaries of psychoanalysis, political economy, and sociology.

In *Eros and Civilization* (1955), which is his most relevant text for my purposes, Marcuse undertakes a critical reading of Freud in which he develops the grim social and political implications of the latter's work while also reading him against the grain to uncover persistent impulses to liberation in psyche and society. Marcuse argues that the individual and collective repression of the instincts (the *reality principle*), which Freud argues is the precondition for civilization proper, becomes in modernity a systematic and social process, in which repression functions to preserve the power of elites. In this process, Freud's reality principle becomes identified with a capitalist *performance principle* that transforms labor into a virtue and an inevitability. The aggressive and erotic instincts that are sublimated into the work of culture, according to Freud, in Marcuse's account animate the exploitation and destructiveness of the contemporary administered society, even as the technological innovations of this society in principle progressively liberate human beings from the need to work and to suffer. Ultimately, against Freud's insistence on the civilizational necessity of repression, Marcuse argues that the life-affirming and productive power of Eros can be unchained and come to ground a non-repressive and free society.

The most important theoretical innovation of his work, in this context, is Marcuse's notion of *surplus-repression*. Marcuse distinguishes this process from the "basic" repression of the instincts that Freud argues is required for the development of culture. For Marcuse (1955), "the specific historical institutions of the reality principle and the specific interests of domination introduce *additional* controls over and above those indispensable for civilized human association" (p. 37). Marcuse contrasts the historical nature of surplus-repression with the primordial character of the modification of the instincts described by Freud:

> In introducing the term *surplus-repression* we have focused the discussion on the institutions and relations that constitute the social "body" of the reality

principle. These do not just represent the changing external manifestations of one and the same reality principle but actually change the reality principle itself. (Marcuse, 1955, p. 44)

The specific form of the reality principle varies along with the specific history and structure of the society in question. In societies organized on the basis of the division and exploitation of labor, in which work becomes alienated, surplus-repression works to restrict the libido and organize consciousness such that this alienation appears as an objective and rational law, and such that controlled and constrained desire appears as normal and natural. What we call "work" in the present—the *daily grind*—is the site of exactly this quotidian alienation and constraint. The important point, for Marcuse, is that the social organization of repression is not an unchanging and "natural" consequence of the need to manage the biological instincts but rather always a historically specific and fundamentally cultural structure.

Ironically, as technological development potentially makes possible greater freedom and multiplies the possibilities for the constructive and liberatory investment of libido (as a result of automation, medicine, and other developments), surplus-repression must intensify in order to support the performance principle and the alienated society organized around it. It is important to note that repression for Marcuse is not always coercive in a simple sense; rather, it is a process of restriction and rearticulation in which "the organism must be trained for its alienation at its very roots" (1955, p. 47) in accordance with the demands of the reality principle. In comparison with Freud's account of repression, then, Marcuse's account of surplus-repression emphasizes its *excessiveness* (vis-à-vis the instinctual repression necessary for cultural development in the first instance), its historical *autonomy* (vis-à-vis organic psychic forces), and its *irrationality* (with respect to the liberatory potential of social development that it seeks to forestall). While Marcuse's reading initially follows Freud in retracing the "biological" roots of social domination in the primary repression of the instincts, in the second moment of his analysis he inverts Freud's schema, demonstrating that the historical development of society as domination then works in turn, and *for its own purposes*, to reorder the very economy of desire that for Freud is the unchanging substrate of culture.

A crucial effect of the historical dynamic described by Marcuse is that domination shifts from being a central instrument of the powerful to becoming, in industrial capitalism, coextensive with society: domination becomes this society's very form and content. (As Marx [1973, p. 460] puts it in relation to the development of capital itself, "These presuppositions, which originally appeared as conditions of its becoming . . . now appear as results of its own realization.") Thus, not only does capitalism work to naturalize alienation and exploitation; in addition, production becomes itself a means of control of dangerous libidinal energy. Likewise, leisure and its pursuits are managed and massified. In fact, Marcuse (1964) elsewhere describes a process of "repressive desublimation," in which the loosening of prohibitions on sexuality, as well as transgressive cultural expressions, allow for a "liberation" of the personality that actually binds desire even more tightly to the matrix of the performance principle, since these transgressions do not challenge the basic alienation and reification of culture and subjectivity. (Consumerism, the culture industry, and middle-class counter-cultural forms are examples of this repressive liberation.)

For Marcuse, then, in the first place, domination in contemporary society cannot be separated from production: *capitalist production is destructive in its very productivity*. Second, domination cannot quite be said to operate upon a preexisting subject, since the sense and shape of that subject (the self) only emerges in and through the historical context of repression. So not only does domination act deeply and intimately within the person; it also functions to organize persons in the first place:

> This state of ossification also affects the instincts, their inhibitions and modifications. Their original dynamic becomes static: the interactions between ego, superego, and id congeal into automatic reactions. Corporealization of the super-ego is accompanied by corporealization of the ego, manifest in the frozen traits and gestures, produced at the appropriate occasions and hours. (1955, p. 103)

Marcuse exposes a fundamental alienation at the roots of both necessity and freedom in contemporary society, a kind of impossibility that lives within our very habits and personalities, our pains and our pleasures. As Pierce (2013) notes, Marcuse is interested in how being itself is organized in capitalism. Indeed, we might say that Marcuse exposes an ontological violence that simultaneously produces and destroys, makes and unmakes.

Marcuse's account implicitly challenges any perspective, including in education, that sees an uncomplicated path to freedom. Nevertheless, his reframing of repression as an essentially political and historical problem makes it possible to imagine (against Freud) a liberation of Eros that is not incompatible with culture. In fact, one central purpose of *Eros and Civilization* is to show the traces of this possibility in Freud's work itself, to the extent that

Freud's analysis—as well as psychoanalysis and memory-work more broadly—preserves and brings to light repressed promises and potentialities in the individual and society. Marcuse argues that the tension between a conservative impulse to renunciation on the one hand and a fundamental drive for freedom and fulfillment on the other runs through the history of Western thought, even as this tradition tends ultimately to collapse into an affirmation of domination. The challenge is to refuse that surrender, and to stand on the side of Eros and liberation against the unnecessary suffering that engulfs humanity: "With its striving for eternity, Eros offends against the decisive taboo that sanctions libidinal pleasure only as a temporal and controlled condition, not as a permanent fountainhead of the human existence" (1955, p. 234).

Marcuse's hopefulness and emancipatory vision have influenced critical pedagogy through the work of Freire and others (e.g., Giroux, 2001), and yet the specificity of his account of domination, and the difficulties it implies, are too often glossed over. While he preserves a dialectical sense of contradiction and contention, the antagonists of the struggle he traces do not stand rigidly apart from each other. As in the work of his Frankfurt School fellow-travelers (see especially Horkheimer & Adorno, 2002), Marcuse shows how the apparently liberatory may repeat a profounder repression, and how the subjective and objective grounds of critique and struggle may be already captured and alienated. In this context, any methodology of liberation has to be thoughtful, careful, and *ambitious*—in order to be able to properly investigate the actual and obscure origin of domination.

Rethinking Marcuse from the Perspective of the "Periphery"

Marcuse undertakes an immanent critique of Freud's work, showing how it betrays its own central insights and emancipatory impulses. Similarly, I argue, Marcuse's ideas need to be pressed beyond the limits imposed by his own method and standpoint—which is at the same time to argue for a kind of translation or transposition of his ideas, in which they come to rest on a different foundation. In *Eros and Civilization*, Marcuse detaches the antagonism between the pleasure principle and the reality principle from the confines of the narrowly psychic and traces the operation of the reality principle as a historical and social process of domination. He shows that this process constitutes the inner logic of capitalism's administered society. However, domination retains in Marcuse a particular instrumentality tied to its role in Freud's philosophical anthropology and the battle of the instincts underlying it. Thus, Marcuse's account of surplus-repression extrapolates Freud's description of a basic and primordial repression of the instincts. This link limits the usefulness of Marcuse's analysis of domination, even if the continuity between the psychic and the social in his account remains central. In other words, the notion of surplus-repression moves the struggle of the instincts to a different stage and gives the story a more ominous shading, but the *form* of the drama remains essentially the same. In addition, Marcuse reproduces the inward-facing orientation of Freud's narrative, in which the struggle between domination and emancipation is assumed to belong essentially to Western culture and history. This makes it impossible for Marcuse to see the centrality of colonial reason in the operation of domination and the impact of coloniality broadly on the structure and meaning of repression itself.

Marcuse's demonstration of the intimacy between violence and production (both economic and cultural) illuminates the organization of power globally. However, the story of civilizational progress which frames his account constrains his argument and his understanding of the nature of the *surplus* in surplus-repression, as I will describe. Confronting Marcuse's account with analyses of domination developed from the perspective of the Global South reveals different itineraries for repression, reality principle, and Eros itself, and recasts the temporality of these processes beyond the Western dialectic of myth and enlightenment described by the Frankfurt School. In addition, juxtaposing Marcuse's account with perspectives that have witnessed up close the genocide that inaugurates modernity suggests a different analysis of the "civilizational" logic of the West. Such perspectives also shift the ground for critical philosophy, showing that it must be explicitly and immediately an ethical project, since it is through the commitment to witness that the structure of reality can become visible (Menchú, 1984).

The concept of *surplus-repression* in *Eros and Civilization* refers to the extra violence—beyond that minimally required to suppress the instincts and to allow for the development of culture—that dominant classes and institutions produce to secure their continued power, even (and especially) when increasing productivity should theoretically allow for a lessening of repression and for progressive liberation from the performance principle. It is important to highlight two aspects of this concept here: (1) "surplus" in Marcuse's formulation is defined relative to the baseline of a culturally necessary degree of repression (in accordance with Freud); (2) domination as *repression* evokes a force aimed above all at holding down or keeping back rebellious impulses. Thus, even as he challenges the lack of distinction in Freud between the primary repression required for the development of the ego and the historical repression that transforms the reality principle into a principle for protecting particular societies and their ruling classes, Marcuse's account refers back to Freud's anthropology. His account emphasizes, like Freud's, the *functionality* of repression (even if this functionality is now political rather than biological or cultural).

Marcuse's (1955) account seeks to trace these processes from the stage of earliest civilization through to contemporary Western industrial society, in which they are symptomatically hidden by the culture of work (capitalist productivism) and the work of culture (the culture industry). However, firsthand accounts of the birth of Western modernity in and through the experience of colonization challenge this analysis of social domination, even as they also, like Marcuse, underline the centrality of domination in the production of modern society, politics, and subjectivity. Considering the writings of Guaman Poma de Ayala and Bartolomé de Las Casas, I argue here that the excessiveness of repression that Marcuse describes has to be understood, in the context of colonial violence, as more than instrumental. In this shift in perspective, events that were diminished or invisible in Marcuse's account—including genocide, enslavement, and cultural erasure—now loom large. While the truth always looks different from different perspectives, this shift shows that the standpoint of the "periphery" is a stronger foundation from which to elaborate an account of modernity and globality.

Guaman Poma, a seventeenth-century Quechua political theorist, in his treatise *El primer nueva corónica y buen gobierno*, condemned the crimes of the Spanish in Peru in moral and religious terms, building an argument that the Indigenous people rather than the colonizers were the true Christians. Contrasting their virtue with the hubris and cruelty of the Spaniards, he writes:

> See here, you poor, foolish, and incompetent Spaniards, who are as proud as Lucifer: Luzbel became Lucifer, the great devil. You are the same as he. . . . You yearn to be more than what God decreed you should be. If you are not kings, why do you yearn to be kings? (2006, p. 144)

Guaman Poma, throughout his work, exposes the lust for power at the center of the West's "civilizing" projects. Likewise, in *Brevísima relación de la destrucción de las Indias*, Las Casas, a sixteenth-century missionary and critic of Spanish colonialism, vividly described the prolific and pervasive violence of the Spanish in the Americas. He shows that this violence was excessive as a matter of principle, extending beyond a repression aimed simply at securing ruling interests. The colonizers' destruction of Indigenous people in Las Casas' account operates according to a necropolitics (Mbembe, 2003) that makes a virtue of assault:

> First, they have waged war on [the Native peoples]: unjust, cruel, bloody and tyrannical war. Second, they have murdered anyone and everyone who has shown the slightest sign of resistance, or even of wishing to escape the torment to which they have subjected him. (Las Casas, 1992, pp. 12–13)

Las Casas' account registers the outrage of invasion through a moral language of denunciation, describing the evil and treachery of the Spanish attacks. From Las Casas' perspective, far from securing the production of culture, even in an alienated form, this violence destroyed the possibility even of the colonial religious mission to which he remained faithful: "The only rights these perfidious crusaders have earned which can be upheld in human, divine, or natural law are the right to eternal damnation and the right to answer for the offences and the harm they have done the Spanish Crown" (1992, pp. 53–4).

These accounts describe a logic of domination that is different from that described by Marcuse. For Marcuse, building from Freud, repression is the instrument that crucially produces self and society, even if these are distorted by the systematization of guilt and the industrialization of culture. By contrast, Guaman Poma and Las Casas reveal the colonial logic of subjection of Indigenous people which inaugurates modernity. In contrast to Marcuse's uncovering of the *hidden* domination that determines the values of modernity, they narrate a violence that is *overt*, and more than disciplinary. Guaman Poma describes the terrors of the quicksilver mines, where "the poor Indians are so harshly punished, where they are tortured and so many Indians die; it is there that the noble *caciques* of the kingdom are finished off" (2006, p. 179). Marcuse's surplus-repression is turned inside-out in this context, becoming a *surplus-assault* that establishes an external order of truth rather than seeking to master Eros internally. This violence is not simply a collective discharge of destructive instincts at the global margins, a by-product of the rationalization of repression in the European metropole, as Marcuse's analysis would suggest. Such an interpretation ignores the spiritual and historical agency of the Indigenous people of the Americas, and the impact of their *survivance* (Vizenor, 1994) on the meaning of conquest and modernity itself. Challenging the surplus-assault of colonialism, the testimonies of Guaman Poma and Las Casas assert the dignity and humanity of the colonized, and implicitly demand at the same time that this humanity be prioritized at the level of social and philosophical analysis.

I do not believe that reckoning with the forms of violence produced by colonialism means that we should abandon Western critical theory's effort to conceptualize the systematic logic of domination in modernity. However, this reckoning presses us beyond the dialectical and inward-looking schema of this tradition (as Dussel, 1985, and Fanon, 1963, show). Marcuse identifies important processes that work across global contexts; if we begin from the standpoint I have outlined in this section, his categories can perhaps be usefully rearticulated. Thus, Marcuse argues that the ultimate content of the technological and cultural accomplishments of industrial society is a kind of injury, and he shows this society to be alienated at its core. However, considering the context of colonial racism reveals a different kind of injury and a different kind of production built upon it. In this context, the work of progress and "culture" is more perverse and irrational than critical theory has imagined. And "civilization," as colonialism and occupation, collaborates more intimately with capitalism than critical theory usually supposes, as Grande (2004) points out. Guaman Poma writes: "The Spanish Christians . . . imagine everything plated in silver and gold, and that they will have riches. They think of it day and night, both husband and wife" (2006, p. 195). There is no philosophical redemption for this obsession. Even as colonial violence inaugurates modernity, its contingency and criminality cannot be seen as the natural result of any primordial historical dialectic.

Marcuse argues that the performance principle, in which "body and mind are made into instruments of alienated labor" (1955, p. 46), is the historically concrete form of the reality principle—which comes into its mature expression within capitalism. From this perspective, the colonial plunder of the non-Western world can be seen as deriving from the economic imperative to accumulation, to the extent that the appropriation of resources in colonialism supported the development of Western society. (This is precisely the argument that Marx [1867/1976] makes in his analysis of "primitive accumulation" as the material foundation for early capitalist manufactures.) The same historical process, however, looks different in Guaman Poma's and Las Casas' accounts. For Las Casas, the greed of the colonizers suggests a demonic cosmology in which gold has become God; it is less a matter of *accumulation* per se and more a matter of *plunder*. Similarly, Guaman Poma describes the monstrous voracity of the Spanish, as encountered by the Incas: "Wayna Capac asked the Spaniard what was it that he ate. He replied in the language of the Spaniards and by signs, pointing at things, that he ate gold and silver" (2006, p. 103). For the most part the wealth captured by the colonizers made its way through Spain to fuel the emerging Northern European economies, as Galeano (1973) recounts.

But to only understand the process of "primitive accumulation" and plunder in terms of its endpoint is to neglect the meaning of its first moment—it is to emphasize the *stomach* of capitalist manufacturing and to de-emphasize the *mouth* of invasion. Marcuse's performance principle by itself cannot grasp this complex phenomenology in which colonial violence is not only for the sake of seamless accumulation.

Considering the specific context of settler colonialism is helpful here, even if there are differences in relation to the colonial societies that Guaman Poma and Las Casas described. Settler colonialism, like the system of violation analyzed by Guaman Poma, operates not simply as a brutal expedient toward the goal of establishing a foundation for accumulation in "mature" capitalism, but rather according to its own logic and *settler grammar* (Goeman, 2014) which determines the legibility or illegibility of Indigenous peoples in relation to land, body, and spirit. As a grammar or articulated system of meaning, settler colonialism retells the world in its own terms and proposes annexation as necessary and virtuous (Calderon, 2014). In this context, the gold and silver in Guaman Poma's narrative might be seen as a metonym for the land itself. As Wolfe (2006) describes, while the seizure of the land serves the interest of capitalism and the state, it is usually undertaken in the first instance by an irregular and extra-legal "frontier rabble." Naked greed in this context collaborates in the first place above all with a project of elimination of Indigenous peoples and sovereignty rather than in service of the progressive and even development of capitalism and its performance principle.

In this context, liberation is more than a matter of setting Eros free, a fulfillment in which being can finally be in and for itself. Marcuse seeks to rescue the dream of liberation from Western philosophy's surrender to pessimistic realism (Freud's foregrounding of the reality principle) and idealism (Hegel's vision of reconciliation within the Idea itself). But Fanon (1967a) and Wynter (2006) show that in the colonial encounter, the racialized Other is made to lack even ontological consistency; the Eros of the West can only misrecognize or assimilate it. Therefore, liberation cannot simply mean uncovering the truth beneath the alienation of the administered society. Rather, the assaulted and erased truth of the colonized has first to assert itself again—and to be reconstituted in this assertion, as Wynter (2006) shows in relation to the discipline of Black Studies. In this way, we shift the ground of Eros, reimagining who it is that might love and be loved. The testimony of Guaman Poma and Las Casas is distinct from the return of the repressed that Marcuse envisions; this testimony is rather the admittance into the circle of truth of that which has been discounted: "Look,

Christian reader . . . the shadowy understanding [the Incas] had of the Creator *was no small thing*" (Guaman Poma, 2006, p. 28; italics added). Marcuse refuses to capitulate to the renunciation and bad faith that runs through Western philosophy, but his analysis of the possibility of liberation needs to pass through the historical prism of coloniality. In this context, liberation must take the ontologically and historically specific form of decolonization (Coulthard, 2014; Wynter, 2006).

Conceptualizing Domination: From Alienation to Violation

Critical theory begins from a belief that in order to struggle against oppression and injustice, we need to understand their inner logic. In this chapter, I start from Marcuse in working to understand the structure of domination, but in this effort the very meaning of structure is called into question. In tracing the logic of domination that I call *violation*, I build from the foundation offered by Marcuse while also challenging it through a consideration of colonial violence; the result is an inversion or reimagination of Marcuse's dialectical narrative. Even as he confronts Freud's ahistoricism, Marcuse develops his analysis of contemporary society through a story that at least notionally ties this society's contradictions to an originary struggle at the heart of culture between the impulses of repression and liberation. In this account, even as repression is institutionalized and technologized in the modern period, it expresses a historical reason that emerges at the interior of culture and develops through a series of interior negations (as the struggle at the instinctual level is transformed into a properly social process): "Domination becomes increasingly impersonal, objective, universal, and also increasingly rational, effective, productive" (Marcuse, 1955, p. 89). And yet, if we locate the colonial encounter at the center of the history and meaning of modernity, we have to reckon with the primacy of the condition of *exteriority* (Dussel, 1985)—with regard on the one hand to the Western construction of the non-Western world as unintelligible *Other* and on the other hand with regard to the experience of interruption and *imposition* that colonialism has produced for non-Western peoples.

Marcuse understands domination as ultimately inward-turning, since it arises from a need in the first instance to exorcise the guilt of desire and the impulse to emancipation. In domination as repression, the community turns against itself, and even society's external aggressions represent forms of instinctual release that derive from this primal dynamic. Marcuse's exposure of the basic link between Western cultural and technological development and violence is crucial, and yet his account ignores the centrality to modernity of exteriority (colonized peoples and lands) as a structuring principle. In order to understand modernity's particular violence, we need to consider it "analectically" (Dussel, 1985)—that is to say, as referring to and depending on an irreducible *outside* which, in its very externality, at the same determines the logic of the interior. In addition, against the tendency of critical theory to understand domination as the effect of a totalizing and internal dialectic, we should recognize, as Dussel puts it, that ultimately "every person, every group or people, is always situated 'beyond' (*ano-*) the horizon of totality" (1985, p. 158). That is, even as power seeks to occupy every outside (and every psychic region), persons and peoples, as such, remain ultimately uncaptured.

An account that builds from the analyses of Guaman Poma and Las Casas should recognize the radical contingency of modernity as an effect of the colonial encounter, and the impossibility of understanding it in terms of a primordial or universal process of cultural development. Furthermore, if Marcuse's dialectical analysis is unable to comprehend the structure of colonial violence, this argues for an approach to this structure from the standpoint of ethics (Maldonado-Torres, 2008). To the extent that the development of the West depended on a process that both consolidated and violated a civilizational Other, then the question of ethics should be at the heart even of political-economic investigations of modernity. In rethinking Marcuse's notion of surplus-repression in terms of surplus-assault, we can consider the colonizers' brutality (exposed by Guaman Poma and Las Casas) in the context of structure. The systematic organization of colonial violence in this sense "functions" not just in the service of accumulation of power and capital but also ontologically to separate and exalt the West as against its colonized Other and Exterior. I use the term *violation* to name the intertwining of repression and assault in modernity, and therefore of political and ethical processes and problems. Violation, in this sense, refers to a spiritual violence connected to the materiality of domination, a complex process of subjection (Hartman, 1997) that works beyond the imperative of merely securing elite power.

On this basis, in relation to the colonial context, we should rethink Marcuse's performance principle. Recognizing the widespread exploitation of Indigenous communities in the Americas through forced labor in the colonial period up to the present means reconceptualizing the performance principle to include the experience of colonial terror at the edges of production (Menchú, 1984). This condition shows up in the present in the economic exclusion of racialized, immigrant, and refugee groups globally (Balibar, 2002). Crucial to Marcuse's explanation of the performance principle is the idea that it extends the moral and libidinal command to labor beyond the degree that is socially necessary. This domination is "exercised by a particular group or individual in order to sustain and enhance itself in a privileged position. Such domination does not exclude technical, material, and intellectual progress, but only as an unavoidable by-product while preserving irrational scarcity, want, and constraint" (1955, pp. 36–7). However, contemporary conditions of superexploitation, permanent unemployment, and mass incarceration, all of which are complex legacies of the early history of racial capitalism (Davis, 2005), arguably expose a performance principle that works beyond even the *political* necessity that Marcuse foregrounds. These ongoing exclusions, which paradoxically press the condition of marginalization to the center of contemporary capitalism's logic, reveal the basic compulsion for power to reproduce, in the present, the condition of economic and ethical violation that is central to coloniality.

Critical theory exposes the scene of alienation that is hidden beneath the happy surface of consumer capitalism. Indeed, for Marcuse, even evasions of and rebellions against the status quo are often themselves captured by the deep logic of the performance principle. He argues that "repressive desublimation" (Marcuse, 1964) allows for the expression of aggressive and sexual impulses in ways that were previously taboo (in popular culture and private life) but that even these expressions ultimately accommodate subjects to the underlying terms of the given and betray Eros as emancipatory desire. However, this account assumes a basic ontological integrity for social subjects (e.g., the worker or the consumer) as well as a universal condition of alienation in which they are enveloped in modernity. An analysis in terms of the process of violation, by contrast, foregrounds (1) the fragmented, ambiguous, and precarious orders of being within which the globally oppressed are allowed to become; and (2) the particular logic of injury (as opposed to mere alienation) which organizes the West's plunder and peripheralization of non-Western and nonwhite peoples.

As Quijano (2008) shows, colonial plunder and the violation of the Other proceed through a global racial system, a system that ultimately reaches into the interior of metropolitan societies in addition to the Global South. Understanding these processes means drawing on a *sociology of absences* (Santos, 2014) in order to look beyond metropolitan society to the "empty" spaces it constructs and depends on. The erased identities and experiences of non-Western peoples, in global terms, become the material and discursive ground for the privileged protagonists of critical theory (i.e., for the white consumers and workers that the alienated metropolitan society represses and exploits). Not only is the consumerism that the administered society promotes made possible by the exploitation of workers outside the core; even the distorted subjectivity of the alienated subjects of the metropole takes shape against the background of what is thought of as an inert and undifferentiated mass of non-Western peoples. Critical theory secures its image of the abundance that emancipation might realize through an expansive philosophical gesture that runs unseeingly over *other* standpoints and histories. Instead, theory needs to learn to perceive more than one dialectic and more than one register of domination, and to see that behind the *repressive* impulse at the center of Western modernity stands the *colonial* imperative (Césaire, 1955). From this more complex perspective, we can see that domination, as a global problematic, demands but also refuses, incorporates but also excludes, and alienates but also injures.

Coloniality, which begins with the colonial space and encounter proper, nevertheless shapes modernity as a whole—the "core" as much as the "periphery." Racialization, which begins with this encounter, centrally organizes the metropole, and not just in cultural or symbolic terms. Racism has been the material foundation for capitalist accumulation in North America and around the globe (Du Bois, 1935/1998). To the extent that Western society has been in this way constituted by coloniality, we cannot understand its evolution—even on its own terms, if such a formulation is possible—without understanding its Other or Exterior. And just as the center is produced out of the margins in this way, by the same token anticolonial and decolonial analysis is indispensable for carrying out even the delimited intellectual project that critical theory sets for itself in relation to Western culture. An adequate critique of the logic of capitalism and the dominative dialectic of enlightenment, including in Western educational contexts, has to start from an analysis of coloniality and has to confront the latter's planetary diffusion and impact.

This reconceptualization of domination also suggests a different view of the process of liberation. While Marcuse argues that the performance principle is rendered increasingly irrational by technological development and that the logic of scarcity connected to this principle will be replaced by a logic of abundance as humanity is freed from material necessity, a sensitivity to the process of violation at the heart of modernity suggests that emancipation must proceed equally through a process of healing (hooks, 2003). Modernity is founded on and fueled by the plunder of the (cultural, geographical, racial) periphery; overcoming domination is then not just a matter of challenging technological reason but also of reckoning with systematic violence—and of creating a horizon for *becoming differently*. Without this horizon, the collective emancipated libido that Marcuse (1955) imagines as the principle of a non-repressive society in which "socially useful work is at the same time the transparent satisfaction of an individual need" (pp. 209–10) will itself become the agent of violent assimilation of the Other. By contrast, a decolonizing Eros, committed against violation, will allow for and respect assertions of difference and autonomy on the field of politics and identity (Alcoff, 2006), as well as supporting the processes of confrontation and dialogue that must be the basis of any non-repressive solidarity.

Education: Injury, Exteriority, and Emancipation

The point of the foregoing analysis is not to reject Marcuse or critical theory more broadly but rather to rearticulate their central ideas within a broader conceptual horizon. Indeed, the specific understanding of domination that I have outlined in this chapter comes out of the confrontation between a Marcusean critical framework and a specific set of anticolonial/decolonial analyses. In the process, Marcuse's notions of (surplus-) repression, performance principle, alienation, and liberation are transposed and inverted. In this shift, *discontinuities* are exposed in critical theory's ostensibly continuous categories of subjectivity and history. Simultaneously, through this analysis we can get a better grasp of the underlying and *complex continuity* across time and space of the libidinal economy that lies at the heart of capitalism and coloniality.

Education is a crucial site in which to investigate this economy. Oriented to growth and formation, education centrally participates in the dialectic that brings together culture and control, as Marcuse's account describes. At the same time, historical processes of demoralization and exclusion in schooling globally point to a colonial logic that works beyond the condition of alienation. All of these processes have been described as separate strands of educational experience. I believe, however, that the framework that I have set out in this chapter can allow us to make sense of them together and to understand their common determination and purpose. In this section, I develop this analysis through a consideration of several contemporary moments—in theory and practice—that have been central to investigations in (and projects of) critical education.

Progressive Pedagogy and the Politics of "Empowerment"

Within educator circles and teacher education programs, if not always within official policies and standards, there is widespread acceptance of constructivism and criticality as guiding principles for teaching. Indeed, these principles could be called hegemonic among North American education professionals. In university schools of education, there is near universal disdain for reductionistic and authoritarian modes of pedagogy and curriculum, and broad recognition of the necessity for progressive and culturally relevant education. At the same time, these same institutions are reluctant to take concrete actions that would actually impede longstanding processes of stratification and carceralization in schools. In this regard, educational researchers and university-based teacher education demonstrate a consistent bad faith, as they insist on "inclusion" without seriously confronting endemic processes of oppression in schools. In short, liberal calls for progressive pedagogy do not reckon precisely with the ways that Marcuse's surplus-repression (e.g., as structural racism) and performance principle (e.g., as punitive assessment and accountability) work through education—even in progressive and constructivist classrooms.

However, even genuinely *critical* forms of teaching need to more directly confront the depth of injury experienced by Indigenous students and students of color. These experiences are different from familiar processes of stratification and alienation in schools, reaching to the level of being itself (Brown, 2018). My rearticulation in this chapter of Marcuse's arguments highlights the excess and irrationality, with respect even to the logic of social reproduction, of social domination. Education for "empowerment" that does not confront this reality amounts to little more than a distraction. The notion of *banking education* developed by Freire (1996), which refers to an authoritarian and dehumanizing pedagogy that cannot recognize the voice and knowledge of students, is a crucial tool in this work, which has been widely taken up in teacher education. However, I believe we need to develop our conceptual vocabulary beyond this starting point, since the authoritarianism of banking education may not comprehend other modes of control. Even progressive forms of pedagogy can also insidiously control and normalize (Bourassa, 2019). On the other hand, Freire's (1996) insistence on the importance of challenging the paternalism and "false generosity" that constructs marginalized populations as "need[ing] to be 'integrated,' 'incorporated' into the healthy society that they have 'forsaken'" (p. 55) sometimes forgets the ways that power also *refuses* and violates. After all, even pedagogy that is committed to unveiling the oppressiveness of dominant ideologies can exclude students at the level of their ways of being and knowing.

My reading of Marcuse suggests an analysis of disempowerment that looks beyond the petrification produced by banking education. My analysis allows us to see, beyond the authoritarianism that works to "minimize or annul the students' creative power and to stimulate their credulity" (Freire, 1996, p. 54), the way that mainstream education in both the global North and South also refuses and marginalizes populations, producing a disposability that is different from the effect of control per se. Even moments of educational "growth" take place within this context. Thus, even in educational environments oriented to project-based and student-centered learning, students of color in particular are simultaneously enrolled and excluded, "empowered" and demoralized, within a pedagogical experience characterized by oscillation and fragmentation rather than simple alienation (De Lissovoy, 2012). These dynamics proceed from a process of *surplus-assault* (as I have reframed Marcuse's *surplus-repression*) that secures the integrity of the colonial center, in ontological and epistemological terms, against its excluded and fragmented Other.

Racialization is a central process across contexts, in a way that progressive education does not always emphasize. On the other hand, in contrast to the analysis of many Northern race-critical accounts, the notion of violation places racism in a multidimensional and global frame. Race is the central axis not only of educational disparity (as even liberals recognize) but also, on a global scale, of exteriority (Dussel, 1985), invisibilization (Santos, 2014), and disposability (Balibar, 2002). Critical pedagogy, in this context, cannot simply expose the political character of mainstream curriculum and instruction. It also has to start from the experiences and identities of marginalized students (that is, from what Walsh [2015] calls the "decolonial cracks" in the current moment), and it has to engage in its own principled refusal of the knowledges and ways of being that exclude them.

The Performance Principle and Neoliberal Education Reform

In addition to pressing us to look beyond a critique of alienation in pedagogical theory and practice, my reflections in this chapter also suggest a more complex understanding of contemporary school reform. Neoliberal educational policy globally has focused on privatization and charterization, choice systems, punitive accountability frameworks, and an unrelenting competition for resources and rewards. Even as global politics has taken a turn toward a more right-wing authoritarianism and national chauvinism, these neoliberal educational projects have proceeded apace. Furthermore, even as it has exposed crucial disparities in resources and access to digital technology and broadband between different communities, the disruptions caused by the Covid-19 pandemic have so far failed to fundamentally alter the neoliberal status quo in educational policy and organization.

Neoliberalism in education is often described in terms of "free-market fundamentalism," in which the human processes of teaching and learning and the subjectivities of students are quantified, calculated, and forced to justify themselves in terms of a return on investment (Saltman, 2012). Nevertheless, as many have also observed, the neoliberal ideological emphasis on efficiency and competition is also characterized by consistent bad faith, since in the competition of the educational market, the deck is stacked against less affluent schools and communities, and since even the failure on their own terms of corporate schools and initiatives (i.e., in terms of test-based measurement of achievement) does not soften the antipathy of elites toward public systems. In this connection, just as we can rethink Marcuse's *surplus-repression* in terms of a process of injury in the context of teaching, we can also rethink his *performance principle* in the context of the contradictions of neoliberal schooling.

Marcuse (1955) describes the performance principle as the historical form of the reality principle, in which the renunciation of Eros is expressed in a commandment to toil within which "body and mind are made into instruments of alienated labor" (p. 46). This commandment to toil seems at first to underlie the focus on back-to-basics instruction, "grit," and responsibility in contemporary schooling, which present themselves as a return to a virtuous discipline in education. But neoliberalism takes this commandment to work to extremes, *converting performance into performativity*, and emptying the promise of renunciation of real content (Ball, 2003). Not only are students in the present not rewarded, at the material level, with the security that compliance with the educational regime is supposed to guarantee (as the gig economy displaces stable jobs and as income disparities become increasingly stark). At the psychic level as well, the integration of the personality that is supposed to be the reward for the sacrifice demanded by the reality principle is likewise elusive, as students experience an encompassing anxiety and psychic instability (National Institute of Mental Health, 2016). In neoliberalism, in exchange for students buckling down, the reality (performance) principle fails to deliver on reality itself, offering students instead a kind of *glossy brochure*—an *image* of virtue, accomplishment, and social contribution. In school, the training of the body conceals the absence of intellectual life; at the university, the shiny credential carries behind it a mountain of debt.

Furthermore, the audit culture that pervades neoliberal schooling is part of a deeper racial project. Neoliberal reform refines this project, discovering new ways of stigmatizing communities of color (Dixson, Buras, & Jeffers, 2015). We fail to understand neoliberalism if we do not recognize the force of white supremacy within it, just as Marcuse's elaboration of Freud's notion of repression misses the decisive moment of the colonial encounter in shaping histories of violence globally. For instance, in the United States, it is overwhelmingly students of color who confront the punitive pedagogy of "no-excuses" charter schools. In this regard, too, the performance principle (which shows up in classrooms in the emphasis on individual responsibility) is emptied of even its distorted rationality, since it works to dominate students rather than to integrate them. Likewise, neoliberal education refuses non-Western and participation-based forms of learning that characterize many Indigenous communities, as Urrieta (2015) describes. In this way, neoliberal accountability retraces the partitions of coloniality and reconstructs the racial Other as Exteriority (Dussel, 1985) at the interior of the school itself.

Public Pedagogy in the Context of Crisis

In recent years, the Black Lives Matter movement has focused attention on systematic police violence against Black people. These efforts culminated in 2020 in global uprisings and protests following the murder of George Floyd by police in Minneapolis. Taylor (2020) describes how the protests against police violence, taking place in the context of the social and economic crises created by the Covid-19 pandemic, linked the issues of racism and anti-Blackness to the health and economic disparities produced by the capitalist state. In community organizations, educational institutions, and across social media, people have engaged in crucial conversations about the nature of white supremacy and state violence. Black people have interrupted casual allyship by white people in these forums (e.g., Johnson, 2020), and white people have challenged each other to confront their own whiteness and its implication in structural violence against Black people, Indigenous people, and other people of color. There are many detours in these conversations; nevertheless, they can be seen as a widespread project of collective public pedagogy and popular education. The protests themselves have also worked as a kind of uncompromising instruction for elected officials, who have found themselves struggling to keep up with a movement that is calling into question familiar assumptions regarding the indispensability of the police and the gradualism of policymaking around racial justice.

As I have described, the notion of *violation* provides a framework for challenging the inward-facing orientation of critical theory and its relegation of the problematic of colonial and racial violence to the margins of history. In the same way, the analysis I have outlined can help to foreground the revolutionary potential of the process of dialogue and movement building against state violence and white supremacy. In addition to street protests and marches, this process has included the production of position statements and petitions, efforts on social media and in workplaces to amplify the voices of Black people, study groups on antiracism, interventions in city council and official meetings, and other projects. Beginning from the ethical and political priority of uprooting white supremacy, Love (2020) argues that these projects must refuse to subordinate antiracist struggle to white liberal reformism. In addition, recognizing the centrality of racial injury within capitalism, these conversations have argued for frameworks and occasions for healing for people of color, both for individuals and as a larger political project.

The framework that I have elaborated in this chapter can also help to contextualize debates within socialist circles in the context of the recent uprisings. On the one hand, socialists have usefully challenged shallow conceptions of allyship as opposed to comradeship (Dean, 2019). It is important to understand the systematicity of racism within the broad context of class struggle. However, socialist pedagogy has to center antiracist struggle not simply as a strategic matter, and not simply from immediate ethical necessity, but also because antiracist struggle confronts the *center* of the system of capitalism-coloniality, as Kelley (2020) explains in relation to the current uprisings. Indeed, the recent uprisings against racist violence call out the anti-Blackness that lives in the heart of US and global society. In recognizing this force, we recognize an impulse to violation that organizes the capitalist imperative to accumulation at its core, and on the other hand the centrality to anti-capitalist politics of struggle against white supremacy. The space of possibility created by this struggle has allowed for consideration of unprecedented policy initiatives (e.g., the defunding and abolition of the police) as well as sudden shifts in popular culture (e.g., the toppling of statues memorializing the Confederacy). The job of a liberatory public pedagogy in this moment is to open this space of possibility even further, and to invite people to demand not merely the attenuation of white supremacy but its definitive destruction—which is of course to demand a different society altogether.

Conclusion

In contrast to those who argue that we should take up a "post-critical" orientation in intellectual work, I believe that critical theory remains indispensable— including as it has been elaborated in the canonical works of the philosophers associated with the Frankfurt School. Among "classical" critical theorists, the work of Herbert Marcuse in particular remains especially useful. Marcuse's work opens a window on the inner determination of capitalism and modernity by a structure of domination that links libidinal, material, and political registers. His notions of *performance principle* and *surplus-repression* develop the Freudian categories of reality principle and repression, respectively, in a way that historicizes these categories and that illuminates their function within the capitalist mode of production. However, in order to make good on the emancipatory promise implicit in the project of critique, critical theory needs to rethink the nature of social domination, in particular through a confrontation with the history of coloniality. Marcuse's analysis adapts, from Freud, an interiority that sees the impasses of contemporary society as emerging from a historical logic internal to the West. This account cannot grasp (1) the reality of an Exteriority vis-à-vis this Western narrative; (2) the essential agency of colonized peoples in shaping modernity from the moment of its inauguration in the colonial encounter; (3) the nature of social violence, emerging from but not limited to the context of racism, as constitutive of modernity and as unredeemed by any dialectic of enlightenment.

The concept of violation that I have elaborated in this chapter seeks to name the logic of systematic injury intrinsic to capitalism-coloniality. My argument builds from Marcuse's crucial insight that in certain ways exploitation and repression have become, in modernity, ends in themselves to the extent that they affirm a ruling morality that has become untethered from necessity. But the conception of violation describes an excess that is different from the one described by Marcuse. For Marcuse, actual historical repression is excessive in relation to the primary psychic repression outlined by Freud, since repression in fact secures a system of domination rather than the simple possibility of culture. My account, by contrast, points to the way that social violence *exceeds the operation of repression itself*, insofar as the latter is always an instrument of control and hegemony. The context of coloniality exposes the extent to which violence operates as the inner content and meaning of modernity rather than simply as a bulwark for the power of elites (Quijano, 2008). In order to grasp this dynamic, we need to start from a vantage point at the margins, a vantage point from which a phenomenology of domination can be sketched that is free from the teleology of the metropole. The testimony offered by Guaman Poma and Las Casas shatters this teleology, showing that in ethical terms the "morality" of the rulers *leads nowhere*, and that it must be inverted or evaded in solidarity with those whom it injures. Starting from these thinkers, my framework in this chapter describes a system of domination made as much out of plunder and decomposition as out of production.

These reflections have important implications for educational theory and practice, as these respond to contemporary conditions that are nonetheless continuous with capitalism's earliest determinations. In the current moment, police violence in particular exposes the essential racism of capitalism and how this racism becomes an organized principle of the state. In this context, the critical dialogue long recommended to educators by theorists of critical pedagogy needs to go beyond just looking underneath official knowledges; it needs to expose and denounce specific histories of colonial and racist violence. This pedagogical work is revolutionary. In fact, the struggle against racism uniquely illuminates the architecture of capitalism's rule and rationality. In the process of this struggle, we can deepen our analyses of neoliberal precarity and responsibilization, including as students experience these conditions in schools within stripped-down pedagogies of discipline, and we can reconnect critical pedagogy to its natural base in social movements and vernacular analyses of power. From this theoretical and practical base, I believe, we might create an enlivened criticality that proceeds from the understandings and desires of those who have been most marginalized, and points toward a process of collective healing that repudiates both alienation and injury.

5

Critical Pedagogy and a Generative
Thematics of the Global

This chapter takes up a set of linked questions that are urgent in the present: (1) How do we respond, in critical education, to social forces and forms of oppression that are global in scale? As economic, ecological, and cultural processes increasingly act immediately at the planetary level, what does this mean for a critical pedagogy that would seek to understand and respond to them? More specifically, what does the planetarization of the "limit-situations" that confront communities mean for the critical education tradition inspired by Paulo Freire, which emphasizes the contextualization of "epochal" processes in local struggles (Freire, 1996)? (2) How can a critical pedagogy oriented against capitalism and coloniality recognize the validity of plural epistemological standpoints, and imagine an enlarged criticality built from dialogue between them? If a *pluriversal* and place-sensitive perspective informed by Indigenous, non-Western, and alternative standpoints is central to decolonial projects in theory and practice (Justice, 2016; Mignolo, 2011), what might this look like in the context of critical education articulated at the scale of the global? (3) Since, in education, forms of knowledge are embodied in both curriculum and pedagogy, how might a pluriversal critical education, concerned with challenges shared across different communities, learn from and draw on diverse sites and modes of teaching, especially those beyond the school itself? These three questions are connected to the extent that considering the scale of the global requires attending to disparate understandings while also looking across experiences for what is shared between them. Even as conditions differ in different locations, accumulation's assault on being, which the preceding chapters have described in historical and contemporary context, is planetary and pervasive. In addition, a rich criticality must be responsive to the range of counter-knowledges that oppose themselves to power (De Lissovoy, 2008); in teaching and learning, understanding is inextricable from collective action even if that action looks different in different cultural and institutional spaces.

In response to these questions, this chapter sketches out a form of curriculum articulated midway between a theoretical analysis of system-level logics (e.g., capitalism and racism) and the elaboration of concrete site-specific educational projects. I describe this mid-level articulation as a *meso-curriculum*. This term describes my proposal in formal terms; at the level of content, I inflect Freire's (1996) curricular organizing principle of *generative theme* to emphasize the level of the global. In critical pedagogy, the global is often taken as a distant reference point for national or local themes (which are analyzed as expressing broader and more abstract antagonisms), but I argue that in the present, global social forces have a concreteness and immediacy that we must recognize and respond to, and I sketch out several key generative themes that work across diverse global sites even as they show up differently for different communities. The distinct ways in which these themes are expressed across sites cannot be separated from the ways in which communities understand them, and so a dialogical and open epistemology has to ground the exploration in this regard. This openness should extend to considering different moments and kinds of teaching in schools and beyond them, and I conclude this chapter by describing how the diverse forms of practical reason that live in alternative pedagogies can collaborate as we confront the central challenges facing us as a planetary community.

Conceptualizing Critical Pedagogy to Scale

The critical pedagogy tradition, starting from the work of Paulo Freire (1974, 1994, 1996, 1998), problematizes social conditions that are generally taken as given and unchangeable. This tradition argues that social domination is anchored in alienated modes of being and understanding and therefore that dialogue that explores these modes is crucial to challenging oppression and creating possibilities for transformation. To the extent that education is a space in which knowledge of the world and forms of subjectivity are constructed, struggle and imagination in teaching are deeply consequential to political movements. However, Freire and those who have followed him understand the political as involving much more than public contests over resources and representation. Politics is just as much a question of which classes or cultures have the authority to *narrate* the world and to organize the possibilities for meaning for both dominant and subaltern groups (Giroux, 1988; McLaren, 2007). A radical political commitment in this context means an exploration and challenge at the level of knowledge, the subject, and consciousness. This commitment also means that education, as it works with students to explore their existential, material, and epistemological worlds, cannot reproduce the familiar forms of either authoritarian or liberal pedagogies if it is to be faithful to a revolutionary project oriented against oppression (Darder, 1991). Building from Marxist philosophers like Lukács and Althusser, who showed the fundamental determination by capitalism of bourgeois science and ideology, and from anticolonial thinkers like Fanon, who exposed the violence and imposition of colonial society, Freire (1974, 1996) argues for a pedagogy that struggles against the fragmentation of knowledge, the dehumanization of the oppressed, and the necrophilic possessiveness of elites.

Freirean critical pedagogy is inherently attuned to the politics of knowledge and subjectivity. In Freire's later work (1998), he argues for a radical "epistemological curiosity" as the basis for authentic dialogue in education. Likewise, he describes education as a process of becoming in which "unfinishedness" is an ethical virtue. This orientation makes critical pedagogy an important starting point for engagements with diverse understandings of the world and with disparate cultural and historical experiences. Critical pedagogues often point out that this approach to teaching has to be reinvented in different circumstances and in response to the historical conditions of different sites of teaching (Darder, 2002). In fact, Freirean approaches to literacy and social movements have been powerfully taken up in response to specific constellations of "limit-situations" in many different countries and continents. At the same time, both Freire and critical educators following him have been criticized for reproducing a universalizing and decontextualized framework for politics—as in, for example, Freire's *oppressor-oppressed* schema—that can erase complex and consequential differences in identity. Some have argued that this problem is connected to sexism and Eurocentrism at the level of epistemology (e.g., Esteva, Stuchul, & Prakash, 2005), to the extent that Freirean pedagogy is organized around a Western dialectical framework and a developmentalist understanding of both consciousness and society even as it proclaims an openness to diverse understandings.

There has been much debate over these questions; there may be a certain bad faith in such critiques given Freire's formidable contributions to global anticolonial struggles at both the material and cultural levels. Regardless, at this point it would be a serious distortion to characterize critical pedagogy as an imperial, race-blind, or masculinist project. This characterization fails to appreciate the important efforts undertaken by many scholars to address epistemological problems and to reinvent critical pedagogy in dialogue with critical theories of race, coloniality, and patriarchy. Thus, Jennings and Lynn (2005), Zavala and Golden (2016), and many others have built on and reframed the Freirean tradition to construct powerful critical pedagogies attentive to race. Brock (2005), Evans-Winters and Piert (2014), and others have articulated critical pedagogy to feminist of color analyses. Gandin (2007), Pereira (2020), and Vally and Motala (2017) offer critiques of neoliberalism inspired by Freireanism and constructed from vantage points outside of North America. Kahn (2009) and Evans (2012) have shown how critical education needs to be conceptualized in the context of a critique of ecological destruction. Elbih (2018), Fregoso Bailón (2015), and others find in critical pedagogy a crucial conceptual basis for pedagogy against both empire and Islamophobia. Perhaps most importantly, Sandy Grande (2004) has undertaken a systematic rethinking of critical pedagogy in the context of the struggle for decolonization and from the starting point of Indigenous intellectual and political traditions. Grande's work simultaneously rearticulates critical pedagogy's materialist politics to recognize the imperative of Indigenous sovereignty (against the narrow discursive frame of "democracy") and renews the critical pedagogy tradition's revolutionary commitment against capitalism (vs. liberal and postmodern appropriations). Thus, in accordance with bell hooks' formulation, "from the margins to the center," the vital core of the contemporary critical pedagogy tradition is located decisively outside and against whiteness and patriarchy.

Nevertheless, my proposal in this chapter aims to stretch even this extended conversation, in certain key respects, so that critical pedagogy can serve as a starting point in building properly *global* educational and social movements against and beyond capitalism. First, although Freire's conceptual framework has been rearticulated to respond to diverse oppressions, the Western epistemological *proyecto* (Dussel, 1985) that partly inhabits the logic even of critical pedagogy remains to be fully confronted, and the reality of epistemological difference remains to be systematically taken into account, though Grande's work crucially opens this conversation. That is, we need to recognize and build from an epistemological *pluriversality* (Mignolo, 2011) that itself corresponds to global geopolitical variegation (and interconnection).

In addition, I argue that critical pedagogy needs to construct frameworks and concrete projects at larger scales. Starting from Freire's discussion of the way that crucial themes for education need to respond to experience at various levels, from the local to the global, I outline here a critical-pedagogical framework at the planetary scale. The insistence in much scholarship on the fact that critical pedagogy needs to be reinvented for diverse local contexts is important but risks overlooking the increasing importance of transnational and global forces in the everyday experiences of individuals and communities. Freire's (1996) methodology for developing literacy projects points to the existence of crucial challenges at the regional and global levels, but critical pedagogy has yet to fully explore projects explicitly articulated at these higher levels.

Finally, as part of building frameworks that can work regionally and globally, critical pedagogy needs to learn from the broad range of radical, alternative, and subaltern teaching practices that diverse traditions propose. Other powerful forms of teaching and learning beyond Freire's problem-posing methodology also address central historical themes and challenges. (For instance, autonomously organized and student-led educational projects have been effective without the authoritative leadership of the critical pedagogue.) Engaging radical understandings and practices beyond the formally "critical" and considering their common participation in anti-capitalist struggles at regional scales can deepen this process of reorganization. It can also extend the antiracist, decolonizing, and ecological emphases in contemporary critical pedagogy scholarship toward a more unified articulation and toward a more systematic negotiation with the Marxian epistemology at the root of the Freirean tradition. Teaching is deeply philosophical work, since in opening and reorganizing knowledge for students it constitutes a thoroughly epistemological intervention. If the underlying organization of capitalist society only becomes visible through the process of the workers' struggle against it, as Lukács (1971) argues, perhaps it is also true that the underlying organization of dominant knowledge only becomes visible in the process of the educational struggle to open up more complex, critical, and pluriversal ways of knowing. If so, that process of discovery would be an indispensable contribution of a reimagined critical pedagogy to radical theory more broadly.

I aim in this chapter to look beyond local problems and to sketch broad challenges, and in particular to consider themes that extend beyond the North American context that has framed much of the work in critical pedagogy. As I have mentioned, I also point to and draw on plural epistemological frameworks and challenge the provincialism of dominant standpoints. Nevertheless, it is important to acknowledge that I write from a geographical position located in the United States and from a personal body-political perspective that is rooted, at least in the first instance, in an intellectualism of the North. Thus, the outline I offer here will need to be extended by others who are differently positioned in order to fully fulfill its epistemological and political commitments.

Planetary and Pluriversal Thematics for Critical Education

Generative Themes at the Level of the Global

One of the most valuable contributions made by Freire (1996) is his notion of the *generative theme* as a conceptual pillar for critical education projects. In starting from generative themes, educators respond to the historical situations and challenges that students confront:

> An epoch is characterized by a complex of ideas, concepts, hopes, doubts, values, and challenges in dialectical interaction with their opposites, striving towards plenitude. The concrete representation of many of these ideas, values, concepts, and hopes, as well as the obstacles which impede the people's full humanization, constitute the themes of that epoch. These themes imply others which are opposing or even antithetical; they also indicate tasks to be carried out and fulfilled. (p. 82)

The key themes of an epoch crystallize the urgent contradictions lived by the people and imply the historical tasks of critique and transformation. In this regard, as Freire puts it, the themes are connected to concrete and specific *limit-situations* or challenges that constrain communities while implicitly inviting a praxis that would critique and transform these situations. From this perspective, for critical pedagogy to be meaningful, it has to apprehend the crucial themes that work through these local challenges and that organize experience and understanding for students in a given time and place.

"Generative themes," according to Freire, "can be located in concentric circles, moving from the general to the particular" (1996, p. 84). At the broadest level, "epochal" themes point to universal and fundamental contradictions shared by everyone living in a particular historical moment. Below this level, there are "continental, regional, [and] national" themes—nested in a series of diminishing concentric circles, as they get closer and closer to local spaces. This framework of generative themes provides a basis for educators to connect immediate conditions with broader and even global processes: for Freire, the most general and fundamental theme of our epoch is "*domination*—which implies its opposite, the theme of *liberation*" (1996, p. 84). Most of the practical work of critical pedagogy in the Freirean tradition has involved uncovering this fundamental epochal theme in local experiences and problems, a process that is not always straightforward. Freire gives the example of the way that the theme of exploitation emerged within a workers' "thematic investigation" circle that was considering the issue of alcoholism, as participants pointed to drinking as an understandable response to disempowerment and low wages, themes that the facilitator had not originally intended to investigate (1996, pp. 99–100). Recent educational projects in the Freirean tradition have exposed the underlying theme of domination-liberation in contemporary processes of curriculum differentiation (Souto-Manning, 2010), gentrification (Heiman & Yanes, 2018), Islamophobia (Elbih, 2018), and many other conditions.

The work of connecting universal and epochal themes to local challenges is essential to any critical-pedagogical praxis rooted in a particular place and time (i.e., every critical educational project). At the same time, I suggest that it is also urgent in the present to attend to the larger circles of Freire's thematic system in their own right—that is, the regional, continental, and global levels that bring together local and national experiences within shared problems and challenges. First, people everywhere are increasingly connected through economic, cultural, and technological processes and networks, as well as through the shared experiences of global environmental degradation and public health crises—as the Covid-19 pandemic has vividly demonstrated. Second, these shared processes and problems are intensifying, making transnational thinking and action more and more urgent. While it is true that it is only through local experiences that fundamental themes can become visible and understood, it is also true that the continental and global economies we inhabit determine broad themes that in some cases only emerge through investigations at these larger scales and yet which act with brutal immediacy across diverse local contexts. In addition, considering themes at broader scales implicitly invites forms of collaboration that work across familiar boundaries and that create new collective counter-subjects, as can clearly be seen, for instance, in the contemporary global climate justice movement (Dawson, 2010).

In this chapter, I propose a framework for generative themes at the global level (as well as an explicit set of themes) as a foundation for contemporary critical educational projects and curricula. Thinking at the global level presses us beyond the national boundaries that typically limit our conceptual framing of social struggles; the challenge is to retain at the same time a meaningful, if still very broad, specificity with regard to key themes. Furthermore, focusing on the global as the unit of analysis throws into relief the reality of interconnected histories and challenges that is often obscured—primarily because of the global power projected by the regimes of the capitalist core and the ideology of exceptionalism that they cling to. Finally, this global framing responds to pan-Indigenous perspectives that highlight the continuous geography and cultural imbrication of regions; for instance, reconfiguring the Americas as

Abya Yala displaces the fragmented and Northernist geographical mapping as the basis for understanding and acting on shared challenges on this continent (Third Continental Summit, 2011). The notion of *Abya Yala* begins from the continuities and communities of the land rather than from the divisions and abstractions of it that make up the formal political sphere. Concentrating on the global level means considering processes that work across states and regions, including those that are asymmetrically "shared" within a relation of oppression or exploitation. This framing invites an imagination that can look beyond dominant constructions of community, development, and identity. However, the ultimate criterion of validity for this project is less a narrowly scientific one and more a curricular one: In what ways does the consideration of global themes in education open up new understandings for students and new possibilities for local, regional, and continental praxis?

Pluriversality against Racism and Epistemicide

A global orientation to social analysis implicitly challenges the disciplinary divisions of scholarship as well as the popular frameworks that make sense of social problems in media and policy discussions. However, this shift in scale doesn't necessarily alter the *epistemological* foundation of analysis, which generally remains constrained, even in critical scholarship, as it takes on a broader survey of reality. By contrast, I believe that it is important for any investigation of generative themes at the level of the global to begin from a *pluriversal* standpoint—that is, a standpoint that recognizes the validity of multiple, and especially marginalized, knowledges in making sense of the world: "Pluriversal global futures require *epistemic democratization*, which is to say the decolonization of democracy" (Mignolo, 2011, p. 89; italics added). This recognition implies a repudiation of the claim to exceptionality and universality made by Western philosophy and science. Furthermore, even though a pluriversal perspective does not deny Western knowledge projects their own particular validity—instead decentering and provincializing them (Chakrabarty, 2000)—the sense of pluriversality that I want to take up here *is* implicitly opposed to Western epistemology *to the extent* that it is a racist and settler-colonialist knowledge. As racist knowledge, Western epistemology has not only claimed a unique universality but has worked to eliminate Indigenous and nonwhite peoples, cultures, and sciences (Smith, 1999). There are moments in Western and critical intellectual traditions that are at least partly separated from the eliminationist logic of coloniality and colonization; however, that separation (and the potential participation of these critical perspectives in a non-dominative pluriversality) has to be demonstrated.

In his autobiographical account of race and racism in the United States, *Dusk of Dawn* (1940/1986), W. E. B. Du Bois describes a shift in his thinking midway through his career when he came to realize that the racism of white people would not be ended simply through the good work of social science as it revealed the irrationality of race thinking. Du Bois realized that racism is not primarily the result of a set of mistaken assumptions about Black people but rather proceeds from "the vast area of the subconscious and the irrational and especially of habit and convention which also produce significant action" (p. 679). Du Bois came to the conclusion that a broader campaign of cultural and economic transformation would be necessary in order to achieve racial justice rather than simply a narrow educational intervention to correct erroneous ideas. Describing this new understanding, Du Bois outlines an ideological project of reorganizing the conditions of racist thinking, but at the same time he exposes an important *epistemological* rift. Indeed, in a crucial mid-section of *Dusk of Dawn*, Du Bois describes the structure of white racism as based on a set of civilizational judgments about the cultural and intellectual accomplishments of African and African American peoples. Engaging an imaginary (but typical) white interlocutor, Du Bois contradicts the latter's assertion that white people are superior at the level of reason:

> Quite the contrary. I know no attribute in which the white race has more conspicuously failed. This is white and European civilization; and as a system of culture it is idiotic, addle-brained, unreasoning, topsy-turvy, without precision; and its genius chiefly runs to marvelous contrivances for enslaving the many, and enriching the few, and murdering both. (1940/1986, p. 658)

Significantly, Du Bois articulates his denunciation of white racism through a critique of European civilization's flawed and fatal sciences. He shows that the feeling of superiority, for white people, is routed through a spurious appraisal of the cultural and intellectual accomplishments of others. Building from Du Bois' analysis, I suggest that confronting the oppressive limit-situations faced by people globally requires an engagement with the politics of knowledge.

In the same section of this work, Du Bois shows that racist judgments about reason and knowledge are closely connected to racist aesthetic and moral understandings, as Black people are denigrated in their physical and spiritual being. Thus, against the assertions of his white interlocutor, Du Bois maintains that "the black race excels [the white race] in beauty, goodness, and adaptability, and is well abreast in genius" (657). If we take Du Bois' analysis as a contribution to a theory of pluriversality, we can see how it points to the link between racisms at the levels of epistemology and ontology. Struggling against racism means validating and creating space for ways of being and knowing that have together been slandered and refused. Du Bois dramatizes for the reader the way in which the creation of a plural and productive space of culture necessitates dismantling the eliminationist project of whiteness across these domains. In this regard, his analysis accords with more recent efforts in decolonial theory to describe a complex "geopolitics" and "body-politics" of knowledge (Mignolo, 2011). These ideas name at once the terrain of judgments about the *worth* of bodies as well as the *logic* of colonial descriptions: "Body-politics describes decolonial technologies ratified by bodies who realized, first, that they were considered less human, and second, that the very act of describing them as less human was a radical un-human consideration" (Mignolo, 2011, p. 140). This situated geopolitics and body-politics is necessarily at issue in accounts of central challenges for peoples globally, and therefore any broad-level description of key curricular themes in this connection has to be reflective about its own epistemological ground (Paraskeva, 2011).

Scholars in critical Indigenous studies have shown how settler-colonial cultures and knowledges are organized around the dispossession of Indigenous peoples, offering "empowerment" for Indigenous people only in the form of assimilative enfranchisement and inclusion (Coulthard, 2014) and producing social sciences premised on the erasure of Indigenous presences (Byrd, 2011; Smith, 1999). Reckoning with this ongoing history means, on the one hand, that epistemology needs to be *expanded* to recognize diverse knowledge traditions; on the other hand, it means in another sense that epistemology needs to be *contracted* to refuse Western habits of imperious survey and to attend to place-based understandings. Daniel Heath Justice (2016) reframes the critical, in this context, as "an interventionist analytic of transformation committed to and dependent on local specificity within a broader network of relationships" (p. 20). This attention to relationships embodied and embedded in local places might appear to be in tension with the broad scale of a global thematics, but I think what is crucial is the epistemological shift Justice suggests toward an attention to relationships and responsibilities. The dominant nation-state-based framing of society and politics refuses genuinely reciprocal relationships and complex identities that work across and beyond states as well as within them (Urrieta, 2017). In this regard, even at the scale of the continental and the global, our understanding of human societies needs to be "emplaced"—that is, attentive to the deep history of the land and the peoples who have lived upon it (Styres, 2019).

In this light, there is perhaps no tension between the "planetary" perspective that decolonial philosopher Enrique Dussel (1998) argues for and the Indigenous Nishnaabeg epistemology described by Leanne Betasamosake Simpson (2017), rooted specifically in Michi Saagiig Nishnaabeg territory. Both are determined against the predatory and deracinated intelligence of the West. Simpson argues for a sense of knowledge embedded in and produced by a Nishnaabeg place-based economy "fully integrated with spirituality and politics . . . intensely local within a network of Indigenous internationalism that [includes] plant and animal nations" (p. 24). Do we not also need to understand the planet itself in this way: not as an abstract conceptual container for the totality of nature and society but rather as a particular *place* that has been built out of the reciprocal relationships between a multitude of human and non-human communities? *To the extent that the Western knowledge tradition has claimed an exceptionality that erases other epistemologies*—in what has been called a process of *epistemicide* (Santos, 2014)—then it cannot simply exist alongside other traditions but must itself be refused. It is not only bourgeois and positivist science that has participated in this process but also critical theory. Indeed, Byrd (2011) argues that a symptomatic erasure of Native peoples underwrites even the subversive gestures of critical, poststructural, and postcolonial theories. From this perspective, we cannot posit a simple epistemological coevalness between Western and non-Western knowledges but have to recognize a "cacophony" (Byrd, 2011) of cultural collision, misrecognition, and appropriation, as well as a characteristic settler disavowal of colonization itself (Tuck & Yang, 2012).

At the same time, as Grande (2004) has shown, there is a potential collaboration between the Marxist critique of capitalism and decolonizing projects starting from Indigenous perspectives, as long as Marxism can confront and overcome its own participation in processes of political and epistemological assimilation that ignore Indigenous sovereignty. Working through these contradictions is an implicit commitment in Freire's thought, given the centrality of both Marxist and anticolonial theory and practice in his writing. In the case of this chapter's proposal for a critical-pedagogical thematics at the global scale, I note that confronting colonialism in education necessarily means confronting capitalism, and that Marxist traditions are indispensable in this project. Nevertheless, it is important to work through the epistemological problems involved in bringing together different traditions toward a complex and yet coherent account of power.

Toward a Critical Meso-Curriculum
of the Global: Key Themes

In this section, I outline a critical curriculum at the scale of the global, which responds to the "highest" level of generative themes as described by Freire. The point of a curricular framework organized at this particular scale is to be deeply flexible and broadly applicable/appropriable. At the same time, this framework is implicitly an intervention into the terrain of critical theory, since it points to the importance of diverse epistemological starting points as well as to the importance of their juxtaposition, even as it begins from a standpoint outside of and against power.

Conditions for a Global Meso-Curriculum

Curriculum is generally conceptualized either at the abstract philosophical level—for instance, in the academic context of the field of curriculum theory—or at the immediate level of the classroom lesson that is the focus of much practical work in teacher preparation. I suggest that there is a conceptual middle level for thinking about curriculum that is too often overlooked in education—what we might call the level of a *meso-curriculum*. In contrast to the immediate level of the concrete unit or lesson, this meso-curricular level, as I conceptualize it, is concerned with broad historical and social problems and themes rather than specific concepts, information, or units. On the other hand, in contrast to the properly philosophical level of curriculum theory, the meso-curriculum works past (or below) purely abstract principles to specify concrete historical thematics. (It is important to note that the *meso* here refers to an *epistemological* level— between the philosophical and the practical—rather than to a *geographic* one; the curriculum proposed here is articulated at the most extended geographic scale.) Informed by theoretical principles, these themes open up for teachers and students the possibility of praxis oriented toward "epochal" problems confronting them. I deploy this meso-curriculum here to explicitly engage the outer circles of Freire's model of the expanding concentric circles of generative themes: those concerned with regional and global limit-situations.

The notion of a globally oriented meso-curriculum challenges familiar partitions that organize curriculum, knowledge, and identity. First, thinking within a Freirean frame about education organized on the basis of historical *problems*—and especially so at the broadest geographical scales—challenges familiar disciplinary divisions that organize knowledge in schools and higher education, since confronting these problems (for instance, gender-based oppression) requires the resources of many disciplines as well as shifting the center of inquiry from an arbitrarily defined *field* to a historically determined *situation*. Second, this curriculum's identification of broadly shared generative themes looks beyond the national imaginary and opens up the possibility for students of reconfiguring their identities in relation to more extended political/geographical terrains (De Lissovoy, 2011). Third, since popular struggles are also often captured by the framework of the nation-state, the curriculum proposed here might create a space for thinking about disparate movements together, and about the ways they may be part of the same larger project to the extent they are concerned with the same underlying limit-situations.

If we understand curriculum in these terms, we have to complexify the familiar framing of curriculum in terms of educational *environment* (Au, 2012; Dewey, 1997a), since this environment would have to include not just different tools, content, and forms of engagement but also different knowledge traditions. This framework should stay faithful to the principle of starting from marginalized communities which is common to the traditions of critical pedagogy (Freire, 1996), feminist standpoint theory (Harding, 1993), and philosophy of liberation (Dussel, 1985). However, as there are plural standpoints connected to diverse communities, the criticality that emerges from them is not singular. Global society is not a single abstract polity but rather an extended overlapping set of places and communities of beings, both human and more-than-human (Nxumalo, 2015), and critical education needs to reflect this condition.

Key Themes

In the following, I sketch out several crucial generative themes, for critical educational projects, that I believe emerge in the present at the level of the global. (This is of course a provisional list. Other themes might be proposed, though it is important at this level that each theme clearly works across a broad range of geographic and cultural sites.) These themes are complex, since they operate both *within* social categories and *on* them: For instance, as I describe later, *ecological destruction* threatens the natural environment while also forcing an epistemological reckoning with the conceptual category of "nature" itself. These themes also intersect; for instance, the forces of *extractivism* and *precaritization* clearly depend deeply on each other. I offer these themes as starting points for diverse local curriculum projects that would take them up as they are expressed in local limit-situations—though to some extent they are also *experienced* globally (for instance by transnational students) as I describe at the conclusion of this section. The emergence of the planetary as an urgent frame for praxis is connected to the fact of epochal change in the context of systemic crisis. As Mignolo (2020) puts it, this means we are experiencing not an "era of change" but rather a "change in era."

Extractivism

Plunder and extraction of resources from the Global South have been central to capitalism from its beginnings—indeed, Marx (1867/1976) describes this plunder as capitalism's founding moment. The theft of natural resources and labor from Latin America fueled the development of modern European societies even as these societies laid waste to Indigenous economies across the continent (Galeano, 1973). Europe's colonial plunder of Africa from the first moments of colonial encounter up to the present have constituted a process of "underdevelopment" (Rodney, 2011) even as they have been rationalized in terms of economic "progress." The persistence of direct (neo-)colonial appropriation of wealth into the contemporary era marks the clear continuity between an original extractivism and a contemporary "neo-extractivism" (Acosta, 2013). Harvey (2003) understands this process of plunder as an "accumulation by dispossession" that works continuously to jump-start a global capitalist economy in persistent crisis. While the seizure of natural resources has usually been the focus of critique in this regard, we can also see the intensifying and asymmetric exploitation of labor-power globally as another moment of extraction—for instance in the superexploitation of workers in the technology industries.

Starting from Quijano's (2008) analysis of the way that processes of appropriation, servitude, and wage labor operate simultaneously within colonial economies, we can see the increasing inequality that characterizes capitalism globally (Piketty, 2014), including in the North, as a reflection of a desperate drive to increase the rate of production of surplus value. Even if workers in the capitalist core do not yet confront the absolute forms of immiseration anticipated by Marx in his projections of the future of capitalism, in relative terms workers have experienced a decline that contradicts the growth predictions of apologists for the market. Below-poverty wages in the expanding service industry, de-professionalization of skilled labor (e.g., teachers), and exploitation of prisoners all point to a class offensive being waged by capital against workers. These trends reveal the simultaneity and interpenetration of direct appropriation and exploitation, as labor-power is purchased below its value and as the pillaging of places and peoples sends capitalism on an unsustainable and sociocidal trajectory.

Understanding land as the source and unity of human and natural being (Simpson, 2017) can also allow us to see settler-colonial appropriation and exploitation as moments of the same underlying process. If in Marxism the specificity of exploitation as an offense against a uniquely human capacity (to create value) separates human beings from the background of nature and from the process of plunder that works across land and resources, an Indigenous understanding of the relationality and sense of purpose (Deloria, 1999) that binds together human and non-human worlds might reveal the underlying violation that operates across diverse moments of extraction. Juxtaposing exploitation and appropriation in this way can allow us to see the insurgent global "class" that is the planet itself and all its communities—in struggle against a capitalist system that is at once assaultive and assimilative.

Precaritization

In addition to the intensification of exploitation, recent decades have seen an increase in insecurity for global populations. This can be noted in the global growth of informal settlements and informal economies at the margins (Davis, 2006) and in the increasing casualization of labor associated with post-Fordism. Indeed, neoliberalism could be said to make precarity a central economic and social principle rather than a peripheral condition. As capitalism has become more flexible, it has become more *predatory* (Duménil & Lévy, 2005), algorithmically varying its mobilization of labor from moment to moment, and content to abandon excess workers (and populations) to the literal and figurative outskirts of production. Racism is both a tool and an effect of this process, as race-based employment discrimination and incarceration produce a condition of disposability for Black, Brown, and Indigenous communities in the capitalist core (Davis, 2005). Furthermore, permanent indebtedness in neoliberalism constitutes both a continuous source of accumulation for capital and a continuous source of vulnerability for households.

Precarity is not only economic but also existential and ontological. War and permanent low-intensity conflicts have led to massive migration globally, uprooting communities and threatening their survival. At the same time, the cruelty and violence faced by vulnerable populations are made invisible through systematic dehumanization and through a discursive derealization that disqualifies vulnerable populations from *being* to begin with (Butler, 2004), and that renders their suffering "unremarkable" (Cook, 2021). The process of *illegalization* is crucial in this context (De Genova, 2004): that is, a criminality that is constructed as belonging internally to the condition of being an immigrant. In the immigrants who risk their lives to join the metropole, Europe and the United States confront the legacy of their own imperial despoliations, but the racist illegalization of refugee populations is also a global phenomenon, as Syrians in Lebanon fleeing war, Central Americans in Mexico, and immigrants in South Africa face state-sanctioned hostility and vulnerability. At the same time, these processes show the coincidence of the racist judgments against global civilizations and knowledges that undergird imperial identity (as described by Du Bois, 1940/1986) and global circuits of capital and labor. Where societies outside of the capitalist core participate in the dehumanization of those who arrive from outside, they seek implicitly at the same time to share in the privileged ontological status of the West.

Gender-Based Violence

Discrimination against women by men globally is undergirded by systematic sexual and gender-based violence that is complexly intertwined with exploitation, colonialism, and economies of racism. For instance, the epidemic of femicides in Mexico and at the US-Mexico border is overdetermined by processes of patriarchy, capitalist accumulation, and spatial domination (Morales & Bejarano, 2009). Likewise, Indigenous activists have shown that the murders of Indigenous women and girls in Canada are part of the broad historical project of settler colonialism and must be addressed within that context (National Inquiry into Missing and Murdered Indigenous Women and Girls, 2020). At the same time, the familiar cisgender and heteronormative discursive framework within which gender-based discrimination is usually understood under-emphasizes the disproportionality of harassment experienced by LGBTQIA people (Flores et al., 2020) and in particular the violence perpetrated internationally against trans women and men (Trans Murder Monitoring Update, 2019). The dominant material and immaterial investments that solicit violence against women and LGBTQIA people in this way fortify ontologies of gender that are allied with diverse registers of domination.

Furthermore, the current resurgence of authoritarianism and proto-fascism in global politics, linked directly to the failure of liberal and neoliberal governance, is also deeply shaped by a violent masculinity that works within and beyond individual men, shaping cultural landscapes and political ideologies. Feminists of color have long pointed out the way that sexism, racism, and capitalism mutually reinforce each other (hooks, 2000; Mohanty, 2003). In the present, it would appear that *patriarchy* does not quite do justice to the gender-based resentment that supports rightist formations in the United States, Brazil, India, and elsewhere. Gender-based violence participates in the broad historical process of coloniality, not only as a subsidiary influence but as a crucial register of domination at the level of ways of being—what Lugones (2008) calls a "coloniality of gender." In addition, the challenge to orders and understandings of gender posed by diverse forms of gender-expansiveness and queer identity reveal the depth of psychic/social investment in these orders, as many putatively progressive intellectuals participate in a moral panic in response to the visibility of transgender women and men. Young people are increasingly remembering/discovering different genders, gender expressions, and subversions of gender; these are not just identities but also alternative knowledges of self and other. The fault-lines in the Western epistemology of gender point to the need to learn from Indigenous traditions in this regard (Driskill, 2010). Overall, the terrain of gender reveals the stakes of identity and identification as a political problematic that crucially ties individual ways of being to global systems of rule.

Ecological Destruction

In the present, confronting the problem of ecological destruction means engaging with the scale of the global. It is clearer than ever that local ecosystems are immediately dependent on and responsive to a planetary ecology. Furthermore, the process of climate change reveals the extent to which environmental harms are the inevitable result of the fundamental logic of capitalism (Kovel, 2002). Nature, as economic "externality," remains the resource for and condition of capitalism's necessary expansion, whatever the balance of industries the system comprises, and the devastating effects of this expansion continue to accumulate (World Meteorological Organization, 2020). Furthermore, pollution, habitat loss, and "natural" disasters work across the interface between human communities and non-human beings. It makes little sense to describe ecological degradation as a process primarily affecting the latter; the human suffering caused by these processes teaches us our absolute belonging to the earth. Migrating from bats to humans, the Covid-19 virus demonstrates the importance of attending, in education and public policy, to our intimacies with other species (Nxumalo,

2015) and also to the single and extensive *tissue* that is the planetary human community.

In this context, the epistemological separation of the human and natural is perverse and irrational. Simpson (2017) describes how Indigenous epistemologies teach the assemblage of relations that constitutes an extended family of human and non-human beings and that foregrounds land not as object of knowledge but rather as context and condition of learning. Escobar (2008) shows how Black and Indigenous knowledge traditions in Colombia reframed conservation projects, challenging the overarching framework of *development* as the paradigm within which the relation to the environment is articulated. In the current moment, these conceptualizations are not just optional alternatives to the dominant but rather indispensable foundations for research and action. While theorists have noted an essential transition in the postmodern era in which "Nature . . . has systematically been eclipsed from the object world and the social relations of a society whose tendential domination over its Other (the nonhuman or the formerly natural) is more complete than at any other moment in human history" (Jameson, 1991, p. 170), we confront in the present an even more profound collapse in the *economy of being*, as the very survival of forests and fisheries globally is threatened. This is a threat to both a material and ontological *"espacio de vida"* (Escobar, 2008).

Surveillance and Control

The rise of the internet led to fears and fantasies of a collapse of the real into the virtual. The real problem, however, is the near-absolute indexing of experience to virtual data maps that are largely inaccessible to individuals and communities. The truth-content and meaning making of human interaction and communication begin to appear as secondary to the function of generating information which can be tracked and analyzed. This is a different problem than that described in Marcuse's (1964) notion of technological rationality, which reduces thought to flat and instrumental ratiocination. Instrumental reason still proposes a kind of thinking, however one-dimensional; in the contemporary datafication of communication, on the other hand, the algorithm operates autonomously to describe and organize reality (Means, 2018). This raises the twin specters of total state control through big data (e.g., "predictive policing") and the privatization of government itself through the expanding and flexible governance of technology corporations. While local conditions vary, the "digital divide" does not mean that this is an issue affecting only wealthy people; for many communities, including displaced people and migrants, social media is an indispensable means of communication (Dekker et al., 2018). It is often pointed out that the social media environment creates information bubbles that enclose communities in their own hothouses of (dis)information, but it is important to analyze this effect not just as an artifact of technology but rather as central to a new governmentality that depends on a weakening of the public sphere (and a corresponding ascension of private brokers of information).

Furthermore, a flexible racial capitalism, in the era of digital technology, creates networked hate as both a twenty-first-century repudiation of the struggle for racial justice and as a profit-generating hub of online activity. On the other hand, for liberatory projects, the tools of digital technology have to be used somewhat at cross-purposes and with an awareness of the risks, even as they offer spaces, in spite of themselves, for new forms of community. However, the specter of total technological control that frightens libertarians is not new; colonial maps have asserted the same claim on space and time since the beginning of modernity (Smith, 1999). Digital technology refreshes and ramifies the process of surveillance, though the control of imagination that knowledge capitalism aims for depends in the last instance on settler occupation of the land. In this regard, it should not be surprising that the contemporary flows and webs of the digital landscape coincide, in the non-virtual world, with the proliferation and hardening of walls, borders, and enclosures that ironically "consecrate" the porosity of the contemporary nation-state (Brown, 2010).

Thematic Decoding: From Vertical to Horizontal

In critical pedagogy, teachers and students work together in a process of dialogue to *decode* central generative themes (as they are represented in curricular texts or codifications) in a process that moves from immediate to more critical understandings and that links local experiences to more global contradictions (Freire, 1996). However, in the case of the global themes I have just described, students' experiences of them are often *already* geographically extended and deeply sophisticated. For instance, Sánchez (2007) shows how second-generation immigrant students from Mexico felt deeply connected to their families' regions of origin and how they constructed a form of critical global citizenship on this basis informed by an intuitive understanding of interculturalism and of the risks and politics of migration. In relation to the theme of precaritization earlier, then, these students' understandings of vulnerability are characterized not by a paralyzing immobility but rather by the energy of literal and conceptual border-crossing. Similarly, with regard to the theme of ecological destruction, the simultaneous effects of climate change globally and the immediately transnational adversary faced by affected communities (in the form of fossil fuel industries and infrastructure) motivate disparate struggles that nevertheless have to operate transnationally in order to mitigate even local threats. And with regard to digital technology and the theme of surveillance, we might note that while social media users, including youth, are not generally aware of the tracking and datafication of their activity, they increasingly deliberately navigate information webs on a global scale, as their communication networks extend far beyond the limits of their own communities, countries, and continents.

This suggests that in relation to these broad global themes, the task for critical education is less to support students in making *vertical* connections between local challenges and epochal themes and more to collaborate in fleshing out in dialogue, *horizontally*, the already felt fabric of the regional and planetary. Forging links with differently situated relations and comrades is crucial to accomplishing this. Similarly, in epistemological terms, the task may be less to help ingenuous local understandings to grow into "developed" and universal ones and rather to offer to those challenged globally by a particular limit-situation the resources of diverse communal-critical knowledges. For instance, the determination of the Zapatista movement to remain rooted in the standpoint of its constituent Indigenous nations, even as it addresses itself to international allies (Marcos, 1995), at once disavows a vanguardist perspective that would speak for others while at the same time providing models of revolutionary praxis that are deeply instructive. In relation to the theme of extractivism described earlier, the analysis and action the Zapatistas have undertaken in relation to the state and non-state agents of capital powerfully communicates—without dictating— to others internationally who confront the same processes and forces in their own contexts. This suggests a loose formula for critical-pedagogical decoding at the level of the global: In learning from others *about how they understand their struggle*, we might come to know more about our own.

Conclusion: Pedagogical Difference in the Context of Crisis

The generative themes I have described constitute what I call a meso-curriculum, in that they are broader than practical projects that focus on the local level and yet still name specific social forces that work below the level of truly systemwide logics. Thus, capitalism and coloniality do not figure as such as themes in this meso-curriculum, since they name underlying systems rather than situations. As I have mentioned, the themes must be connected in curriculum projects to local conditions and experiences since it is in these experiences that the themes are present to people and also because they show up differently in different sites (Freire, 1996). For instance, precaritization takes the form of economic casualization in the service economies of the North; in the context of war or pervasive social violence, precarity impinges more starkly and existentially. These differences also signal that what these themes name are deep processes with a complex phenomenology, working at both the material and immaterial levels. This complex *condition* of oppression and struggle is also the *occasion* for curricular richness, since it means that experience can and should be examined at many levels and from different geopolitical vantage points.

Themes also need to be articulated differently for different educational spaces and groups of students. Age, identity, and location make a difference in how social processes are present for people, and teaching needs to start from these differences. This does not mean that there is not a concrete reality to these processes that works across contexts. However, social reality is complex in a way that extends even beyond the effects of positionality in that it is felt and figured from the standpoint of different ways of knowing. As we support students in constructing a deeper criticality in relation to their analysis of their experiences, as the tradition of critical pedagogy has insisted we should do, we also need to introduce them to a decolonial "otherwise" (Walsh, 2015)—that is, to the possibility of plural epistemological frameworks for this criticality.

In this context, it is crucial to note that curriculum comes alive *pedagogically*, which means that different pedagogies articulate curriculum differently, making it into distinct projects/experiences. Describing the lessons contained in a traditional story, Simpson (2017) explains how context becomes the form and site of curriculum, as land, family, and community are the indispensable condition of knowledge and learning in Nishnaabeg epistemology. Core to this epistemology, she writes, are "practice" and "visiting." If action and relation are the center of teaching and learning in this way, then approaching the previously described theme of ecological destruction would look very different from describing the condition of an isolable and objectified "natural environment." Likewise, if we think of education in the context of the cooperation of a community comprised of adults and children working together on a project of interest or necessity (Rogoff, 1990, 2001), then curriculum is both enacted and distributed among participants. Urrieta (2013) describes the participatory education practices of Indigenous communities in Michoacán in terms of "cooperative belonging" and "responsible coordination." Recognizing the necessary specificity of community-based education, could we not also see the global movement against climate change as a site for this kind of learning on the grandest scale, as students, activists, scientists, and farmers work together to confront and study a global network of elite power tied to extractive industries? In this instance, social movement itself is the variously organized site of pedagogy. Furthermore, if pedagogy is conceptualized beyond the bounds of *learning* itself (to the extent that learning is dependent on familiar forms of educational authority), as an "exopedagogical" choreography of curricular possibilities (Lewis & Valk, 2020), then the biopolitical management of human being is foregrounded across the generative themes described earlier—as power works through surveillance, violence, and even identity to appropriate the commons of social possibility. This perspective presses us to recognize autonomous moments of study and imagination (in art, political activism, and elsewhere) as important sites from which to approach global limit-situations.

On the one hand, considering the different contexts of and approaches to pedagogy that I have described suggests that education is dependent not only on epistemological standpoints in the abstract but also on cultural-practical sites and situations. On the other hand, recognizing the validity of these different *teaching situations* suggests that we need a notion of critical education that is limited neither to the school nor to out-of-school spaces. From this perspective, education would need to start from the epochal tendencies that produce experience and then work across different institutional and extra-institutional spaces. Mignolo (2020) speaks of a contemporary "third nomos," within which planetary society is beginning to depart from the rule and grammar of the European modernity/coloniality paradigm; this is a shared and global project, even if different communities approach it through different paths. Can we not likewise imagine a broad and shared project on the terrain of pedagogy that aims, in different ways and from different starting points and conditions, to confront a set of themes that crystallize the leading edges of the system of capitalism-coloniality? Elsewhere, with Means and Saltman (2014), I have proposed this project as a decolonial "new common school movement," though *school* here has to refer to informal and community-based teaching spaces as well as formal schooling.

The 2020 pandemic forced people into their homes and out of public spaces. On the other hand, it also forced students out of the confinement of formal schooling and into the alternative spaces of family-based, virtual, and self-directed learning. The ordeal of this shift should not be underestimated, given the tremendous disparities in access to technology experienced by students and the stripped-down and isolating lessons made available through official remote learning for those who were able to access it (Layne, 2020). However, this shift has at least created a rupture in our curricular habits and perhaps opened the possibility for imagining projects that more powerfully link school and community knowledges. Furthermore, in bringing education more immediately into the space of families, and in taking place under the sign of shared and global crisis, this involuntary educational experiment might serve as a starting point for efforts to explore and confront the global generative themes that I have outlined in this chapter as they are diversely experienced in different locations. While the pandemic has worked against in-person collaboration, it may be possible to preserve the experimentalism of the current moment even as we reconnect; in this way, families, social movements, community organizations, arts projects, and schools themselves might become networked sites of learning and linked moments of divergent pedagogies. In collaborations between these spaces, we would explore not just new forms of curriculum but also other kinds of thinking.

Differences in pedagogical practice make vivid the differences in ways of knowing and being that critical education has to start from and respond to. At the same time, global challenges connect peoples across these differences. The shared generative themes that I have described are shaped at once by common problems and by the diverse ways in which they are understood and imagined. Collaboration across societies—collaboration that refuses the finality above all of nation-state boundaries—is necessary in order for regular people to be able to confront the ruling elites whose inhuman and unreasoning administration is destroying lifeworlds everywhere. Education is the foundation for this work, and critical pedagogy can be its guiding framework—if this tradition is enlarged and unfolded, and if it can be directed by the plural needs and knowledges of communities. Starting from this framework, educators can play a central role in working with students to name the world in old and new ways—against the forces that seek, incessantly and unthinkingly, to plunder and exploit it.

Part III

Practicing Emancipation

6

Pedagogy of the Anxious

Critical pedagogy, and the work of Paulo Freire in particular, understands the struggle for emancipation as centrally involving the emergence, as historical agents and subjects, of those who have been marginalized. This process of subjectivization for the oppressed is not a prologue to social transformation but rather a crucial dimension of this process. In this regard, the tradition of critical pedagogy could be said to foreground a *politics of the subject* as central to its philosophy and program. It is for this reason that the organization of dialogue in classrooms and beyond is so consequential, since the occasion of teaching makes possible an intervention not merely in ideological space but also in the very trajectory of identity production. In his foundational writings, Freire (1974, 1978, 1994, 1996, 1998) describes how transformative work in politics and pedagogy involves a challenge to the modes of cognition, affective structures, and constitutive relationships that delimit the ways of being of students and teachers. Exponents of the tradition of critical pedagogy, following Freire in this respect, have pointed to empowerment as a process of identity formation (Darder, 1991), coming to voice (Giroux, 1992), and construction of agency (hooks, 2003). This tradition is a crucial starting point from which to extend the analyses articulated in the first two parts of this book and to take up the question—on which Part III is focused—of emancipatory practice in contemporary capitalism. Chapter 5 laid the groundwork for this investigation in setting out key themes that might organize critical curriculum in the present; in this chapter, I pivot from that chapter's thematic and curricular focus to a central consideration of orientations to teaching within the context of neoliberalism.

I believe that in any consideration of critical pedagogy, Freire's work is an indispensable starting point. However, even as Freire's central emphasis on becoming—and the process of conscientization that accompanies it—remains a crucial pillar in critical pedagogy scholarship, the specific challenges posed to his conceptualization of the subject by the contemporary context, and neoliberalism in particular, have not been fully addressed. Thus, while there are many critiques by critical educators of neoliberalism's social and political program with regard to marketization, commodification, and privatization (e.g. Buras, 2011; McLaren, 2007; Saltman, 2012), Freirean scholars have not fully attended to the reorganization of subjectivity that neoliberalism proposes—that is, to neoliberalism's own politics of the subject. In addition to undertaking a reorganization of policy, political economy, and ideological common sense, neoliberalism also reframes the discursive and symbolic organization of subjectivity (Brown, 2003; Read, 2009). This reorganization takes place against the backdrop of a shift from earlier forms of alienation to the contemporary condition of anxiety that is associated with destabilization, precarity, and fragmentation—conditions that characterize the experience of the majority in the present. In the context of this anxiety, neoliberalism asks us to understand ourselves on the basis of principles of individual responsibility, autonomy, competition, and calculation.

As I describe, this neoliberal politics of the subject poses a challenge to certain key principles and figures that are assumed in critical pedagogy and Freire's work. Thus, Freire's account of the paralysis that characterizes the oppressed, whom he describes as immobilized by a "fear of freedom," is challenged by the specific kind of autonomy that neoliberalism demands, which arguably results in a hypermobility of the subject rather than a petrification. Likewise, the privileging of the sphere of consciousness and cognition in Freire may overlook neoliberalism's work at the affective and corporeal levels, as well as the structure of libidinal investments within neoliberal circuits of consumption and communication. In this chapter, I explore these tensions and others, as well as outlining key implications of this investigation for critical-pedagogical principles and practice. I am aided in this effort by a set of concepts drawn from theoretical traditions that have been especially sensitive to the politics of the subject in neoliberalism: namely, the Foucauldian notion of *governmentality* on the one hand (Foucault, 2008; Rose, 1999), and the Lacanian notions of *drive* and *desire* on the other hand (Lacan, 1978; Dean, 2012; Žižek, 2008a). These theoretical tools allow me to highlight crucial aspects of the deep structure of neoliberalism and to explore the challenges it poses to the conceptualization of subjectivity in critical pedagogy.

I begin this chapter by describing these theoretical starting points and then move to an account of the sociopolitical context that conditions contemporary neoliberal subjectivity. These sections set the stage for my subsequent interrogation of central aspects of Freire's account of the politics of the subject, and following this, for my description of the implications of this analysis for contemporary projects in critical education. The goal of this investigation is to consider how key emphases in Freire's work might be rethought in the context of neoliberal autonomy and responsibilization, and to outline on this basis a set of reconceptualized principles for critical pedagogy. While I consider his oeuvre as a whole, my emphasis is on Freire's key text, *Pedagogy of the Oppressed* (1970/1996), which most powerfully explicates his central philosophical principles. It should be clear in the context of this book that my investigation starts from a belief in the enduring value of Freire's work and the tradition of critical pedagogy more broadly, in the context of which I place my own scholarship. It is because his analysis is indispensable that I believe we must also seek to reinvent it in the context of conditions that he was not able to fully foresee. In that regard, this chapter aims to contribute to the larger effort among scholars both to reimagine critical pedagogy and to carry this tradition forward.

Theoretical Starting Points: Governmentality, Drive, and Desire

More than a matter of doctrine or policy, neoliberalism is a particular historical organization of the meaning of human relationships and human being. The kinds of responsibility and freedom that it proposes are not meant merely to reorient systems of values; beyond this, they are assumed as the unstated discursive and symbolic parameters for coherent decision-making by individuals, states, and institutions. To understand the relationship of subjects to this grammar of the social, and the meaning of critical analysis and action in this context, I draw on two crucial critical lenses for analyzing the meaning of the subject in neoliberalism. Together these frameworks provide important starting points for a reconsideration of Freire's account of the politics of the subject.

First, the notion of *governmentality*, indicating a rationality of government that works across both the state and civil society, is very helpful in understanding the meaning of neoliberalism. Foucault (2008) shows that beyond simply functioning as a policy or ideology, neoliberalism, in the figures of *homo economicus* and the notion of human capital, comes to serve as a matrix of intelligibility for the organization of social and political life. On the one hand, against an old-fashioned laissez-faire position fundamentally hostile to regulation of the economy, the state becomes an important arena for the enactment of neoliberal governmentality, as the market is understood as requiring intervention in order to secure its efficiency (Brown, 2003). On the other hand, the state is just one site of governmentality among many others (Rose, 1999), and this is no less the case in the instance of neoliberal governmentality, which institutes itself as the governing logic across diverse social terrains, including health, education, and the economy itself. In this context, at the same time that a market-oriented accountability is demanded of institutions, likewise the fundamental rationalities of competition and entrepreneurialism increasingly organize our relationships as individuals to others and to ourselves, as we are encouraged to continuously assess our qualities and accomplishments both at work and in private life. This is more than an ideological common sense; below the level of morals and values, neoliberal governmentality sets the ways of knowing and being that can construct coherent identities.

The notion of governmentality foregrounds the problem of subjectivity and points to the historical production of a kind of subjectivity that coheres with and expresses the rationality of *homo economicus* (Foucault, 2008; Read, 2009). In this regard, this framework intersects in important ways with the emphasis in critical pedagogy on the politics of the subject. Perhaps Freire's most urgent intervention, both as an educator and a Marxist, was his central focus on the process of *becoming* for both teacher and student and on the emergence of a historical agency that inaugurates what he considered an authentic subject— against the objectification and paralysis of the oppressed that banking education supports (Freire, 1996). However, an analysis of subjectivity in terms of neoliberal governmentality allows us to consider, beyond the absolute problems of alienation and objectification, specific discursive matrices of intelligibility underlying different historical formations of selves, and in particular the kinds of anxious subjectivity that neoliberal reason both produces and supports. Critical pedagogy in the present has no choice but to work on the terrain created by this reason and in the context of the politics of the subject that is associated with it.

In his propositions regarding the emergence of the subject and the alienation that structures the identity of the oppressed, Freire also depended on a psychoanalytic framework that came to him from the tradition of critical theory—particularly through the work of Fromm (1964) and Marcuse (1964). For this reason, it is also very useful to bring to bear on his theses a second set of conceptual tools that is responsive to this psychoanalytic emphasis. Specifically, drawing from the Lacanian tradition that has been influential in recent analyses of capitalism and neoliberalism (Lacan, 1977, 1978; Dean, 2012; Žižek, 2008a), I start from the notions of *drive* and *desire*. These concepts provide alternative figurations of both the logic of domination in capitalism and of the revolutionary imagination that would contest it. In Lacan's work, as Dean (2012) explains, while both drive and desire are associated with loss, drive achieves a kind of enjoyment through a compulsive repetition or enactment of loss, while desire remains by definition unsatisfied, a desire for desire. This basic distinction allows us to understand, in a political frame, the kinds of compulsion to communicate and consume, both offered and demanded by neoliberalism, in terms of the incessant loop of *drive* (Dean, 2009). At the price of an accommodation with the given, drive supplies a certain limited enjoyment. On the other hand, the principle of *desire* points to a revolutionary project that exceeds and overwhelms the compulsions of neoliberalism. Thus, in abandoning desire, we give up the possibility of fundamental transformation, but in exchange we are offered a compensation in the form of the small pleasures of consumption, communication, and cultivation of self that are ever more ubiquitous in capitalism's real and virtual worlds.

This Lacanian analysis, as extrapolated in contemporary Marxian critiques, shares Freire's commitment to a revolutionary horizon, and for this reason is very useful in evaluating the political status of his central concepts. The notion of desire, in particular, insists on the radical break and openness that are central to Freire's notion of liberation. At the same time, this framework shifts the frame of analysis away from familiar critical-theoretical conceptualizations of ideology and social control. While critical pedagogy has generally thought about these problems in terms of a colonization of consciousness by the powerful (following both Gramsci and the Frankfurt School), the notions of drive and desire point beyond the category of consciousness to the basic structure of self and society in capitalism. The Lacanian perspective describes the ideological organization not just of the individual but of "reality" itself, which only becomes intelligible to us in the context of the libidinal economy that is capitalism (Žižek, 2008a). These conceptual tools can allow us to rotate Freire's psychoanalytic apparatus toward an engagement with the specific organization of subjectivity that neoliberalism creates.

The theoretical frameworks underlying the notion of governmentality, on the one hand, and the notions of drive and desire, on the other, are distinct, and to a certain degree in tension. The notion of governmentality works as a construct enabling us to trace dispositifs (such as human capital) that work continuously across scales and registers of the social, while the notions of drive and desire refer conjunctures of subjectivity and society to the framework of a fundamental libidinal economy. However, my purpose in drawing on these theoretical traditions is not to synthesize them toward a unified account of subject or society. Rather, my aim is to start from the specific insights within each of these approaches on the *organization of subjectivity in neoliberalism*—toward a multipronged interrogation of the Freirean conceptualization of the relation between politics and the structure of the subject. In this way, the analyses of the logic of neoliberalism that are offered within the Foucauldian and Lacanian traditions expose related and yet different aspects of the theoretical and practical problems that confront critical pedagogy in the present. The notion of governmentality illuminates the project and postures of the subject as an expression of and response to power and its reason; the notions of drive and desire point to the circulation of pleasures and the constitutive disavowals that sustain the possibility of the subject within capitalism. These processes are in each case particularly inflected in the context of neoliberalism in ways that are consequential for critical education's purposes and prospects.

Anxiety, Autonomy, and Education

These theoretical principles serve as starting points for my consideration of critical pedagogy's politics of the subject, and this investigation takes place within a contemporary social context that is defined by a condition of pervasive insecurity and anxiety. In contemporary capitalism, freedom is lived as an anxious navigation of difficult economic and social challenges or "choices." At the same time, the fear that characterizes neoliberal landscapes of competition is praised as a spur to initiative and innovation. This landscape of responsibilization and autonomy is the backdrop against which identities are constructed at school, at work, and in a range of social relationships (Lemke, 2001). This is the decisive symbolic and discursive terrain on which education has no choice but to operate in the present, and in order to remain generative, I believe that critical educational interventions must be responsive to the processes that I outline here.

Neoliberal Insecurity and the Topography of Anxiety

Capitalist society in the neoliberal era is characterized by a condition of instability, precariousness, and risk. The subjective supplement to this landscape of insecurity is an extended and complex topography of anxieties. At the existential level, increasingly global and unpredictable flows of capital, information, and technology threaten stable senses of community and identity (Appadurai, 1996) and inaugurate a basic condition of "liquid modernity" (Bauman, 2000), in which familiar social institutions and solidarities dissolve, setting individuals free to navigate social reality as best they can. At the material level, the casualization and fragmentation of the labor market introduce a condition of insecurity and precarity for youth and workers (Standing, 2011). This economic security is accompanied by a carceralization of society that seeks to discipline the unemployed and to warehouse those cast off by neoliberal downsizing (Gilmore, 2007; Wacquant, 2009). This turn to punishment produces a very concrete anxiety in relation to the punishing state for the poor and marginalized, especially people of color (Alexander, 2010).

In education, the topography of anxieties connected to these themes is associated with processes of competition and accountability. As students, teachers, and schools confront a race for rewards and credentials, within which they are persistently assessed, audited, and ranked, education becomes an unceasing effort to achieve above the cut score (Hursh, 2007). However, as researchers have shown, the essential problem is not simply an external pressure that acts to depress imagination or interest. Rather, as students are made increasingly responsible for their educational portfolios (O'Flynn and Peterson, 2007), and as work is reconceptualized as requiring a process of lifelong learning, education is reconstructed in terms of a "learning apparatus" in which agency and empowerment are themselves a form of capture (Simons and Masschelein, 2008). Likewise, accountability and auditing schemes for the evaluation of teachers, in the neoliberal era, partly insinuate themselves into the very mode of being of educators, resulting in a condition of "performativity" (Ball, 2003), in which teachers find themselves reorienting their practice and affect in accordance with systems of curricular standards, even as they partly refuse the pedagogical limits and control that characterize these systems.

Furthermore, these complex ideological and subjective effects should not obscure the straightforward increase in levels of clinical anxiety that has been remarked among school-age children. According to the US National Institute of Mental Health (2016), up to 25 percent of children have a diagnosable anxiety disorder. It has been observed that these levels of anxiety cannot be attributed simply to experiences in school; indeed, as I have described, the kinds of material and immaterial precariousness that are lived in school are continuous across social experience in neoliberalism. Seeking to patch up the anxious identities that such conditions produce, parents and educators have turned to a range of interventions. Notably, along with the rising use of medications for other mental and behavioral conditions such as attention deficit hyperactivity disorder (ADHD), the rate at which antidepressants are prescribed for anxious children has risen significantly in recent years (Griffith, 2016). These medications might be said to act in the context of schooling like the patches that neoliberalism places on the economy as a whole in order to secure the ongoing process of accumulation.

The anxieties introduced by life under neoliberalism should not be understood as mere discomforts. They are connected to a reorganization of subjectivity that cuts across the psychic, somatic, symbolic, and ideological registers (Rose, 1999). In this way they express a fundamental rationality, or governmentality, organizing the intelligibility of the actions of individuals, as instances of human capital, as well as states and other institutions. Anxiety names the subjective and objective tension—expressed both in the fears of individuals and in the crises of institutions—that characterize a way of being organized on the basis of competition. The anxiety that is associated with neoliberal governmentality is important for us to confront, then, not simply as a pathology to be negotiated, but as a basic social condition—as a grid within which the responses of students and the pedagogies of teachers should be crucially contextualized. Moreover, as I argue, the prospects for a contemporary critical pedagogy have to be gauged in relation to this context. Teaching that does not centrally confront this problematic of anxiety will have little chance of reorganizing possibilities for students in an emancipatory frame.

Responsibilization and Autonomy

Neoliberalism channels this experience of insecurity, and the anxieties that accompany it, via a set of ideological processes that obscure the horizon of the social whole and the relationships that organize it. In the first place, the theme of *responsibilization* makes individuals responsible for the social conditions they confront and for their ultimate destinies in this context (Lemke, 2001). As society is restructured in terms of the market, the theme of *choice* comes to be fundamental both to moral frameworks for judging individuals and their fates and to rationales for public policy. Thus, systems of choice are favored in the apportionment of social services. At the same time, one's happiness or unhappiness is understood to be the effect of a sequence of individual decisions in relation to the arenas of education, work, and family. Furthermore, the theme of *punishment* emerges as a supplementary ideological pillar, enforcing discipline and allowing the system to rationalize its own neglect of those on the margins (Melossi, 2008). Within this theme, which is deeply racialized, we see the appearance of an "objective cruelty" (Balibar, 2002) in which the abandonment or incarceration of specific communities is taken as a proof of the virtue of those who are spared and protected.

Against the backdrop of individual and collective crisis, neoliberalism prescribes a greater level of choice and autonomy. We are assured that greater choice in and responsibility for our own destinies is the answer to the social ills that increasingly afflict us. According to the perspective which sees, as neoliberal economist Milton Friedman (2002) puts it, "freedom as the ultimate goal and the individual as the ultimate entity" (p. 5), freedom as choice will allow us to pressure service providers to raise the quality of their product; it will force us to exercise and strengthen our own self-discipline; it will make possible the elimination of superfluous bureaucracies. In this way, neoliberalism offers us the source of the illness (the market itself) as the privileged remedy (Žižek, 2008b). From the earliest grades in school, to the tech-dominated twenty-first-century workplace, to the sphere of moralizing spaces of public discourse, freedom as choice and responsibility is offered both as a cardinal principle and as a solution to persistent crisis. Thus, elementary school children are urged to take ownership of their progress through the educational pipeline, consumers are taught to blame themselves and their imprudent financial choices for the stagnation of the economy as a whole, and citizens are remonstrated with over the failures of the policies of elites.

The outlines of this theory of neoliberal freedom were articulated by F. A. Hayek, whose work served as a touchstone for the pioneering neoliberals of the Chicago school. For Hayek (1960/2011), efficiency and growth were made possible by a basic freedom from state coercion that would allow those with the necessary talent and resources to innovate. Inequality for him was not an obstacle to freedom, but a crucial condition. We can see an expression of this notion of freedom in the choice movement in education, which does not begin from an assumption of equal outcomes for all students. Rather, an unevenness of outcomes is supposed to allow the educational consumer to distinguish "high-performing" from "low-performing" schools. The thrill of school choice is inseparable from the anxiety that attends the risk of a bad bet (on the part of parents and families); this risk is taken as a necessary effect of the judgment of the market even as it leaves unlucky individuals to make their way in sub-optimal educational spaces and reinforces stratification (Ball, 1993). In this way, in the ideological organization of neoliberal freedom, misfortune and failure are the necessary accompaniment of liberty, proving the virtue of those who succeed (De Lissovoy, 2008).

In neoliberalism, the responsibilization of the individual serves as the framework for decision-making. In Lacanian terms, in exchange for the disavowal of *desire* (for *liberation* itself), we are allowed a determined field of *autonomy* within which *drive* can be mobilized; at the same time, an objective anxiety circulates as the residue of this compromise. In this way, neoliberal freedom works as an ideological fantasy which at once fetishizes the proliferation of communication and consumer/lifestyle choices that we confront while obscuring our actual relationship to capitalist society (Dean, 2009). For instance, Boltanski and Chiapello (2005) describe how business management discourse and practice since the 1970s has increasingly sought to emphasize values of employee autonomy and initiative as opposed to structures of top-down control. They argue that this shift worked to head off anti-systemic movements in the 1960s that were directed against both state bureaucracies and capitalist economic exploitation. In moving toward working environments of greater choice, enterprises sought to respond to the cultural critique while evading the political-economic one, and to frame autonomy as a strategic mobility of the employee, rather than as a political category.

Economies of the Subject: Rethinking Freire in Advanced Neoliberalism

How then can critical educators confront this condition of anxiety, and the neoliberal responsibilization and autonomy that accompany it? I argue that in order to respond adequately to the recomposition of social domination and subjectivity in the neoliberal moment, we must reconceptualize central principles in the tradition of critical pedagogy, and in the work of Paulo Freire in particular. At the same time, we should preserve the radical commitment and imagination that has characterized this tradition, and rediscover this imagination in new modes of praxis. Following Freire (1974, 1996, 1998), any adequate critical pedagogy has to rest on analysis of the social logic that holds together subject and society. Education intervenes on this terrain, opening up in dialogue the possibility of reimagining investments and relationships that structure the self. However, Freirean critical analysis in the present should be partly rethought in several crucial respects, in light of the context and processes that have been previously described.

From Alienation to Fragmentation

For Freire, the essential historical and political problem is alienation—the alienation of human beings from themselves, from society, and from their vocation as historical agents. This alienation, expressed in the authoritarianism of the workplace and the school, denies the humanity of the oppressed, reducing them to quasi-objects, detached from the historicity of the world and from the solidarity in which individuals can emerge as integrated subjects: "The oppressed have been destroyed precisely because their situation has reduced them to things. In order to regain their humanity they must cease to be things and fight as men and women" (Freire, 1996, p. 51). Against alienation, problem-posing education recovers the world as a space of possibility, and recovers for the oppressed the special task of restoring an authenticity to human being. In the processes of conscientization and praxis, the oppressed undergo a transformation, an emergence out of mere existence and into subjectivity itself, as they become "permanent re-creators" (1996, p. 51) of the world. In existential terms, problem-posing education makes the world present authentically, as the dialectical counterpart of a humanity that aches to intervene and to push back against the inauthenticity that is expressed in relations of oppression and domination.

In neoliberalism's regime of anxious autonomy, however, it may not be the distance from the authentic that constitutes the inner meaning of the self; rather, an atomization and fragmentation keep the self perpetually off-balance and incoherent (Fisher, 2009). For instance, the emergence of the theme of "multitasking," which is simultaneously valorized and disparaged in popular discourse, points to the reorganization of both work and leisure in terms of the management of an incessant stream of small assignments or distractions (Wallis, 2006). Likewise, neoliberalism does not aim at a paralysis of the subject; rather, the self becomes incessantly mobile (Dean, 2009), as it aims to establish its presence or assert its image across multiple sites and networks. In contrast to the stunting of subjectivity diagnosed by Freire, the anxious subject of neoliberalism is *obsessively cultivated*—and disperses in multiple directions. It is prolific and promiscuous, responsible for a multitude of subject-effects. For a literal example we can look to the proliferation of identities that individuals manage across multiplying social networks, both personal and professional (Facebook, Twitter, LinkedIn, Instagram, etc.). In this way, rather than suffering from a lack of subjectivity, in neoliberalism we might be said to suffer from an *excess* of subjectivity. This neoliberal self anxiously seeks to manage the expectations and requirements that come with its obsessive enlargement. Plugging into the social network at multiple points, individuals must attend continuously to each of its nodes. In neoliberalism, the cathexis of energies that makes possible the emerging subject contemplated by Freire is confounded by the incessant dispersal of the self, and the recuperation of its fragments by the social network.

Both school and higher education in neoliberalism's contemporary "enterprise culture" (Peters, 2001) endorse and reproduce this condition in their obsessive embrace of technology, their reframing of curricula and courses of study in terms of "entrepreneurship," and their outsourcing of auditing onto students in the form of assessments required by accreditation and accountability processes. US public school students now take an average of 112 standardized tests between pre-kindergarten and twelfth grade (Hart, et al., 2015). Furthermore, students are encouraged to develop habits of self-surveillance through behavior management systems (García & De Lissovoy, 2013). These initiatives take for granted that the multiplication of modes of engagement and the habits cultivated by continuous auditing are beneficial for students. These new educational processes may support skills of self-presentation that are increasingly expected in education and at work (Simons & Masschelein, 2008); at the same time, they result for students in a dispersal of the self and a fundamentally anxious orientation.

Reconsidering the "Fear of Freedom"

Likewise, it is against this backdrop that we ought to reconsider the critical-pedagogical diagnosis of social oppression in terms of a "fear of freedom." In this idea, central to his argument in *Pedagogy of the Oppressed*, Freire argues that marginalization and domination work primarily through an ideological process of assimilation, which paralyzes the oppressed and leaves them unable to imagine themselves as political and historical agents:

> The "fear of freedom" which afflicts the oppressed, a fear which may equally well lead them to desire the role of oppressor or bind them to the role of oppressed, should be examined. One of the basic elements of the relationship between oppressor and oppressed is *prescription*. Every prescription represents the imposition of one individual's choice upon another, transforming the consciousness of the person prescribed to into one that conforms with the prescriber's consciousness. Thus, the behavior of the oppressed is a prescribed behavior, following as it does the guidelines of the oppressor. (Freire, 1996, pp. 28–9)

The goal of Freire's problem-posing pedagogy is to overcome this paralysis through a demystification of the authority and power of the oppressor, and through an unveiling of reality as an open space of historicity. For the student, the recognition of oneself as a subject in history makes possible a new freedom to intervene in the world. Against the narrow reality of the given, freedom in Freire's problem-posing education is connected to a basic remaking of social and educational relationships (Freire, 1998). His emphasis on the ideological, psychic, and symbolic registers represented in the notion of the "fear of freedom," and the project of *demystification* which must confront this fear, has been inherited by the tradition of critical pedagogy, and continues to organize its diagnoses and proposals (e.g., hooks, 2003; McLaren, 2003).

However, given neoliberalism's pervasive processes of responsibilization and its retraining of the understanding, body, affects, and personality in accordance with an anxious performativity, is it indeed a psychic immobilization that primarily afflicts the oppressed? I argue that the critical diagnosis should be at least partly rethought in the current context. In the present, it might be said that the oppressed suffer less from a *fear of freedom* than from an *anxious autonomy*. In advanced neoliberalism, a pervasively entrepreneurial governmentality directs subjects to optimize their performances (Ball, 2003). What confronts the majority is the prospect of falling through the cracks, not just of the social safety net but of society itself—as this latter notion becomes increasingly frayed (Bauman, 2000). For instance, those who have given up looking for work are not counted in unemployment statistics; in effect, within the official accounting, they have ceased to exist. The marginalized are increasingly thrown back, materially and ideologically, on their own devices, while being asked to participate in a retraining of their ways of being. The form of control at work here is distinct from the internalization of authority that Freire (1996, 2005) emphasized, and from the fear of transgressing it. The authoritarianism with which Freire was concerned reserved a position for the oppressed within its system, however abject; neoliberalism threatens to pull the rug out from under the subject altogether, as individuals and communities are made dispensable through downsizing and incarceration (Sudbury, 2002; Wacquant, 2009). After all, from the perspective of neoliberalism, liberation from the claims (and guarantees) of society itself represents the purest form of autonomy.

Being Neoliberal

Anxiety also differs from alienation in terms of its point of attack on the subject. As Foucault (2008) describes, the neoliberal installation of the figure of *homo economicus* at the heart of social and political reason means that we confront the world as fundamentally a condition of risk which necessitates a calculating and strategic orientation. Internalizing the competitive logic associated with the market, we understand our agency in society in terms of an entrepreneurialism that seeks to accumulate economic and symbolic capital and outperform others on diverse indices of value and achievement. In education, this entrepreneurial rationality is produced through systems of accountability and assessment, discourses of lifelong learning, and the proliferation of certificates, diplomas, and credentials of various kinds. Anxiety in this context works not simply as the effect of a race to the top but also as a crucial spur to activity, a pressure toward self-control and exertion. From this perspective, anxious autonomy becomes not just a way of thinking but a way of being. It is incorporated into our habits, interactions, impulses, and social rituals (Davies & Bansel, 2007). Thus, in contrast to the "necrophilic" gaze of banking education, which immobilizes the subjectivity of the oppressed and "transforms students into receiving objects" (Freire, 1996, p. 58), anxiety is not only or primarily a psychological syndrome. Rather, it is a discursive, affective, and corporeal field that works as much across the surfaces of the self as it does within the ideological core.

In psychoanalytic terms, we can understand neoliberalism's anxious autonomy in terms of the theorization of drive. As neoliberalism displaces the horizons of revolution, history, and utopian ideals with a micro-politics of local interventions, we accommodate by sublimating our desire to a manageable democratic politics of drive that returns partial victories and pleasures. Through drive, the subject enjoys "in another way," as desire gives up and turns back on itself, and as we replace solidarity with self-surveillance (Dean, 2012). In this bargain, we are afforded an identity that has its place in the network, and its private itineraries of struggle and success. While the Freirean notion of alienation points to a subject cut off from society as agent and actor, the neoliberal subject by contrast is offered a watered-down or simulated agency at every point—as a consumer choosing among products, a parent choosing among charters, a young person choosing a persona on social media, or even an activist choosing among local interventions. Given this condition of preoccupation that plagues the neoliberal subject, it may be that even the truncated subjectivity of the *oppressed* that Freire (1994, 1996) describes is in some respects potentially more potent. Denied and dominated by power, the self of the oppressed, for Freire, nevertheless remains an incipient whole, and its experience of alienation can serve as the ground of critique. The dispensable and distracted neoliberal subject, on the other hand, is plugged in at multiple points to a temporality constructed as a perpetual present (Fisher, 2009), and must devote its energy to managing these fragments toward a provisional and shaky unity.

This condition is both ideological and material. Increasing insecurity at work and the stagnation of pay mean that many people must continually struggle to secure additional employment. In this regard, the tendency to fragmentation in neoliberalism confronts people as an objective condition. Not only do the kinds of identity that are attached to a settled vocation become increasingly tenuous but also the amount of energy that must go into securing a basic entry into the labor market—one might say the very opportunity to be exploited—increases significantly, especially for those at the bottom of the scale (Van Oort, 2015). Everyday life is in this way pervasively reframed in terms of a strategic orientation. In education, we can see a similar process in the growth of alternative schools that are emerging both outside and in the interior of the public school system (Grady, Bielick & Aud, 2010). In the spread of magnet programs, special academies, and districts within districts, not to mention the growth in dual language programs, career and technical education, and other forms of curricular differentiation, students and their families confront a complex terrain that demands very significant attention and calculation. These boutique programs are not all geared toward affluent families; rather, the fragmentation of the system takes place across diverse levels of educational stratification.

Beyond Anxious Autonomy: Critical Principles

The process of *conscientization*, as described by Freire and the critical-pedagogical tradition that has followed him, aims to awaken persons at once to the social and political conditions that surround them and to cultivate a historical subjectivity and agency that can act against these conditions and create transformative praxis. This critical awakening pierces the veil within which the world appears inert and immovable and in which history shows up as the property of the powerful, and as already determined in its reflection of their interests and understandings. This is what Freire (1996) refers to as the "narrative" character of oppression, which paralyzes the oppressed within a story not of their own making and within which they appear as no more than quasi-objects (pp. 52–4). Freire's methodology aims to crack open the fixity of this narrative, through a collective process of interrogation, critique, and self-reflection, and to uncover reality as an existential and historical problem:

> Problem-posing education affirms men and women as beings in the process of becoming—as unfinished, uncompleted beings in and with a likewise

unfinished reality. Indeed, in contrast to other animals who are unfinished, but not historical, people know themselves to be unfinished; they are aware of their incompletion. In this incompletion and this awareness lie the very roots of education as an exclusively human manifestation. (1996, p. 65)

This methodology challenges the objectification and paralysis of subjectivity that prevailing and dominative forms of education produce. It proposes an exploration and development of knowing and being within which the oppressed might emerge as active and authentic subjects and authors of their own realities.

Freire's emphasis on the need for intervention on the terrain of subjectivity, and the centrality of pedagogy in this process, remains essential: he shows that the organization of the imagination is a decisive political task. Likewise, Freire's (1998) insistence on an emancipatory horizon in teaching should remain as a touchstone for critical pedagogy in the present, against the prevailing narrative that social transformation is impossible. At the same time, it is also necessary now to partly rethink the processes of conscientization and problem-posing centered by Freire. In the context of a "communicative capitalism" (Dean, 2009) that demands constant motion and extension of subjectivity, and that atomizes and disperses subjects through neoliberal modes of autonomy, I argue that it is as necessary in the first instance to unravel the proliferating selves that operate us as it is to focus on an amplification of subjectivity. In teaching, we should work to break through the loop of drive that constitutes students as the subjects of accumulating and accelerating pleasures. In this way, the authentic being together of students and teachers, which includes passages of both silence and discomfort (not just talk), should pull students away from the habitual selves that insulate and isolate them. Refusing the compulsions that tie both teachers and students to an autonomy built from individualized decision points, we need to discover a collective subjectivity and agency that liberates us from the "freedom" of fragmentation.

Betraying Anxious Subjectivities

Neoliberal governmentality institutes competition and entrepreneurialism as the central truths of self and society. Not only beliefs and ideologies but identities, habits, and affects are recreated in neoliberalism as effects of the need to valorize one's capacities as human capital. Networked with the captured imaginations of others, our human creativity becomes an engine of surplus value in the era of knowledge capitalism, including within education (Olssen & Peters, 2005). Hardt and Negri (2004) argue that in this context what is necessary is an *exodus* from subjectivity as given and a production of new identities that threaten the regime of material and immaterial accumulation. We can also understand this exodus as a withdrawal from the circuits of communicative capitalism that trap us in the loop of drive. From this perspective, the emphasis in Freire's formulation should be somewhat altered: rather than aiming in teaching at the consolidation of an imposing figure of authenticity (the oppressed as historical Subject), critical pedagogy might recover *desire* as the "collective subjectification of an irreducible gap" (Dean, 2012, p. 199). Here Dean describes a basic impasse within being that our compulsive communication and consumption practices seek to evade. We need to be faithful to this gap, which is the very site of emancipatory possibility in self and society, including in education (Ford, 2017), and in this way seek to cleave the subject from the structure of anxious accommodation that neoliberalism produces.

Students in Freire's account are invited to reflect on and overcome their own fear of freedom: "To surmount the situation of oppression, people must first critically recognize its causes, so that through transforming action they can create a new situation" (1996, p. 29). Rearticulating this process of *overcoming* in the context of the precariousness that organizes possibilities for being in school and society in advanced neoliberalism, we might instead invite students to *betray* their anxiety. It is not that this anxiety is unfounded, but rather that it inscribes precariousness as the truth of being and refuses the possibility of reflection. In the context of the contemporary "learning apparatus" (Simons & Masschelein, 2008), the race for credentials that infects even the early years of schooling and crowds out educational experiences not geared toward bolstering students' academic portfolios is both a response to an objective condition and a determined cultivation of a particular form of subjectivity. Likewise, as Vassallo (2013) shows, the current fetishizing in educational psychology of "self-regulated learning" ostensibly aims at empowerment while actually demanding of students an anxious dependence on and adaptation to their environments.

Betrayal, as a critical strategy, would mean delinking from neoliberalism's ideological, psychic, and affective economies. Against neoliberalism's logic of scarcity, which is manifested in schools as a relentless competition for symbolic capital and self-driven human capital development, critical pedagogy might propose collective projects premised on a revolutionary plenitude (Hardt & Negri, 2004)—the plenitude of students' desire and imagination. Autonomy in this context would be refigured not as individual freedom to choose among determined alternatives but rather as collective imagination against the given

(Love, 2019). Radicalizing the familiar progressive emphasis on collaborative educational experiences, the pedagogical projects proposed here would depart from the decided curriculum of the school and would refuse validation on the basis of the earning of credit or qualification. The many social movements in which youth are currently involved (for example for immigrant rights and ethnic studies, educational equity, and freedom from police violence, among others) propose exactly this kind of praxis-based education that works outside of the official spaces of learning (see for instance Cabrera, Mesa, Romero & Rodríguez, 2013).

The betrayal of anxiety is at the same time a betrayal of the *isolation* that is the foundation of neoliberal autonomy. Neoliberalism figures the accumulation of choices as freedom and replaces collective power to act with an individualized tactics of navigation through the landscape of the given. Students experience this as a proliferation of ostensibly elective (but in fact required) experiences, both curricular and extracurricular. Indeed, for college applicants the entrepreneurial ethos now often demands, as part of the overall resume, a record of altruistic volunteerism—and service opportunities are sought as a way to enhance the applicant's package (Morimoto & Friedland, 2013). Against this relentless entrepreneurialism, how might students find instead a collective and emancipatory subjectivity and imagination? Beyond the familiar call for solidarity in progressive pedagogy, we need to build a new pedagogical subject and project. Inviting students to turn away from themselves as anxious, exhausted, and isolated entrepreneurs of their own talents and capacities—a logic which prevails in working-class schools as well as in more affluent ones— we should point the way at the same time toward an organized and collective subjectivity within which the singularity of each individual imagination becomes a privileged moment of the whole (De Lissovoy & Armonda, 2020).

This means the constitution of a collective that refuses the atomization, anxiety, and narrow autonomy that is offered by neoliberal education. For instance, struggles by students, parents, and teachers to protect community schools and against the proliferation of charters, as in Chicago, New Orleans, and elsewhere, are usually analyzed in terms of opposition to privatization. While this is correct, it is also important to see these struggles as rejecting the narrow framing of freedom as freedom of choice, and also as refusing the individualization of the social that neoliberalism insists on. These movements implicitly propose a collective and community agency and subjectivity in place of the atomized agency of the individual educational consumer (see for instance Buras, et al., 2010). Similarly, the recent resurgence of a militant and community-oriented teacher unionism (as represented in such disparate instances as the Chicago Teachers Union and its Caucus of Rank-and-File Educators, United Teachers Los Angeles, and the struggles by the teachers union and affiliated movement in Oaxaca, Mexico) refuses the terms at once of teaching, politics, and subjectivity that neoliberalism offers. In their place, these movements embody a *dangerous* subjectivity (from the perspective of power)—a subjectivity that collects the singularities of individual actors into a potent collective that refuses to perform according to the rules of neoliberal reason. These movements are both defensive efforts to preserve places and possibilities for public education and offensive efforts to assert new political protagonists and identities.

Practical-Pedagogical Starting Points

In practical terms, for educators my analysis suggests that we should be skeptical about the current fetishizing of pedagogical tactics and learning modalities connected to technological innovation. Teachers are increasingly encouraged to exploit the latest apps, presentation platforms, virtual discussion and polling sites, and other innovations, and in this way to update to what we might call their *pedagogical operating system*. However, in the first place the novelty of these innovations is mistaken for educational improvement, as has been pointed out (Burbules, 2016). More importantly, these proliferating platforms cohere with the trends in neoliberalism described above toward the fragmentation and incessant mobilization of the learning subject. This bloom of educational technology often takes the place of collective dialogue and prevents the developed critical analysis that dialogue makes possible. The movement of teaching and learning online during the Covid-19 pandemic was necessary, and in breaking (in part) from the familiar routine, pointed to new possibilities. At the same time, this shift has accelerated the technologization of education. If the obsession with apps and learning modes represents a culmination of the progressive tradition's emphasis on experimentation in constructing educational environments, the refusal of this fetishism would mark the point where a genuinely critical education would chart a different course. Even the move toward "social justice" in schools sometimes results in a series of ephemeral experiences for students, as opposed to engaging them in a theoretical and practical struggle aimed at basic transformation (De Lissovoy, 2013b). Here too, the solicitation of temporary subject-effects is substituted for the constitution of a collective and critical agency.

A more fundamental problem for educators is how to escape an economy of classroom communication in which more is always thought to be better, and in which the proliferation of discourse is taken as proof of the vigor of dialogue. In this case, we ought to insist once more on Freire's notion of dialogical communication (2005) and *communion* (1996), which should be distinguished both from the relationships underlying banking education and from those expressed in indifferent talk. Communion depends on an economy of speech and silence that involves interlocutors in a dangerous intimacy. In Freire's framing, dialogue brings people together in a shared attention to the world as a historical problem. However, in contrast to the paralysis of the oppressed that Freire described and sought to break through, critical educators in the present must work through a collective compulsion toward incessant communication and interactivity. Thus, the pedagogical challenge in the present may be first of all to reveal the possibilities that incessant communication refuses, and to *clear a space for dialogue* (which is different from speech) in the first place. This means a departure not only from test-driven teaching but also from a more general fear of unscripted or unanticipated gaps in classroom discourse.

The distinction between the anxious autonomy of neoliberalism and the commitment to collective critique and action is not the same as the opposition between insecurity and safety. Emerging from neoliberal governmentality is not a safe process nor does it imply any automatic hopefulness. On the contrary, the recomposition of subjectivity that the exodus from neoliberal freedom implies is an ordeal, to the extent that it challenges the habits and grounds of the self that sustain our intelligibility (Žižek, 1999). However, radical dialogue and critique can also open a horizon of ethical commitment and collective identification that is fundamentally enlivening. The task of critical educators is to make that option, which is obscured by the dispersal of identity and attention that neoliberalism sets in motion, present and concrete for students. More than an ideological investigation, critical pedagogy has to undertake a reorganization of being.

Conclusion: The Practice of Emancipation

The tradition of critical pedagogy following Paulo Freire has insisted that the site of teaching, and the process of becoming of students and teachers, is deeply political (Freire, 1996; Giroux, 2001; hooks, 1994). For Freire, the authenticity of critical pedagogy is proven by its revolutionary commitment; conversely, social transformation depends on a democratic and pedagogical engagement with the oppressed. In this regard, Freirean critical pedagogy shares with the Foucauldian and Lacanian perspectives I have started from here an emphasis on the centrality of a politics of the subject. The notions of governmentality on the one hand, and drive and desire on the other, point to the coincidence of the subjective and systemic, just as critical dialogue in Freire is both an individual and a collective process of transformation.

At the same time, these perspectives differ in how they understand the subject, and these differences are important for their ability to make sense of the context of neoliberalism. For Freire (1996), consciousness is the crucial site of struggle in the process of liberation, and conscientization (or consciousness-raising) is the essential form that this struggle takes; problem-posing education "strives for the *emergence* of consciousness and *critical intervention* in reality" (p. 62; italics in original). By contrast, the notion of governmentality, often described as the "conduct of conduct," points to a rationality that is realized in *performance* (Ball, 2003). Thus, *homo economicus* is not simply the name for a subject dominated by a market-oriented common sense but rather indicates an agent that is coherent with the matrix of intelligibility of neoliberalism. Likewise, the notions of drive and desire point beyond the interiority of the subject toward the *practices* that produce political reality. The neoliberal subject is realized in its compulsive networking and virtual communication (Dean, 2009). On the other hand, the reality of desire is proven in a break with these compulsions, in acts that work as a cut in the libidinal economy of capitalism.

These distinctions are important in a neoliberal context that is partly defined by power's sidestepping of traditional hegemonic struggles. Neoliberalism's ultimate message is that *there is no alternative* to its organization of society. Its victory is in our surrender, in practice, to its inevitability. In accordance with what Žižek (1999) calls a contemporary "decline in symbolic efficiency," political protests are increasingly experienced in the present as moments of self-expression that circulate like other opinions within capitalism's communicative circuits, no longer capable necessarily of demanding a response from power (Passavant, 2014). Similarly, in education, control works increasingly through apparatuses of testing and standards and the pervasive anxiety that accompanies them rather than through ideological limits on permissible discourse. The Freirean emphasis on consciousness runs up against an economy of practice (the rituals of accountability) that proceeds in spite of our determined critiques of its premises (De Lissovoy, 2013a). In this context, the demystification of power, and the process of consciousness-raising, can only go so far; radical politics and pedagogy ultimately have to prove themselves through a set of practices that break from neoliberal governmentality and the compulsions of drive.

Anxiety in neoliberalism is a response to real insecurities and instabilities. At the same time, anxiety becomes the privileged mode and limit of response, as neoliberalism presents itself as the solution to the crises it has created (Slater, 2015). While political leaders seek to capitalize on widespread anxiety to justify retrenchment, the prevailing moral pedagogy makes this anxiety into a virtue in representing it as a spur to self-improvement. In education, this turn can be seen in the recent celebration of student resilience and "grit," as Saltman (2014) describes. But the responsibilization which blames students for the system's failure obscures its dominative rationality while also demanding a difficult inflation of the subject. While the prevailing discourse insists that individuals become aggressive entrepreneurs of whatever cognitive and symbolic capital they can muster, critical pedagogy in the present should seek by contrast to betray the anxiety that fuels this obsessive entrepreneurialism. As we turn away, in schools and elsewhere, from an identification with the exhausted and fragmented agent of neoliberal freedom, we should turn instead toward an identification with a collective and emancipatory political subject. In this effort, we stay faithful to Freire's radical project while also reinventing it for the present. If critical dialogue cannot now be counted on by itself to initiate a political sequence in the way that Freire at times seems to assume, the collective determination that he outlined, against a form of power that is both an ideological system and an ontological order, remains indispensable. In this project, as I have described, subjectivity is an essential political category and its ways of being are a crucial site of contest.

7

Constituent Power, Ethics, and Democratic Education

Democracy is a vexed question in the present. Progressive and critical visions of democracy struggle with the burden of tired rhetorics of engagement. The language of democracy is appropriated continuously for efforts at empire building. Meanwhile, democratic education is increasingly marginalized under the pressure of educational accountability regimes. While the question of democracy is implicit in the investigations, in preceding chapters, of the politics of the subject in capitalism, this chapter is an explicit intervention in this regard and an effort to specify the meaning of democratic education in the current moment. In this investigation, I start from two contemporary philosophers—and two radical philosophical traditions—to understand democracy in an alternative frame. The first of these is Antonio Negri and autonomist Marxism; my focus is on Negri's interpretation of the concept of *constituent power*. My second starting point is Enrique Dussel and his philosophy of liberation; within Dussel's work, I focus on the notions of *obediential power* and the ethics of *exteriority*.

Negri and Dussel share an emphasis on the originary power of the multitude (or *pueblo*, in Dussel's terms), from which constituted and institutional power derives. They also both foreground the revolutionary potential of relationality, a condition that Dussel analyzes in terms of a decolonial ethics. In the course of my analysis of these ideas, I offer a critique of prevailing progressive conceptions of democracy, and I outline several important philosophical starting points for democratic education in the present. I argue that the resources these two radical traditions make available for conceptualizing democracy should push us, against the image of democracy as unity and reconciliation, to rethink teaching and learning in terms of a basic (political) trauma, as well as to look past familiar senses of criticality toward an affirmation of the agency of students and communities. Building from these principles, I conclude this chapter with a discussion of a pedagogy of radical *longing*—faithful to students' imaginations and desires—that might animate contemporary democratic education.

I develop these positions along the way by juxtaposing them with John Dewey's conceptions of democracy and democratic education. Dewey's ideas stand in contrast to the cheapened models of engagement that official politics offers us. He shares with Negri and Dussel a focus on communication and relationship as central criteria for democracy. Mobilizing complex processes of social coordination and organization, democracy for Dewey (1997a, 1997b) is an active principle, not a detached index of institutional procedures. At the same time, I argue that the ambivalence and enervation of the principle of democracy in the current moment also find an echo in Dewey's work. His philosophy fails to register the irreducible antagonisms that extend across social life and forgets the revolutionary desire that works past the limits of his own project of reconstruction. To this extent, Dewey's philosophy is complicit in the assimilation of democratic education into the structure of the given. By contrast, I argue that if we start from the emphasis on relationality, solidarity, and collaboration that he shares with Negri and Dussel, and yet develop this emphasis in a way that is sensitive to the radical ethics, creativity, and desire that are centered in the latter, we can propose a model of democratic education that is responsive to the particular challenges of the historical moment.

Constituent Power and the Crisis of Politics

The notion of *constituent power*, as it has been developed in the work of Antonio Negri, including in his work with Michael Hardt, is an important starting point for conceptualizing democracy in the present (Hardt and Negri, 2000, 2004, 2009; Negri, 1999, 2003). Building on a long history in political philosophy of engagement with this idea, Negri understands constituent power as the force that brings political life into being—the generative power, or *potenza*, from which democracy springs as a basic and open need. However, in contrast to many thinkers who focus on the way in which constituent power is absorbed into and constructs established political orders, Negri emphasizes the permanence and absoluteness of constituent power:

> In contrast, the paradigm of constituent power is that of a force that bursts apart, breaks, interrupts, unhinges any preexisting equilibrium and any possible continuity. Constituent power is tied to the notion of democracy as absolute

power. Thus, as a violent and expansive force, constituent power is a concept connected to the social preconstitution of the democratic totality. (Negri, 1999, p. 11)

Democracy, from this perspective, is not located in the juridical realm but in the ontological power of the multitude. Constituent power is an omnipresent creative and irruptive force, and this innovativeness and revolutionary determination are the essence of democracy. Constituent power, for Negri, is not exactly equal to *the people*, as a political subject, but is rather found in life itself, in the biopower of living labor. In this regard, Negri's understanding of constituent power is a Marxist one, since he sees the basic antagonism that splits politics as ultimately rooted in the dominion of capital, as dead labor, over human life and creativity. Emerging within and against capitalist exploitation, "constituent power is established politically on that social cooperation that is congenital in living labor" (Negri, 1999, p. 33). Negri's work understands the revolutionary movements that have always threatened rulers as much more than oppositional; as expressions of constituent power, such movements are generative of politics in the first place, and inassimilable to any order that would freeze them within a logic of institutions and constitutional representation.

There are important echoes of Dewey in Negri's arguments. Most importantly, like Dewey, Negri locates the source and meaning of democracy outside the structures of the state, electoral politics, and official advocacy with which this category is usually identified. Dewey's criteria for democracy are also, in the first instance, social ones:

> The first [element] signifies not only more numerous and more varied points of shared common interest, but greater reliance upon the recognition of mutual interests as a factor in social control. The second means not only freer interaction between social groups ... but change in social habit—its continuous readjustment through meeting the new situations produced by varied intercourse. (Dewey, 1997a, pp. 86–7)

Thus, Dewey's description focuses on interest, interactions, and habit, within a broader definition of democracy as "conjoint communicated experience" (p. 87). Likewise, for Negri, democracy is a social and ontological process—a "becoming-common" in which the inherent creativity of the collective, materialized in cooperation and communication, threatens the relations of production of economic and political life. Dewey's celebration of democracy's "widening of the area of shared concerns" (p. 87), and the way that it cultivates ever more complex networks of relationships and processes of coordination, is close to the emphasis in Hardt and Negri (2004, 2009) on the autonomously developing creativity of networks and the webs of communication that bring singularities together into a multitude. Indeed, as for Dewey, the multitude for Hardt and Negri is the subject of democracy not through any particular program of civic action, but rather in its very being. The "kaleidoscopic" character of this subject, in which difference is built on rather than subsumed, recalls the bridging of differences (of class and culture) in democracy so emphasized by Dewey. Constituent power draws on the capacity for relation and communication which produces the richness of experience that Dewey saw as being at the heart of both democracy and education.

Nevertheless, the notion of constituent power as articulated by Negri differs from (and presses against) Dewey's sense of democracy in several important respects. In the first place, whereas Dewey understands richness of experience as grounding democracy and providing the rationale for processes of governance, Negri emphasizes the essential antagonism toward institutions and sovereignty that animates constituent power:

> Everything, in sum, sets constituent power and sovereignty in opposition, even the absolute character that both categories lay claim to: the absoluteness of sovereignty is a totalitarian concept, whereas that of constituent power is the absoluteness of democratic government. (Negri, 1999, p. 13)

For Negri, the creativity inherent in constituent power directly confronts the limits of constituted power, and this challenge is immediately the criterion for democracy. A *crisis* lives in the heart of politics which reveals the democratic force of constituent power; the point is not to solve this problem but rather to "better identify its critical characteristics, its negative content, and its unsolvable essence" (1999, p. 12). While Dewey seeks to create political and educational spaces open to experimentation and change, crisis itself can hardly be said to be a productive category for him, and he celebrates a form of social control that regulates democratic social life and which wards off its antagonisms and aporias. Control is very different for Dewey (1997b) from simple authority, referring instead to the organic direction of activities that is affirmed by participants rather than foisted upon them; however, it is precisely the rules and habits that organize social life from the inside that Negri's vision of democracy most urgently confronts. Negri (1999) describes an "ontological accumulation" (p. 32) that characterizes the evolution and growing strength of the multitude in its resistance to domination, and that challenges the existing order even at the level of the habits and identities within which subjects are intelligible.

Furthermore, the process of struggle foregrounded in the notion of constituent power is directed above all against capital itself, which is not merely a limit to creativity but, in fact, a process of absorption and transmutation of life, strength, and *potenza*. Just as capitalism feeds off the natural creativity of life at the level of the exploitation of labor, so too, at the level of its institutions, it exploits and subsumes the history-making force of constituent power's permanent revolution. By contrast, for Dewey, the evil of class society is understood in terms of a condition of isolation. An antisocial spirit, Dewey argues,

> marks nations in their isolation from one another; families which seclude their domestic concerns as if they had no connection with a larger life; schools when separated from the interest of home and community; the divisions of rich and poor; learned and unlearned. (Dewey, 1997a, p. 86)

If Dewey's analysis of the harms of class polarization in terms of the *estrangement* of social groups is usefully unconventional—exposing, for instance, the distortions even of elite culture that result—the notion of democracy is at the same time attenuated in his account, and its agonistic dimension is foreclosed. By contrast, for Negri, the struggle of life against capital marks the point at which political revolution intersects with social emancipation, an intersection which is the matrix of democracy itself. It is not simply that Dewey's notion of democracy is exposed, in a formal sense, as too placid; it is that his perspective refuses the necessary determination of democracy as insurrection—within a history organized by the conquest of dead labor over living labor.

Within a temporality of democracy registered as an impetuous present (Negri, 1999) rather than a simple continuity of experience (Dewey, 1997b), education needs to expose the constitutive crisis that lives as much in the habits and categories of ordinary experience as in the visible confrontations of politics itself. Education does not provoke this crisis but rather uncovers it. Dewey's injunction to educators to test thinking against the evidence of the world, and to connect academic work to life outside the boundaries of the school, might in this regard be pressed against itself. If constituted power, like the constituted experience of education in schooling, is written in letters of domination and assimilation, as Negri's analysis suggests, then a democratic pedagogy will have to be directed in the first place against the given, if only to mobilize the power of relationships and collaboration that Dewey so ardently insists on. In this history—the history we in fact inhabit—the richness of experience at which Dewey's philosophy aims can be nothing other than the richness of *revolt*—a rebellion against a form of rule that aims not merely to sideline constituent power but rather to refuse and defeat it.

Obediential Power and the Ethics of Exteriority

Negri's elaboration of the notion of constituent power, juxtaposed with Dewey's work, might be said to reveal the missing element of the *political* in the latter's notion of democracy—where the political is understood not in the sense of the constitutional or institutional but rather as a terrain of antagonism, insurrection, and dissensus (Rancière, 2010). On the other hand, the work of philosopher of liberation Enrique Dussel (1985, 2003, 2008), and in particular his notions of *obediential power* and *exteriority*, might be said to expose the attenuation of the *ethical* in Dewey's philosophy, even if, just as is the case with Negri, there are important concerns and commitments shared by Dewey and Dussel.

For Dussel, the possibility of democracy depends on a responsibility to ethical principles that are the framework for authentic forms of intersubjectivity at the existential level as well as for civic action and governance at the level of politics. Relationships are foundational for Dussel, just as they are for Dewey. However, from Dussel's (1985, 2003) perspective, to specify ethical relationships properly means to confront the historical facts of Eurocentrism, conquest, and cultural marginalization. Dussel argues that within Western philosophy and politics, tied genealogically to imperialism, the world as totality of meaning excludes the reality and dignity of the oppressed, and this totality as Being affirms itself against the non-Being of the (Indigenous, exploited, and impoverished) Other. As Dussel describes it, the true ethical moment is not that of a responsiveness to an already intelligible Other as interlocutor, but rather that of a traumatic impinging, on the given, of the Other as exteriority:

> Others reveal themselves as others in all the acuteness of their exteriority when they burst in upon us as something extremely distinct, as nonhabitual, nonroutine, as the extraordinary, the enormous ("apart from the norm")—the poor, the oppressed. They are the ones who, by the side of the road, outside the system, show their suffering, challenging faces: "We're hungry! We have the right to eat!" (Dussel, 1985, p. 43)

Thus, the ethical moment profoundly disturbs the world as settled organization of sense through the epiphany of the alterity of the Other—above all, through the gaze of the oppressed.

Likewise, in political life, the people (*pueblo*)—the community of the oppressed and marginalized—becomes a political actor not in being incorporated into the system, but rather in tearing down its walls, affirming the will to live against a fetishized and dominative politics (Dussel, 2008). Although for both Dussel and Negri the source of politics is the transformational power of the *pueblo/ multitude*, Dussel argues further that the liberatory potential (*potentia*) of the people must realize itself on the terrain of feasibility and practicality and become institutionalized in some form (*potestas*). The challenge is for *potestas* to remain accountable to the *pueblo* and its liberatory vocation. The form of this democratic accountability, this refusal of the fetishization of politics, is a power that "commands by obeying"—what Dussel (2008) calls "obediential power." Fulfilling the mission of obediential power means being attentive to a call and vocation in which "the one who 'calls' is the community, the people, and the one who is called feels 'summoned' to assume the responsibility of service" (Dussel, 2008, p. 25).

For both Dewey and Dussel, democracy crucially means overcoming social distance and division. As is often remarked, central to Dewey's vision of education as a democratic process is his emphasis on the way that it can overcome differences and bring people from diverse backgrounds together within the framework of a common experience (Moses and Chang, 2006). For Dewey, overcoming distance and division does not just follow from an arbitrary throwing together of learners, but is rather the result of engagement in a "constant reorganizing or reconstructing of experience" (Dewey, 1997a, p. 76), a process that remakes both impulses and desires (Dewey, 1997b), and that works at both the individual and institutional levels. Likewise, for Dussel, liberatory struggle depends on a solidarity that also aims to overcome distance, though in a way that is different from that described by Dewey. Solidarity, for Dussel (1985), refers back to a primordial condition of *proximity* (in the first instance, of mother and child). Both romantic love and comradeship, for instance, work across the distances that organize the world to recall this original proximity— not the ontic closeness of separate beings (or of separate bodies in a classroom), but the ethical closeness of subjects in "face-to-face" relation (Dussel, 1985, p. 19).

Furthermore, this ethics of proximity means more than particular persons encountering each other; it extends to encompass the social, historical, and physical environment. Thus, human beings remake themselves in their interventions in and in their responsibility to their material surroundings. For Dewey, this worldly dimension is represented in his expanded notion of practical or industrial education, an education that refuses to divide mind and body. On the other hand, Dussel (2008) highlights this practical dimension in terms of a basic responsibility to the reproduction of life in economic, cultural, and ecological terms. Dewey's empiricism is echoed in Dussel's (2008) insistence, against an idealistic orientation to politics, on "the heterogeneous differentiation of functions through institutions that allow power to become real, empirical and feasible" (p. 20). The space of democracy is in this way at once transformative and practical, its ambitiousness guided by a responsiveness to materiality.

However, just as Negri's work exposes a basic antagonism—between the constituent and the constituted—that cuts across the space of politics and which Dewey's account obscures, Dussel points to the ethical space subtending politics as a space of confrontation and radical struggle rather than merely of negotiation and coordination. In a history given by imperialism and alienation, the ethical recognition of the Other is at the same time the intrusion of *exteriority* into the world as given (see also Maldonado-Torres, 2007; Mignolo, 2011). For Dussel, the oppressed stand out against and beyond their assimilation by the system. In this context, the epiphany in which others are recognized (against their reduction to mere instruments) is not an indifferent step forward for democracy, but rather an interruption of the sense and order of Being: "As other than the system, that one is beyond Being. Inasmuch as Being is and non-Being is not, the other is not. If the other speaks, provokes, or demands, it is the verbal expression of non-Being" (Dussel, 1985, p. 51). From Dussel's perspective, then, the ordeal of ethical recognition must devastate the social coordination and control that remain desiderata for Dewey within a process of reconstruction (by citizens and/ or students). Put another way, for Dewey, education reconstructs the inadequate architecture of society, opening passages where there were only closed spaces and letting light in against the dimness of inertia and prejudice. But for Dussel (1985), this house of the social, indeed of Being itself, rests on the foundation of the non-Being of the Other. We find justice not in improving the construction of this system but rather in breaking its beams and shattering its windows, which offer to the privileged inhabitants only a reflection of themselves. This Western philosophical and cultural projection of the centered self, even as it seems to insist on growth and change, remains a repetition of Being and thus a repetition of the assimilative truth of invasion. In this way, Dewey's vision, not in spite of but precisely in its very progressivism, consolidates what Goeman (2014) calls "settler grammars" that erase the dispossession of Indigenous people and encode a presumed superiority of the settler state—a discursive strategy tied to deeply embedded understandings of citizenship.

Dussel's obediential power opposes the corruption that comes with fetishized power, which is power for its own sake, enclosed in bureaucracy and separated from the people. By contrast, from the vantage point of Dewey's (1997a) criterion for democracy, in which "more numerous and more varied points of contact denote a greater diversity of stimuli to which an individual has to respond" (p. 87), authoritarianism is to be rejected because of its paucity of opportunities for relationship, communication, and collaboration. In an authoritarian system, "stimulation and response are exceedingly one-sided" (Dewey, 1997a, p. 84). However, this argument ignores the active violence of institutional power, which usurps and corrupts the foundation of politics in the people. The everyday contraction of politics to a set of institutional (especially electoral) procedures is not merely a truncation of democracy (West, 2009) but an active denial of the *pueblo* that is the true source of politics (Dussel, 2008). This is more than a matter of pointing to a terrain that Dewey tends to underemphasize. From the standpoint of the oppressed global "periphery," the very virtues of the center, including the norms of established democratic life, are expressions of a dominative ontology and a fetishized politics—in Dussel's (1985) terms, a "legality of perversion" (p. 57). As history has shown, even the Deweyan and progressive impulse to challenge division and stratification can easily be made to cohere with an alienating rationale of mere *diversity*, as opposed to an insistence on the ethical and political *alterity* of the Other. By contrast, the category of the *pueblo* expresses the political and hegemonic agency of the oppressed. Otherness is not mere difference here, but rather exteriority and anti-power, as the starting point for genuine political creativity and transformation.

Rethinking Democratic Education

The accounts I have described share with Dewey and progressive education more broadly an emphasis on the centrality of relationships to democracy, as well as a focus on cooperation and solidarity as foundational to social life. They differ from him, however, in understanding democratic collaboration as essentially revolutionary and partisan—that is, fundamentally oriented against the world as it is given and fundamentally accountable to the oppressed and exploited multitude. Taken together, the arguments of Negri and Dussel propose a reframing of the "conjoint communicated experience" that is the Deweyan criterion for both democracy and education, and it is to the implications of my investigation for education that I now turn. Here I offer a critique of aspects of Dewey's work while also outlining key principles of a critical pedagogy grounded in the notions of constituent power and decolonial ethics. This means considering the meanings of relationship and democracy in the space of teaching, and specifying what are in the first instance political concepts in pedagogical terms.

Against Reconciliation

For Dewey (1997a), the progressive classroom coordinates individual and social development in a unified project of becoming: "It is the particular task of education at the present time to struggle in behalf of an aim in which social efficiency and personal culture are synonyms instead of antagonists" (p. 123). The effective curriculum work of the teacher, which sets out a flexible and yet organized educational environment, allows for a multilevel process of integration: integration of a student's personal capacities (versus one-sided training), integration of different students within the collective space of learning (versus an antisocial and antidemocratic individualism), and integration of local and present interests with social and long-term aims (versus an irrational provincialism). In this way, Dewey arguably stages in his educational program a fantasy of reconciliation. The progressive Deweyan classroom aims to reveal the unity of the apparent antinomies of modern experience: The individual and social, for instance, do not come to a compromise in his account, or collide toward a Hegelian synthesis, but are rather revealed as ultimately identical. Thus, the control exerted by the rules of a game is not a limit on the freedom of the individual child, Dewey (1997b) argues, but rather the condition and occasion of this freedom, since individual agency can only exist in social context. One might even say that, for Dewey, the exercise of individual freedom *expresses* this social organization.

Conceptualizing education in terms of constituent and obediential power means challenging this emphasis on integration and reconciliation. The accounts of Negri and Dussel start from a principle of antagonism that not only opposes the rulers to the ruled but also traverses internally the body of the collective subject of the *pueblo*/multitude—or, in the educational context, the students. For instance, in an extended analysis, Negri argues that the revolutionary force of the early Soviet workers' councils was not in serving as building blocks of socialist society and government, but rather in mobilizing and organizing revolutionary desire—a desire directed against constituted power and the state itself. To the assimilation, by the constituted power of the state, of moments of revolutionary mobilization, "the communists must always answer no; the movement must continue and go beyond itself" (Negri, 1999, p. 292). Revolutionary agency and creativity are in this way in fundamental tension with sites of even "radical" institutional or constituted power, and thus, in order to stay faithful to the gap of revolutionary desire, they must go beyond themselves and aim for the very abolition of constituted power.

Likewise, the group that is the teacher and students together cannot aim simply to actualize the full potentials of the classroom environment, to integrate and coordinate them in the manner suggested by Dewey. Rather, this group must aim to surpass itself toward a set of possibilities already disallowed by the educational institution. The classroom, as the site of constituted and institutional power, does not just hamper the possibilities of teaching and learning, but rather absorbs, exploits, and assimilates them (Lewis, 2012; Means, 2011). The university, for instance, seduces us with the promise of free inquiry, all the avenues of which are nevertheless labeled and catalogued within its diverse programs and faculties (Edu-Factory Collective, 2009). By contrast, where learning is alive and enlivening, it is directed against education as unity and reconciliation. This is more than a matter of a contradiction between authentic inquiry and the acquisition of the symbolic capital of educational credentials. Even the hum of the progressive classroom, at once organized and unpredictable, ultimately expresses the school and society of which it is a part. By contrast, the insurrectionary classroom must imagine and instigate a rupture, both social and educational. The kinds of critical conversation that it opens up should enact a break with the reason of the school, and create the possibility of an unruly and autonomous teaching and learning (Slater and Griggs, 2015). Thus, to the extent that teaching is determined by a decided set of institutional possibilities, democratic pedagogy must in the first instance also be directed against education itself.

Pedagogy and Trauma

We can best capture the temporality in Dewey of democratic education in his principle of *continuity* of experience. The principle of continuity, he argues, means that educational environments should reckon with and respond to accumulated experiences in the past, while at the same time reorganizing the understandings and identities that have been their result with a view to opening possibilities for further growth (Dewey, 1997b). The principle of continuity in Dewey is closely connected to the principle of reconstruction, which challenges the received wisdom of the past, the accumulated habits of students, and the gulf that separates different classes and communities. Reconstruction is more than a simple gradualism that tinkers with ideas and institutions until they are more or less perfected. Nevertheless, the principle of continuity works as a theoretical and practical limit to this process of reorganization. Continuity establishes a temporal coherence; it integrates past, present, and future; and it aims to liberate powers that exist as potentials in the individual and society. This temporal coherence corresponds to the underlying relationship between Dewey's vision of democratic society and actually existing Western modernity. While Dewey outlines a political and pedagogical rearrangement that would reshape this modernity, the principle of continuity nevertheless demands that the new must grow from the inner trajectory and possibilities of the given.

The reframing of the notions of relationship and democracy that I have outlined in this chapter suggests a temporality for pedagogy that is very different. Against the notion of continuity, the radical time of politics that emerges from the autonomist and decolonial accounts I have considered in this chapter might be understood in terms of the notion of *trauma*. This term is popularly used to refer in a general way to painful experiences. However, the Greek root means, more specifically, a *wound* or *blow*—a sense that foregrounds the objective register, whereas the popular usage emphasizes the subjective. Thus, ethics, for Dussel (1985), depends on the effect of the shock of recognition of the Other— the impinging on Being by non-Being or exteriority, as I have described. This is a kind of ontological trauma that is much more than subjective; it points to the abyss that grounds subjectivity (Žižek, 1999). Pedagogy, as a relational and ethical project, should engage the dynamics of this traumatic recognition, a recognition that absolutely confronts settled forces and conditions. This does not mean that democratic education is always concerned with "revolution" rather than "reform," in a narrow sense, but rather that we have to recognize that democracy involves a passage through an essential moment of crisis. Importantly, however, the relation to the notion of trauma is different for different students. For instance, while this is a generative process—in the sense that I outline it here—for white people (for whom an ordeal of disidentification opens on to social and political possibility), for people of color the challenge is for pedagogy to mediate a relationship to a historical trauma that is already well underway; the subjective recomposition that is relevant here is students' creative refusal, in the educational context, of racism's pervasive assaults. Likewise, the revaluation of the notion of trauma I propose here might also be understood in terms of an inversion in perspective: from the vantage point of those who have been oppressed, the wounding of power and whiteness means after all a kind of healing.

In terms of the interactions between students and teacher(s), we can recognize this sense of trauma within the transformation produced by dialogue. Dialogue aims not at reconciliation but rather at the ordeal of intersubjectivity (Freire, 1996). Dialogue does not mean submerging interlocutors within an undifferentiated unity, but rather confronting them with the upsurge of alterity and demanding from them an extension of self toward this otherness. As Dussel (1985) puts it, in the moment of recognition that is the condition of dialogue, "suddenly the glassy stare of the instrumentalized is transformed into a penetrating gaze" (p. 63). Dussel highlights the shock of this encounter and the way that the consolidated identity of the privileged is disrupted, even injured, by the gaze of the oppressed. In the same way, recent work on the dynamics of whiteness in education points to the distance and defenses that white teachers place in the way of recognition of and solidarity with students of color (see, for example, Leonardo, 2009; Picower, 2009), and shows the risk and stakes of these encounters. These defenses aim to ward off the ordeal of recognition and the ethical responsibility it implies—since to defy them is dangerous to the teacher's settled identity. It may seem incongruous to claim that everyday interactions in classrooms or other educational spaces are, or should be, marked by such moments of risk, but that is what is demanded by a genuinely radical and ethical pedagogy (De Lissovoy, 2010).

Just as Dewey means reconstruction to refer both to the reorganization of impulses in the individual student and to the reorganization of purposes in society more broadly, in the same way the particular sense of trauma that I outline here should be understood as a social and cultural process just as much as an individual one. In education, this process is importantly registered on the terrain of curriculum. By curriculum, I mean the epistemological underpinnings of what is taught just as much as the educational resources and environments themselves. It is at this point that the *decolonial* problematic most clearly touches the terrain of teaching. Cultural domination takes place crucially on the terrain of knowledge; in education, this means a "pedagogical alienation" for marginalized students which can even be felt as a "cultural death" (Dussel, 1985, p. 90). From the standpoint of an ethics of liberation, the curricular response cannot be mere reorganization. Rather, the decolonial option proposes a different epistemological order, and *disrupts* the claims of the dominant (Mignolo, 2011). Furthermore, it means listening to different lessons and stories, Indigenous ones in particular, from other cultural, embodied, and "kinetic" standpoints (Simpson, 2017).

To propose a curriculum unmoored from Eurocentric exceptionalism means displacing the "center" (Dussel, 1998); it means privileging the projects and desires—the sciences, literature, and arts—of the "periphery" (McCarthy, 1998). The decolonial option presents a significant challenge to progressive educational philosophy to the extent that it decenters the latter's central epistemological and cultural supports.

The Meaning of Criticality

The progressive conception of democracy in politics and education should be juxtaposed with a properly critical conception; nevertheless, the meaning of the critical has to be specified. In this regard, the theoretical resources I have drawn on here also press on familiar approaches to *critical* education and their conceptions of the relationships that organize teaching and learning. These tensions can be instructive for our consideration of Dewey himself.

For instance, the critical pedagogy of Paulo Freire (1996, 2005) and the tradition that has followed him points beyond the reorganization of impulses and understandings that Dewey proposes toward a more radical project of emancipation. Importantly, the liberation of the oppressed in the Freirean tradition requires and starts from the intervention of the teacher or organic intellectual. From the standpoint of Negri's (1999) analysis of constituent power, however, the constituted power of institutional agents, including teachers, derives ultimately from the originary power of the multitude. This fundamental creativity can be inflected and organized by educators and leaders but it does not depend on them for its emergence or effectivity. While Negri's work tends at times to be overly enthusiastic about this autonomous agency, it does implicitly propose an interrogation of the "epistemological curiosity" (Freire, 1998) that places the critical teacher/leader, in an epistemological sense, in an *advanced* position relative to the students. Without abolishing the figure of the teacher (in the manner of Rancière, 1991, or Illich, 1970), Negri's work challenges critical educators to be more attentive to the centrality and agency of students themselves, and to learn even more profoundly "to speak by listening," as Freire (1998, p. 104) puts it.

Similarly, the permanent revolution of constituent power extends upwards through the register of epistemological authority, challenging the notion of *science* upon which both Deweyan progressivism and critical education have sought to establish their practice. For Dewey, science offers a method for thinking itself, on which pedagogical experiences should be modeled. This method passes sequentially through the moments of "perplexity," "conjectural anticipation," "careful survey," "elaboration of the tentative hypothesis," and "testing the hypothesis" (Dewey, 1997a, p. 150). On the other hand, for critical pedagogy, the alternative science of *ideology critique* lifts teaching and learning out of the realm of the merely ingenuous (Freire, 1998; McLaren, 2007). However, just as the position of epistemological advancement that these approaches reserve for teachers risks obscuring the agency of students, so too does the emphasis on the authority of a scientific method potentially risk obscuring the primacy of revolutionary *desire* (Dean, 2012)—as well as the shock of the ethical encounter, highlighted by Dussel (1985), between teacher and student—as the criterion for radical education. Love is not simply a prerequisite in this regard but rather the essence of method itself, apart from which the methodological science of educationalists fades into a dry recipe.

From this perspective, criticality has to make its way past the *negative* toward a radical *affirmation* of students and communities. The Deweyan and Freirean dialectics of democracy aim at a properly educated subject of praxis; this subject is in a sense the end product of enrollment into an educational program of citizenship and conscientization. However, while not denying the central role played by educators and leaders, we should recognize that the true author and subject of democracy is the *pueblo* itself. Teachers, in accordance with Dussel's (2008) notion of obediential power, which recognizes that "there is no other subject of power except the community" (p. 18), ought to be fundamentally responsible to this original agency in students—not simply as a raw capacity that waits to be effectively molded by the teacher's understanding but rather as the creative power that is already organizing the occasion of teaching and learning.

Conclusion: Democracy and the Pedagogy of Longing

The foregoing discussion suggests that democratic education involves the shock of encounter—with the Other, with desire, with the impossible. The principles of constituent power and exteriority point to an erotics of democracy in which love pulls subjects toward each other and toward a revolutionary project—and beyond the transactionalism of prevailing liberal conceptions of democracy. While Dewey's account of democracy is powerful, positing a shared space of interaction and communication that extends beyond familiar definitions of civic engagement, he nevertheless does not engage the revolutionary and libidinal horizon of politics and teaching. If politics and pedagogy depend on being faithful to radical desire (which, in the Lacanian sense, is always a desire for desire, a faithfulness to the gap that lives within the given), Dewey betrays this desire in his preference for a process of reconstruction that reorganizes reality (the subjective reality of learners and the objective reality of society) without confronting the antagonism between constituted power and the desire of the multitude. By contrast, the ethical and insurrectionary projects of Negri and Dussel are animated by a desire that demands this confrontation, an erotics of democracy that remembers the necessity of love as revolutionary struggle.

Democracy means nothing if it does not engage subjects in a demand for what reality refuses. This is the indispensable kernel of democratic teaching. When we speak of democratic education, we ought to speak of a *pedagogy of longing*. An education for democracy is an education that presents to students what has been refused and invites them to remember their need for and commitment to it. This pedagogy seeks to uncover the ways in which we are fundamentally vulnerable to each other (Butler, 2004), and the ways in which we must desire the end of the processes of domination that exploit these vulnerabilities. To speak of longing is to speak not merely of a personal disposition but rather of a collective and political project. In his notion of *communion*, Freire (1996) proposes a project of this kind; however, to frame critical pedagogy in terms of longing is to emphasize how the communion of teaching catches us up in the most intimate of ways, as well as how it immediately confronts the contrary commandment— from power—to brokenness and isolation.

The proposals of Dewey and progressive education already importantly move the center of gravity of teaching away from abstract lessons in history or civics to engaged and collaborative experiences that mobilize the democratic *capacities* of students. However, a critical and decolonial pedagogy of democracy, as I have outlined it, would invite students to additional and riskier collaborations, in which not merely are their habits of mind unsettled but also their suffering is witnessed, their anger is awakened, and their desire is provoked. It is important to acknowledge that students do not require educators to give them permission for the condition of engagement that I evoke here. However, teachers can crucially participate in furthering this engagement and can lend important resources to it (Adair, 2014). Curriculum, for instance, remains a crucial site of decolonial contestation (Paraskeva, 2011), and efforts (by teachers and faculty) to decenter the Western and Northern authority that has anchored curriculum show that basic reconfigurations of the politics of knowledge in education are possible (Grande, 2004). Furthermore, neoliberalism's increasingly frenetic siphoning of resources from public schooling and its attack on instruction through processes of accountability is a crucial generative theme for teachers to respond to (Au, 2011). In this case, democratic education confronts its antagonist immediately in the ordering of the experience of school itself. Beyond simply exposing these processes, democratic pedagogy should incite the imagination of students toward a different kind of teaching and learning, and articulate, with them, a praxis that can materialize this imagination.

Democratic education, I believe, cannot mean just the inculcation of certain orientations and dispositions. It has to participate in crystallizing for students the contradictions that set the basic conditions for experience: the contradiction between dead and living labor (i.e., between capital and human creativity); the contradiction between the Being of the powerful and the non-/refused Being of the excluded; and the contradiction between an ethics of deferral to constituted or fetishized power and an ethics of revolution (faithful to constituent and obediential power). Beneath the traffic of opinions that constitutes what we conventionally understand as politics, the antagonisms just mentioned produce the real terrain of the political. We ought to feel the real ordeal that these contradictions and this struggle visit upon us, underneath the salves that power's false generosity provides, and we ought to feel (which is perhaps even more difficult) the real desire that captures us when we begin to experience transformation as possibility and actuality. In this pedagogy, the power of collectivity, communication, and relationship becomes concrete rather than abstract, and shifts from an ideal to a material, and dangerous, practice.

8

Notes for a Revolutionary Curriculum

1. Opening

Current crises caused by the coronavirus pandemic and police violence against Black and Brown communities have created an unprecedented social and political shift. The tremendous suffering of this moment is accompanied by new possibilities for change. The pandemic has forced a dramatic reorganization of daily life even as it has thrown working people into economic crisis. At the same time, uprisings against state violence have put the system on its heels while demonstrating an unanticipated depth of solidarity and commitment across communities. These crises reach also to education as schooling is upended for large sectors. The current shock to the capitalist system opens up a space of possibility in education and society. As politics, daily life, and learning are destabilized, shouldn't thinking and theory be as well? This chapter seeks to press the insights developed throughout this volume into a confrontation with the contemporary crisis, and in response to this moment's emergencies and possibilities, suggests a reimagination of the pillars of radical education.

I believe that we are invited by this moment to consider the question of what kinds of curricula, in schools and beyond, might be possible—beyond the habitual and stultifying forms with which we are familiar. As the slate is wiped clean, the questions cease to be purely theoretical: What might we actually want to learn? What might we actually want to be? As the encompassing cognitive envelope of information, education, and ideology is shaken loose, the world, in its particularity and materiality, becomes more vivid and present. It reminds us that there is only the present, which does not belong to old stories. We are called to a dialogue with the world, to listen to what we weren't able to hear before. We might walk out into it in a new way, and find a schema for a new kind of learning.

If all experience is educative, as Dewey (1997a) put it, then the breaks and torsions of experience also teach, unsettlingly. Each moment of aliveness, in its anguish or triumph, is also a teaching. In the current moment, we can feel the historicity of oppression in a new way—its dependence on a set of constructed assumptions and understandings. Even revolutionary movements have insisted on the necessity of strategic compromise in the long march out of the shadow of domination; now, our starting point should be: *no compromise*. No more exploitation, no more rationales of imposition, no more fictitious sciences of hierarchy and degradation, and no more teaching of these sciences. The challenge is that even the critical traditions have formed themselves in relation to the given and its limits. How can we press these traditions beyond that determination, and discover a liberatory knowledge built out of an uncaptured language?

We need new conceptual tools and principles for struggle, which we can use to take advantage of the current historical opening. At the same time, we need to look forward—past this crisis, and capitalism itself—to a radically different kind of education, not bound by the limits of the current dispensation. I do not believe that identifying the commitments and principles of a fundamentally new curriculum (understood in the broadest sense) is wishful thinking. Rather, it is a necessary step both for being able to imagine and believe that we can move past the current system and for being prepared for the moment when we do. In this process, we need to think beyond the current organization of teaching and also beyond its current meanings; we need to consider education's unconsidered registers and possibilities.

Learning is being—being produced in the juxtaposition of sites and moments. Likewise, capitalism is an organization of bodies, movement, materiality, affects, and understandings. If its arrangement of being is interrupted, it ceases to function. Capitalism convinces us that being belongs to it and is impossible without it. But we need to refuse the assertion of its order, in the understanding that actually capitalism *belongs to us*, in a historical sense, as only one social possibility, one arrangement. Teaching might participate in moving beyond capitalism in the arrangements that it evokes. Teaching sets up sequences of events that work as an open coding of ontological and historical potentials. So the *art* of teaching is indispensable, as many have noted, but also the *conscientiousness* that takes responsibility for its potent intervention. This is not only the ethical responsibility that Freire (1998) foregrounds but also a kind of scientific responsibility that is attuned to effects and implications.

This kind of intentional teaching depends on a deep cooperation and mutuality. In capitalism, mutuality is organized through the medium of the market. That is why collaboration in education always gets cashed in for a grade. But an ungoverned mutuality produces strange exchanges and thick cooperation. In education, we almost can't imagine what such collaboration would look like, since the whole logic of school is underpinned by the symbolic capital of the diploma or credential. What would it look like to learn together in the absence of this anxiety? Would the walls collapse? One of the basic logics of capitalism is mutilation—the mutilation of process, relationship, and becoming, which produces the commodity and the settled truth. Is it so radical to want to refuse that mutilation, to want to open the possibility of wholeness? Familiar progressive and critical pedagogies gesture toward that wholeness but they do not give themselves the permission to actually imagine and create it.

Solidarity not only is strength in the face of power but is also the basic condition of survival. In this sense it is unsentimental and indispensable. Solidarity in the context of education means mutual support toward the finding/founding of a truth. We hold each other up because we can't understand without each other. But the shape of solidarity in education is complex. While teachers learn from students even as they teach, the students, collectively, teach the history that encompasses all. That is, the mobilization of the people/students, taken as a whole, *directs* the process of learning and praxis, and sets the parameters for engagement. We need a kind of curriculum that is produced from the living and livid energy of regular people. That would be a revolutionary teaching, obeying the sacred word of the whole. This is more than a constructivist or culturally relevant curriculum. This is a curriculum of commotion and communication, working across quadrants.

I aim in these reflections to undertake the imagination of such a curriculum. This is an anti-capitalist and socialist project. It is also an opportunity to reimagine the limits of these commitments. Revolution is a process that works at the levels of subject and sensibility in addition to relations of production in a familiar frame. We need to create new sites/sights, new orientations, new idioms, new ambitions, new juxtapositions. History already pushes us into some of these on its own. I believe that we can build on those immediate experiences and press them forward toward a more comprehensive and systematic apprehension of revolution. This requires, however, a committed and energetic kind of thinking.

2. Collaboration

Collaboration in the critical traditions is different from the group work that is recommended in conventional approaches to teaching. In the former, learning together takes place under the sign of struggle and aims at transformation. In the latter, collaboration is simply an alternative modality for experiencing the familiar educational environment and epistemology. For Freire (1996), collaboration in critical education is necessary because we become ourselves through dialogue, and because dialogue is indispensable for constructing historical agency. By contrast, in a liberal frame, collaboration is *teamwork*—an appropriation of the creative possibilities of cooperation toward the production of the same learning-commodity that is aimed at in individualized study.

Even critical approaches, however, risk preserving an emphasis on the individual—whose subjectivity is organized and activated by means of dialogue with others. The excitement of the process of *conscientization*, as Freire describes it, is in the way that this process illuminates a particular learner's sense of their relation to the world—even if this illumination occurs at the same time for others. Collaboration in this frame produces an existential shift that changes *our own* sense of ourselves and of historical possibility. The communion that Freirean dialogue envisions in pedagogy and praxis both preserves and transgresses the limits of the individual consciousness.

Is it possible to look beyond this sense of collaboration and the kinds of subjectivity it depends on to a different and deeper sense of collectivity in education and praxis? Might the current moment demand a reconfiguration of these categories in the context of the historical task of collective survival against a desperate capitalism's accelerationism and eliminationism? Can we think of collaboration not so much in moral or even political terms—but rather in an ontological frame? In doing so, can we rescue a revolutionary sense for collaboration—one that aims in the first instance at a material disruption of the given and its ideological and aesthetic *police* (Rancière, 2010), rather than at a moral enlargement of the subject?

The first step in this reconceptualization of collaboration might be to recognize the collective intelligence of people, before the institutionalization of formal processes of dialogue. Recognizing this intelligence challenges the individualism of even critical educational accounts as well as the tendency to center the teacher/leader's pedagogical authority. In his account of the Haitian revolution, C. L. R. James (1963) argues that Toussaint L'Ouverture's ultimate mistake was to lose touch with the desires and thoughts of the mass of Black laborers whose movement he was leading. But James goes even further, arguing that in the context of revolution, the people (and their unknown leaders at ground level) are the actual and authentic directors of the movement, whose implicit or explicit direction the more visible and celebrated leaders must be faithful to, at the risk of betraying the revolution. The task of the leader, in this context, is not to show the people the way but rather to listen to the people in order to discover the way, and to help them in the blazing of that trail. This collective understanding is historical—the product of a deep attunement that can only be possessed by an entire class.

The consolidated image of the masses proposed by James may not adequately respond to the splintering, disorientation, and demoralization that precarity, pandemic, and ecological destruction have produced in the present. But even these processes are class experiences which occasion new kinds of collective communication and learning. Any project for social or political transformation has to begin from the understandings that are created in the context of crisis, and which proceed from the ground up, even where the ground is shifting or broken. Formal political or pedagogical collaboration, as a second order organization of thinking and action, has to be based on the primary collaboration within social being itself—the elemental intelligence of the mass of regular people, in the context of a naked confrontation with history.

Starting from this understanding in education would mean listening to, and living within, the collective intelligence of students. It would also mean recognizing regular people as themselves competent students of their own lives. Instead of simply building from "prior knowledge," as progressive education aims to do, it would aim for unprecedented juxtapositions of experience, understanding, and impulse. For instance, what indispensable insights on contemporary politics and society do *children* possess (Simpson, 2017)? How are we missing out in not taking their insights deadly seriously? What wisdoms exist in the communication between the diverse texts that populate formal and informal educational experience (e.g., video, voice, storefront, chapter, advertisement)? What secrets do teachers know that they aren't telling, because they believe that they don't count against the school's official knowledge? What knowledge is proposed in the accidental sliver of woods beyond the strip mall, filled with trash and saplings and wildflowers?

Capitalism seeks to abolish intelligence, in its most authentic sense—the collective intelligence of being that listens to and converses with the world. Capitalism bends understanding into the distorted forms that are compatible with its distortions of work, relationship, and identity. Collaboration that starts from genuine curiosity has to be directed against these distortions, which limit the possibilities for knowledge even as they regiment experience itself. In this context, collaboration is subversive in reaching past the individualism that is the ideological anchor of capitalist society and in crystallizing the mass intelligence of ordinary people as a powerful subject of learning. Power insists on and clings to ignorance— both the people's ignorance and its own. Collaboration and collectivity threaten the system in a political sense and also in an epistemological sense, since the system is jealous of knowledge that might extend beyond its own flat rationality. From the point of view of education, this means that the most deliberate and dialogical learning is inherently radical at the level of its epistemological commitments.

We might reimagine the space of school as the nexus of diverse collaborations proceeding outward as often from students as from teachers. What if students or parents or community members could propose educational projects reaching across classrooms and generations and professional status? What if the physical space of school were the repository of the artifacts of the imagination of connected communities? What if the school was relevant not only "culturally" but also politically, philosophically, strategically? The public system increasingly serves students of color and poor students, as white and more affluent families exit the system for private education. What if the students left behind, together with teachers, seized this space as a laboratory for the creative, complex, and unpredictable production of an organic class consciousness? This is an inherently contradictory proposition to the extent that schools have always worked to stratify and exclude. That is precisely the reason for the urgency of this dream, which we can only dream in the context of a breach in the given. Such a school is only imaginable in exceptional circumstances, and as the result of a purposeful appropriation (De Lissovoy, Means, & Saltman, 2014).

If collaboration is complexified and intensified, its products—as culture, identity, knowledge—will be too. If the range of connections between people increases, so too will the richness of their communicative accomplishments. The power of collaboration is connected to its social and political horizon, as critical education has stressed; but in addition, I suggest that while the collective intelligence of people has a direction, it might press forward in that direction along a multiplicity of paths, and curriculum might be an intersection in that open landscape.

3. Foundation

Can there be a kind of learning that gathers up the abandoned fragments, that looks past shattering? We are more than ideologically compromised. We are broken in the bones of our being. We are broken in the grammars of our understanding. We can't overcome those hurts through ratiocination. We have to *heal* those hurts, and we have to refuse to be the agent of them.

Fraser (2018) argues that behind the process of exploitation, which is the hidden background of capitalism's foreground of exchange, there are *other* backgrounds, upon which exploitation itself depends—namely, the domains of social reproduction, political constitution, and the appropriation of nature. These are the "non-economic" spheres against which the economy defines itself, and which capitalism obscurely assimilates. The crucial implication is that struggle has to take place on terrains beyond the market and beyond the economic foreground of capitalism. This includes the terrain of social ontology: what the institution of capital allows us, and the world, to come to be. Is there not likewise, behind the background of the ideological hegemony that conditions the official curriculum in schools, *another* background on which this hegemony depends—the ontology of the classroom, the field of violences that makes the classroom possible?

If so, then politics and pedagogy have to start from this first plane, and our refusals have to be refusals not only of framings of the world but of the world itself as physics and history of domination. In this deeper refusal we might move from the alterglobalization motto, "Another world is possible," to "Another world is here." We might be able to see, unraveling, the tissue of injuries that constitutes capitalism and its world. Pedagogy might proceed from and refer to the modulation in being through which a post-capitalist world is emerging. As in the Haitian rebellion narrated by James, there is a revolution underneath the revolution. Just as the rebellion in San Domingo against the planters and for France's Rights of Man concealed a more fundamental revolution against imperialism and for independence, we might say that underneath the surface of contemporary political contests there is an underlying contest of ontologies.

Teaching has to be attuned to this *foundation of the foundation*. The familiar first principles of progressive education fall away in this gap, as the protagonists of teaching and learning change shape and reassemble. For instance, in the context of the pandemic, the teacher splits in two: the virtual authority that emanates from the online school on the one hand and the improvising amateur (parent/sibling) at home or in the neighborhood on the other. Official instruction is hard to sustain for long in this context, but the flux of attention and activity that characterize this moment is its own kind of education. The rebellion that might emerge from this opening is not against the teacher or the school but instead against the certainties—of temporality, identity, knowledge—that have set the parameters of even alternative forms of education.

If familiar critical education uncovers the hidden determinants of disparities and injustices, a new pedagogy ought to uncover the conditions for these determinants themselves. These conditions include the continual collapse of being into the familiar; the violence that makes exploitation possible; the humiliation of spirit, not just psyche; the tyranny of capital over space and time; and the paltry satisfactions of accomplishment and ambition in learning that conceal an emaciated subjectivity.

In *Stalker*, a film by Andrei Tarkovsky, a meteor strike has produced a depopulated terrain of decaying buildings and wild grass (the "Zone"), both dangerous and miraculous. The Zone is a figure for the unconscious and for the terrain of partial objects that are the *ingredients* of assembled persons and realities. In the film, only a journey through this landscape can offer the possibility of true fulfillment and liberation, but the journey is risky. We can also understand this as the terrain that pedagogy has to negotiate—the sub-terrain below the familiar agents and identities of education. Teaching has to learn to see and respond to the incomprehensible elements that inhabit this realm. The impacts of social domination, like that of the meteor in Tarkovsky's film, have penetrated even to this depth, creating fields of pain that liberatory praxis has to come to know through modalities beyond the familiar ones. At this level, the task is less to understand than to listen, and less to overcome than to heal. If Fraser is right that we should extend our definition of capitalism to include its impacts on and assimilation of a set of background sites and experiences beyond the economy, we should also extend our sense of the meaning of struggle against capitalism to include the attunement and healing that works at the level of being and spirit.

This attunement is connected to familiar kinds of caring in education but it is not identical to them. It has to be distinguished from the emotional and intellectual labor that the system itself demands of teachers, and which progressive pedagogies supplement. The attunement I am describing does not contradict familiar kinds of solidarity with students, but it works as a commitment that extends beyond them. It is not a personal quality or principle, but rather a journey into the commons of the political unconscious.

4. Experience

We are used to thinking, in a critical frame, of learning as a process of awakening. But what if it needs to be rather a properly *revolutionary* sequence? What if learning takes place in a condition of extremity? For Dewey (1997a), all experience teaches, albeit in different directions, and his framework describes traditional education simply as less optimal in terms of the experiences it affords (as compared with progressive education). But this overlooks the wretchedness and viciousness of the actual and given "experience" in schools and beyond them. We need to do more than just apprehend that wretchedness. What if learning begins not in the slow awakening to the hidden determinations of "normal" reality, but rather at the moment in which we begin to strike out against this reality?

Conversely, revolution is not a narrow and calculated power play, but rather an experience, an education. As Rosa Luxemburg (2004b) showed, it cannot be scripted and directed by professional leaders but has to be made and lived by the masses, in a process of "spiritual transformation" leading toward socialism. Without this pedagogical aspect, revolution will fail, since it will only remove elites without destroying bourgeois forms of consciousness and authority. The people are taught here not by enlightened cadres but by the procession of events themselves—the brisk twists and turns of the exceptional moments in which history makes a shift. Luxemburg describes the accumulation of knowledge and power within the proletariat in revolutionary Russia, showing that seemingly small actions occasioned sudden leaps forward in militancy and organization. In these historical passages, apparent "failures" prepared the way for deeper understanding and broader action. While this understanding is evident in the minds of individual workers and the decisions of party leaders, the true subject of it is a kind of mass "unconscious."

The uprisings sweeping the United States and the world following the murder of George Floyd represent this kind of revolutionary and educational experience. The unfolding events of this moment, including both impasses and triumphs, teach in a way that no individual teacher can. These struggles, including street protests, direct actions, study groups, and official political campaigns, are analogous to the mass strikes described by Luxemburg. While they depend on determined leaders, they work beyond any single set of political calculations, radically reshaping consciousness, discourse, and historical possibility. They starkly expose determinative contradictions—in particular revealing that the struggle against white supremacy is an essential road to revolution in the United States, bringing together broad swaths of people in a multiracial coalition. Many have learned more in these few months than in many years prior.

The curriculum here is the conjuncture: Tamika Mallory's (2020) searing condemnation of white hypocrisy; the forces of the state encircling masked protesters; the police inflamed in a violent defense of their right to violence; the Slack channels, chants, and proclamations of solidarity; the flooded intersections and embankments; the local elected officials, hiding online; the lethal "less-lethal" rounds, the lethal press conference rationalizations; the webinars of revolutionaries and abolitionists; white defaults and appropriations, the collapse of liberals; the evasions of university administrators; the implicit history lessons, as self-appointed "protectors" guard Confederate monuments; and the beautiful toppling of these monuments.

Experience becomes genuinely educative here because it becomes genuine experience. There are important lessons in this regard for progressive "experiential" education. The craft workshops, gardening projects, and critical historical investigations in familiar progressive education dress up the status quo in *activity* and *authenticity*, but fail to confront the central antagonisms that produce the social reality that they fetishize. In this way, even project-based education can be further from real experience than the most "abstract" and text-centered instruction, as long as that instruction asks students to face the actual historical forces that organize their lives. In addition, just as Luxemburg criticized party leaders for seeking to manage the revolution (e.g., through trying to schedule mass strikes or limit democratic engagement), critical educators need to understand that learning from experience is something that happens essentially outside and independent of school; they can build from it but they cannot control it.

The present moment offers another lesson: Instead of being prudent, measured, and "realistic," struggle needs to be ambitious and *immoderate*. For instance, decades of complaints against police abuse have failed to move the needle. It is only now, with the idea of abolition suddenly on the table, that even modest reform begins to seem possible. As Luxemburg (2004c) put it, "Either the revolution must advance at a rapid, stormy and resolute tempo, break down all barriers with an iron hand and place its goals ever farther ahead, or it is quite soon thrown backward behind its feeble point of departure and suppressed by counter-revolution" (p. 287). The biggest risk is not that activists will go too far in their demands but rather that they will not go far enough, just as the biggest danger in the current political moment is not its unsettledness and unpredictability but rather that it will be folded back into the limits of the normal. A corollary of this insight is that experience, if we are going to appeal to it as the ultimate teacher, has to include experience of the "impossible," of an unfolding and vertiginous history that does not shed itself of risk and joy.

5. Value

Luxemburg challenged Marxist orthodoxies not only with regard to the nature of revolution but also with regard to political economy. Critiquing Marx's restriction of his discussion of colonialism to the period of the initial development of capitalist manufacturing, she argued that mature capitalism also always requires access to non-capitalist strata and countries. Luxemburg (2004a) argued that the enlarged reproduction of aggregate capital is impossible within the closed system of capitalism itself, since the total surplus value in this case cannot be fully consumed (realized) by the capitalist and working classes by themselves. In addition, capitalism depends on access to raw materials and to labor on a global scale.[1] In Luxemburg's account, capitalism is necessarily dependent on its periphery, which absorbs excess capital and consumer goods and constitutes a reservoir for enlarging the stock of constant and variable capital. This means that there can be no capitalism *without those places and peoples that lie beyond it*—and with whom it is always in intimate (and predatory) relation.

We can observe the dynamic that Luxemburg described in terms of economic capital in the sphere of cultural and symbolic capital as well. Doesn't the consolidation of the white and Western depend in the same way on a dominative relationship to the colonized and to Blackness? In *Discourse on Colonialism*, Aimé Césaire (1955) showed that the spurious pronouncements of French intellectuals and the racist knowledges they produced served at once to pathologize the African and to exalt the European. These intellectuals "will prove to you as clear as day that colonization is based on psychology, that there are in this world groups of men who, for unknown reasons . . . are psychologically made for dependence; that they need dependence, that they crave it, ask for it, demand it; that this is the case with most of the colonized peoples" (p. 59). Drawing on the raw materials extracted by the colonizing French social sciences in their studies of African peoples, France then sold back the intellectual products (theories of "primitive" psychology, theology, and aesthetics) to Africa itself—in a cultural metabolism that corresponds to the plunder described in the economic sphere by Luxemburg. In both cases, the accumulation of value at the center depends on an assault on and remaking of the periphery.

Furthermore, drawing out the full implications of this argument, the extraction at the periphery not only enriches the culture and economy of the core but constitutes its very condition of existence—since, for instance, the disciplines of anthropology and psychology (and the intellectuals who adorn them) are produced in the first place out of the colonial encounter. In this way, we can see that (surplus-) value in capitalism, in both its economic and cultural aspects, is (1) produced, (2) the effect of a metabolism involving an *outside*, (3) realized in and through violence. This is the logic that Enrique Dussel (1985) indicates in the category of *exteriority*—which names those peoples who are both beyond the center and at the same time included in it as an unacknowledged and invisible supplement.

We can see the school as another register of this same process. Like whiteness and capital itself, the school works on the raw materials of what lies beyond it (people and ways of knowing). It works up these materials into *education*: the educated and their legitimate knowledges. As in capitalism broadly, the school denigrates these materials even as it depends on them for its own value, since this value accrues from the transformation of consciousness that it undertakes. We usually think of the politics of knowledge in schools in terms of the process of hegemony, but we can also understand it in terms of production: the value of the official knowledge of school can only be accumulated to the extent that it is *realized* beyond the school—that is, to the extent that it is consumed (takes effect) in society as credentials, prestige, and distinction. This accumulation is the effect of a violence against the identities and understandings of marginalized students.

We should not give up on education, or on schools, but the capitalist school must be demobilized. Like the police, the capitalist school as a social system and epistemological order cannot be reformed, only abolished (Love, 2019; Stovall, 2018); however, unlike the police, the school beyond capitalism remains a possibility, a horizon for imagination and experimentation. It is hard to say what a *different* school would look like, since it would be embedded in and operate a social logic different from the one we live in. We can say, at least, that it would be resolute, communal, democratic, solidaristic, anti-oppressive, partisan, and pluriversal. Its value would not be produced from extraction and assimilation—a value then imposed on communities in place of evicted ways of being. But we first have to halt the machinery of the capitalist school in order to begin to see possibilities for teaching and learning that lie beyond it.

6. Canon

Recently there has been a surge in efforts to rethink the canon that organizes core curricula in higher education and secondary education, a process that has coincided with racial justice struggles on university campuses and the growth of movements for ethnic studies courses in schools. While it is ultimately not a matter of censorship of any tradition but rather of making space for marginalized voices and experiences, in the first instance decolonization is a process of replacement or inversion in which the dominant must make way for that which has been excluded, and these dynamics are particularly stark in regard to the canon. This does not mean that there is a rigid dichotomy that separates the Western from the non-Western or the dominant from the subaltern; historical imbrication and intertextuality are central to cultural politics in education (Nakata et al., 2012). However, a revolutionary engagement in curriculum is not clean or cordial, and is proven in actions that concretely reorder structures of power.

At the same time, we can view this process in terms of ferment, dynamism, and creativity. To make a different selection of materials for a course is to tell a different story, and this is an exciting and enlivening process. It is also an occasion to rediscover and make more widely accessible cultural resources that are urgently needed. For instance, in the course of recent popular discussions of antiracism, readers have moved from contemporary texts (often by white people) to foundational writings by Black people—including the work of W. E. B. Du Bois. Du Bois is very well known in the academy and beyond, but he is often not accorded the place at the very center of US philosophy, history, and sociology that rightfully belongs to him. Perhaps white people themselves, in the course of struggles around race, can come to understand that Du Bois' voice (along with the voices of Douglass, Cooper, Baldwin, and other Black intellectuals) is indispensable—for them, for Black people, and for all—indeed more indispensable, in intellectual, spiritual, and aesthetic terms, than the white figures that are consecrated as the central protagonists of US culture. Furthermore, reordering the historical canon in this way is directly connected to contemporary projects to center Black voices in curriculum (see Madkins, 2020).

In addition, the contemporary challenge to the cultural canon is an opportunity to rethink our understanding of the meaning of culture and its relationship to society. Instead of understanding culture as a collection of products of individual imagination, we can begin to see the most powerful accomplishments as powerful precisely in their expression of a collective experience, and even as *the form of* this collective's voice or gesture. This is the point made by Dussel (2018) as a preface to his argument that we need an "obediential aesthetics" in which cultural workers start explicitly from the needs and desires of the community, and in consultation with it.

A socialist curriculum in the humanities and sciences would need to be characterized by this kind of responsibility. It would need to reflect the needs and desires of working people. It would also need to constitute an opening that moves beyond critique to the consideration of a range of possible futures. How can we see the possibilities for a different kind of knowledge and learning as long as we are held by the assumptions that capture the current one? This is not a call for a flight from all organization and authority but rather a call for a basic inquiry into what that organization ought to be. Which disparaged but essential texts/traditions might we recenter in this process? What heterodox or refused knowledges might we invite to unsettle the space of official knowledge? (See for instance projects for restorying place and nature in Nxumalo, 2015.) What reprioritizations of voices might evoke a different tradition and a different set of cultural possibilities in the present? (For instance, dismantling "American literature" courses in favor of hemispherically organized collections of texts.)

Furthermore, a revolutionary curriculum needs to be centrally mobilized by subaltern standpoints, as the necessary and essential signs under which a universal project of emancipation might unfold. A decolonial socialism is not the simple dialectical antagonist to capital but rather the agent of its interruption and unraveling. If elites have insisted on understanding high culture as white and Western, what would it look like to replace that hegemon and to articulate a universal project of culture under the signs for instance of Blackness or queerness, not to the exclusion of their Others but rather as the hegemonizing signifiers to which other senses of identity and struggle would be sutured (Laclau, 2005)? Would this not be a salutary bolshevism on the field of curriculum, just as Lenin imagined the workers' insurgent dictatorship as the form of a reorganization of universal social and human possibilities? These struggles over the canon make educators decisive actors in the cultural and epistemological space of revolution—a space that has historically been under-emphasized in relation to the sphere of the formally political.

7. Difference

Badiou (2001) argues that the play of differences is not useful as a starting point for politics, since there is, in a sense, *only difference*—that is, nothing is identical even to itself, let alone to others. From this perspective, the clever theoretical subversions of poststructuralism collapse like a house of cards, since they only affirm the most banal and basic condition of existence. Similarly, the celebration of differences in liberal multiculturalism is a frequent target of criticalists for the way it obscures underlying contradictions and the possibility of solidarity. From the latter perspective, in the name of affirmation and diversity, multiculturalism collaborates with capitalism in refusing the possibility of commonality.

These critiques are correct but shallow, since they do not engage deeper and more powerful senses of difference as Otherness and pluriversality (Mignolo,

2011). Difference is significant not in itself but as a marker, first of all, of the divide produced by oppression. Second, at a deeper level, difference is significant as the name for a juxtaposition of ways of being and knowing that are substantial and autonomous in themselves, not simply arbitrary nodes in a social or signifying system. These deeper senses of difference are not opposed to solidarity. They are the ground of solidarity, since in their historicity and determinativeness they make the bonds that solidarity forges across difference, through dialogue, authentic and potent. Within this frame, the assertion of oppressed identities, experiences, and standpoints is not a simple valorization of alterity but rather a necessary moment of liberatory struggle (Haider, 2018).

Too often such assertions get misunderstood as the expression of an ungrounded postmodernism. But capitalism is a complex system and structure with many mediations and registers. Furthermore, it is a system that depends on a refused exteriority as well as an exploited interiority (Fraser, 2018). Confronting capitalism means working on many fronts; it also means challenging the divisions that make it coherent. This places anti-oppressive struggles around difference in a different light. For instance, immigrant rights struggles ultimately aim not at abstract inclusion but at ending cultural and economic violence—violence which nevertheless makes use of the discursive matrix of identity. Likewise, as opposed to a politics aimed simply at "troubling" rules and norms around gender, doesn't trans liberation aim at a *decolonization* of gender that reclaims its possibilities for those who have been excluded? Such struggles around difference are essential, since they attack crucial articulations of the spirit of violence that capitalism systematizes and ramifies.

A revolutionary curriculum would aim at "inclusion" (in the sense of a consideration of excluded histories and understandings) not for the sake of representation alone but also in faithfulness to a deeper *rigor*. This curriculum aims to overcome the provincialism and intellectual poverty of the hegemonic standpoint. It also makes a more serious ethical commitment against injustice and a more determined political commitment to liberation. By contrast, US school and university curricula that—for instance—treat Latin America as distant and unimportant (1) fundamentally misunderstand US history, (2) erase continental Indigenous histories that link and differentiate nations across Abya Yala, (3) deprive themselves of the crucial resources of hemispheric philosophical and political traditions (from Mariátegui to Commandante Ramona), and (4) obscure the essential process of coloniality—out of which US culture itself has been decisively formed. The "high expectations" for students ostensibly touted by both liberal and critical pedagogies are a sham if they don't include the expectation that students grasp their location within complex hemispheric and global histories of domination.

This does not mean that the notion of class should not be central to an emancipatory curriculum. Indeed, class histories and cultures, as well as labor history, are among the most marginalized topics in education. Providing young people with the conceptual resources for understanding and affiliating with the global working class is essential. But the meaning and standpoint of this class ought to be fleshed out on the basis of an exploration of a range of revolutionary histories—indeed an exploration grounded first of all in the most marginalized segments of this class. A white- or Western-chauvinist Left is not Left, even in its own narrow terms. Instead, as emancipatory curriculum preserves invaluable and longstanding frameworks for revolutionary identifications for students, it needs to open possibilities for refiguring these identifications in light of new information and events and also in light of disparate revolutionary understandings and figures.

Freire (1998) argued that "epistemological curiosity" allows us to reflect on the ground of our own thinking and to be open to learning from others. Taking this concept one step further, I suggest that an *epistemological humility* would recognize that our own ways of understanding are surrounded by many other organized and legitimate systems. Our efforts to make sense of the world and to isolate its central contradictions might then be more open to learning and also more aware of their provisionality, without thereby having to give up on the project of grasping the truth. This sensitivity is also a recognition of the complexity of the world itself that we seek to comprehend. Far from a disavowal of the effort of comprehension, this is the form of a greater ambition and determination to understand and to act thoughtfully against oppression and exploitation.

8. Spirit

The spiritual register of radical education is often overlooked or discounted. Materialism is not incompatible with a revolutionary notion of spirit. As Dussel (2013) shows, the "will-to-live" of the oppressed, which is concerned in the first instance with the material struggle to survive, is also the ground of ethics. On the other hand, in contrast to some religious conceptions of faith, spirit is not separable from intellect. I am not referring here to the idealist Hegelian unity of unfolding philosophical understanding as world-spirit, but rather to a synthesis in which reasoning is tied to a spirituality rooted in the land, relationships, and social practice (see Deloria, 1999).

Solidarity and comradeship are not instrumental articulations of relationship but rather spiritual commitments and conditions. They ground political work in a frame that transcends the individual and the calculation of gains and losses. Solidarity is both temporal and eternal: temporal to the extent that it implies a responsibility to practical experience; eternal to the extent that it is not contingent on calculation and results. Solidarity belongs to the horizon of Benjamin's angel of history, pointing to the redemption of suffering and defeat even in the face of the world's persistently long odds for liberation. Solidarity flies in the face of bourgeois morality and subjectivity and evokes an ontological entanglement that is disallowed and denied by the dominant grammar.

There is a spiritual intimacy in our collective investigation, within education, of the world. Teaching and learning bring souls together in a profound confrontation with the shape of the material and immaterial conditions they confront around them. We should love our students since we aim for their engagement and thriving. But we should also love our students because they are our partners in crime; together with them, we seek to constitute a community not governed by bourgeois calculation and competition. That impulse is a communist one and also a spiritual one. But this is a profane religion dedicated to the overthrow of all idols. In an alienated and oppressive society, teachers need a *bad attitude*. The spirituality that grounds this teaching is a spirituality of resistance and struggle.

In his films, Abbas Kiarostami ruptures the fictionality of the narrative through an obtrusive presence of the world beyond the film. But this reality itself becomes visible through its systematic re-staging rather than via a simple documentary method. The worker, the village, and the child are present in performing themselves and thereby uncover the sacredness of the ordinary. Kiarostami uncovers a spirit that cannot be detached from things themselves. This spirit is demonstrated through images, but it cannot be captured and owned. These films show the sacredness of the world in its ignominious particulars. That is a spiritual and socialist teaching, which teaches us to love the actual, incomplete, and uncelebrated.

That is the utopian community that teaching ought to aim to create—a community of impossible and wounded beings, beautiful in their invocation of justice. We love each other in loving what is beyond us, as our shared responsibility and horizon. In the light of that collective commitment our individual and particular features are illuminated—they even then become the faces and voices of that beyond. In this way, spirit names not the distant and esoteric but rather the motive force of what is present and anguished; spirit is the energy that passes through that anguish to remake the world as possibility.

Love (2019) makes a distinction between *survival* and *thriving* for people of color. Vizenor (1994) combines these ideas, with regard to Indigenous communities, in the notion of *survivance*. Their argument is that we must refuse the project of whiteness, which seeks to reduce its Others to a form of bare life. But perhaps we can also say that survival itself, as Dussel's *will-to-live*, contains the seeds of this very thriving. After all, isn't spirit itself expressed in the illumination of flesh and earth and event? Politics and pedagogy should be mobilized by this kind of scandalous spirit, which reveres no consolidated power and seeks to raise up all that has been left behind, in the thick of things.

9. Conclusion: Transition

We talk about learning as a blessing, but it is also an ordeal. Isn't learning unforeseen, shocking, and unpredictable? The dominant progressive paradigm for learning is *growth*—a figure which implies a kind of stability within the process of change. But thinking of learning as *transition* is less comfortable, since it implies movement, loss, and replacement. But transition also suggests possibility. I believe that we have to think of learning now in terms of this figure. Capitalism is dominant, but it is also stretched and teetering. The myth of its inevitability is shaken, even if the system still prevails. We can feel other social possibilities waiting just outside the frame. The stresses on the system are not just material ones. They are tensions at the level of being, inasmuch as we can now viscerally feel the difficulty of sustaining familiar imaginaries of history and society. These tensions teach us about the weakness of what we have taken as reality, but they also demand an accelerated and ambitious learning.

Hardt and Negri (2000) write about ruptures at the level of subjectivity, politics, and society in terms of an *exodus* from the given, but this figures the imagination in terms of flight. It is better to think of the shifting ground of revolutionary politics in terms of recomposition. In a process of collaborative teaching-learning, young people in particular are recomposing the frameworks that allow for meaning and movement. The Left tends to be captured by stale debates about "identity politics," as if struggle at the level of subjectivity were disconnected or opposed to material struggle. But revolution has to intervene at the level of *sociogeny*, in Fanon's (1967a) terms, which means the level of the remaking of the basic possibilities for social being. After all, capitalism is a *manifold* order of exploitation and control.

Critique cannot be the central mode of this curriculum, since critique refers itself to what is or has been. Instead, in a moment of transition, emancipatory curriculum can engage the *fact* of rupture, and it can speak from a position of strength. Young people are innovating at the level of sociality and communication. Even as it is not afraid to recall older revolutionary commitments and identities, the Left also needs to absorb and be reorganized by these innovations. The atomization of neoliberalism gives way to the new assemblages of this transitional period. A revolutionary class is crystallized on the street but also online, in political organizing and also in aesthetic experiments.

The pandemic vividly demonstrates that curriculum was never just in school. We learn through our own experiments and initiatives, even as the broader crisis starkly teaches the falseness of the system's pretensions. The empty neighborhood; assignments from the organizing committee; sparrows in the cedar elms; helicopters over the evening vigil—this is an extended and heterogeneous curriculum of being, a being-in-crisis which is also being-in-transition. There is no calm before the storm, only ceaseless calm and ceaseless storms which have to be navigated with a new subjectivity. Urgency is an inadequate term for this condition. We have no choice in this context but to learn.

A revolutionary curriculum is a curriculum of being, not just knowing. It is a curriculum of making, not just of unmaking. It has to be a curriculum of and for the people—and so this means it must be a decolonizing curriculum. It has to organize and also provoke. Against the fetishizing of fluidity, it must consolidate but also improvise. It is a material and a spiritual project. It is an intellectual project that starts from invisible intelligences. It is a project of and for young people who nevertheless remember the wisdom of the elders. This curriculum is not a project that looks up to denounce the distant parapets of capital, but rather one that speaks from the ongoing fact of capital's unraveling. This curriculum needs to be sturdy, but it also needs to be quick: we are traveling fast through history now.

Note

1   Technically speaking, Luxemburg argued that the breakdown of means of production and means of subsistence within the surplus product (in which surplus value is necessarily objectified) is not necessarily in proportion to the ability of these two economic departments—production of means of production and production of consumer goods—to absorb the surplus.

References

Acosta, A. (2013). Extractivism and Neoextractism: Two Sides of the Same Curse. In M. Lang & D. Mokrani (Eds.), *Beyond Development: Alternative Visions from Latin America* (pp. 61–86). Quito, Ecuador: Fundación Rosa Luxemburg.

Adair, J. K. (2014). Agency and Expanding Capabilities in Early Grade Classrooms: What It Could Mean for Young Children. *Harvard Educational Review, 84*(2), 217–241.

Ahmed, S. (2012). *On Being Included: Racism and Diversity in Institutional Life.* Durham, NC: Duke University Press.

Alcoff, L. M. (2006). *Visible Identities: Race, Gender, and the Self.* New York: Oxford University Press.

Alexander, M. (2010). *The New Jim Crow: Mass Incarceration in the Age of Colorblindness.* New York: The New Press.

Alfred, T. (2009). *Peace, Power, Righteousness.* Oxford: Oxford University Press.

Althusser, L. (2009). *Reading Capital.* London: Verso.

Appadurai, A. (1996). *Modernity at Large: Cultural Dimensions of Globalization.* Minneapolis, MN: University of Minnesota Press.

Au, W. (2011). Teaching Under the New Taylorism: High-Stakes Testing and the Standardization of the 21st Century Curriculum. *Journal of Curriculum Studies, 43*(1), 25–45.

Au, W. (2012). *Critical Curriculum Studies: Education, Consciousness, and the Politics of Knowing.* New York: Routledge.

Badiou, A. (2001). *Ethics: An Essay on the Understanding of Evil.* London: Verso.

Balibar, E. (2002). *Politics and the Other Scene* (C. Jones, J. Swenson, & C. Turner, Trans.). London: Verso.

Ball, S. J. (1993). Education Markets, Choice and Social Class: The Market as a Class Strategy in the UK and the USA. *British Journal of Sociology of Education, 14*(1), 3–19.

Ball, S. J. (2003). The Teacher's Soul and the Terrors of Performativity. *Journal of Education Policy, 18*(2), 215–228.

Ball, S. J. (2012). *Global Education Inc.: New Policy Networks and the Neo-Liberal Imaginary.* London: Routledge.

Bauman, Z. (2000). *Liquid Modernity.* Cambridge: Polity.

Binkley, C. (2020). *Survey: Pay for University Presidents Climbs 10.5%.* Associated Press, January 14, Retrieved from https://apnews.com/article/180121a8b1cc99151f5a6b9 d613ae2b0#:~:text=The%20survey%2C%20released%20Tuesday%2C%20finds,9%25 %20in%20the%20previous%20year.

Boltanski, L., & Chiapello, E. (2005). *The New Spirit of Capitalism* (G. Elliott, Trans.). London: Verso.

Bourassa, G. N. (2019). An Autonomist Biopolitics of Education: Reproduction, Resistance, and the Specter of Constituent *Bíos. Educational Theory, 69*(3), 305–325.

Bousquet, M. (2003). The Rhetoric of "Job Market" and the Reality of the Academic Labor System. *College English, 66*(2), 207–228.

Broad Foundation (2016). Our. *Vision.* Retrieved from http://broadfoundation.org/education.

Brock, R. (2005). *Sista Talk: The Personal and the Pedagogical.* New York: Peter Lang.

Brown, A. L. (2018). From Subhuman to Human Kind: Implicit Bias, Racial Memory, and Black Males in Schools and Society. *Peabody Journal of Education, 93*(1), 52–65.

Brown, A. L., & De Lissovoy, N. (2011). Economies of Racism: Grounding Education Policy Research in the Complex Dialectic of Race, Class, and Capital. *Journal of Education Policy, 26*(5), 595–619.

Brown, K. D. (2013). Trouble on My Mind: Toward a Framework of Humanizing Critical Sociocultural Knowledge for Teaching and Teacher Education. *Race, Ethnicity and Education, 16*(3), 316–338.

Brown, W. (2003). Neo-Liberalism and the End of Liberal Democracy. *Theory and Event, 7*(1).

Brown, W. (2010). *Walled States, Waning Sovereignty.* New York: Zone Books.

Buras, K. L. (2011). Race, Charter Schools, and Conscious Capitalism: On the Spatial Politics of Whiteness as Property (and the Unconscionable Assault on Black New Orleans). *Harvard Educational Review, 81*(2), 296–330.

Buras, K. L., Randels, J., & Ya Salaam, K. (2010). *Pedagogy, Policy, and the Privatized City.* New York: Teachers College Press.

Burbules, N. C. (2016). Technology, Education, and the Fetishization of the "New." In P. Smeyers & M. Depaepe (Eds.), *Educational Research: Discourses of Change and Changes of Discourse* (pp. 9–16). New York: Springer.

Butler, J. (2004). *Precarious Life: The Powers of Mourning and Violence.* London: Verso.

Byrd, J. A. (2011). *The Transit of Empire: Indigenous Critiques of Colonialism.* Minneapolis, MN: University of Minnesota Press.

Cabrera, N. L., Meza, E. L., Romero, A. J., & Rodríguez, R. C. (2013). "If There Is No Struggle, There Is No Progress": Transformative Youth Activism and the School of Ethnic Studies. *Urban Review, 45*(1), 7–22.

Calderon, D. (2014). Uncovering Settler Grammars in Curriculum. *Educational Studies, 50*(4), 313–338.

Carpenter, J. (Director). Foster, D., & Turman, L. (Producers) (1982). *The Thing* [Motion picture]. United States: Universal Pictures.

Cervantes-Soon, C., Dorner, L., Palmer, D., Heiman, D., Schwerdtfeger, R., & Choi, J. (2017). Combating Inequalities in Two-Way Language Immersion Programs: Toward Critical Consciousness in Bilingual Education Spaces. *Review of Research in Education, 41*(1), 403–427.

Césaire, A. (1955/2000). *Discourse on Colonialism* (J. Pinkham, Trans.). New York: Monthly Review Press.

Chakrabarty, D. (2000). *Provincializing Europe: Postcolonial Thought and Historical Difference*. Princeton, NJ: Princeton University Press.

Cleary, J., Jr. (2017). Neoliberalism Inside Two American High Schools. *British Journal of Sociology of Education, 38*(3), 325–343.

Clinton Foundation (2016a). About Us. Retrieved from https://www.clintonfoundation .org/about.

Clinton Foundation (2016b). *Consolidated Statements of Activities, Year Ended 31 December 2014*. Retrieved from https://www.clintonfoundation.org/sites/default/ files/2015_ar_financials.pdf.

Cook, C. B. (2021). *Unremarkable Violence and the Politics of Relation*. Unpublished doctoral dissertation. University of Texas at Austin.

Coulthard, G. S. (2014). *Red Skin, White Masks: Rejecting the Colonial Politics of Recognition*. Minneapolis, MN: University of Minnesota Press.

Cusicanqui, S. R. (2012). Ch'ixinakax Utxiwa: A Reflection on the Practices and Discourses of Decolonization. *South Atlantic Quarterly, 111*(1), 95–109.

Darder, A. (1991). *Culture and Power in the Classroom: A Critical Foundation for Bicultural Education*. Westport, CT: Bergin & Garvey.

Darder, A. (2002). *Reinventing Paulo Freire: A Pedagogy of Love*. Boulder, CO: Westview Press.

Davies, B., & Bansel, P. (2007). Neoliberalism and Education. *International Journal of Qualitative Studies in Education, 20*(3), 247–259.

Davis, A. Y. (2005). *Abolition Democracy: Beyond Empire, Prisons, and Torture*. New York: Seven Stories Press.

Davis, M. (2006). *Planet of Slums*. London: Verso.

Davis, O. (2014). The Newark School Reform Wars. *The Nation*, May 28. Retrieved from https://www.thenation.com/article/newark-school-reform-wars.

Dawson, A. (2010). Climate Justice: The Emerging Movement against Green Capitalism. *South Atlantic Quarterly, 109*(2), 313–338.

De Angelis, M. (2007). *The Beginning of History: Value Struggles and Global Capitalism*. London: Pluto Press.

De Ayala, G. P. (2006). *The First New Chronicle and Good Government* (D. Frye, Trans.). Indianapolis, IN: Hackett Publishing.

De Genova, N. P. (2004). The Legal Production of Mexican/Migrant "Illegality." *Latino Studies, 2*(2), 160–185.

De Las Casas, B. (1992). *A Short Account of the Destruction of the Indies* (N. Griffin, Trans.). New York: Penguin.

De Lissovoy, N. (2008). *Power, Crisis, and Education for Liberation: Rethinking Critical Pedagogy*. New York: Palgrave Macmillan.

De Lissovoy, N. (2010). Staging the Crisis: Teaching, Capital, and the Politics of the Subject. *Curriculum Inquiry, 40*(3), 418–435.

De Lissovoy, N. (2011). Pedagogy in Common: Democratic Education in the Global Era. *Educational Philosophy and Theory, 43*(10), 1119–1134.

De Lissovoy, N. (2012). Education and Violation: Conceptualizing Power, Domination, and Agency in the Hidden Curriculum. *Race, Ethnicity and Education, 15*(4), 463–484.

De Lissovoy, N. (2013a). Conceptualizing the Carceral Turn: Neoliberalism, Racism, and Violation. *Critical Sociology, 39*(5), 739–755.

De Lissovoy, N. (2013b). Pedagogy of the Impossible: Neoliberalism and the Ideology of Accountability. *Policy Futures in Education, 11*(4), 423–435.

De Lissovoy, N., & Armonda, A. J. (2020). Curriculum for Liberation in the Neoliberal Era. In M. F. He & W. Schubert (Eds.), *Oxford Encyclopedia of Curriculum Studies* (pp. 1–6). Oxford: Oxford University Press.

De Lissovoy, N., Means, A. J., & Saltman, K. J. (2014). *Toward a New Common School Movement.* Boulder, CO: Paradigm Publishers.

Dean, J. (2009). *Democracy and Other Neoliberal Fantasies: Communicative Capitalism and Left Politics.* Durham, NC: Duke University Press.

Dean, J. (2012). *The Communist Horizon.* New York: Verso.

Dean, J. (2019). *Comrade: An Essay on Political Belonging.* London: Verso.

Dekker, R., Engbersen, G., Klaver, J., & Vonk, H. (2018). Smart Refugees: How Syrian Asylum Migrants Use Social Media Information in Migration Decision-Making. *Social Media + Society, 4*(1), 1–11.

Deloria, V., Jr. (1999). *Spirit and Reason: The Vine Deloria, Jr., Reader.* Golden, CO: Fulcrum Publishing.

Dewey, J. (1997a). *Democracy and Education.* New York: The Free Press.

Dewey, J. (1997b). *Experience and Education.* New York: Simon & Schuster.

Dixson, A. D., Buras, K. L., & Jeffers, E. K. (2015). The Color of Reform: Race, Education Reform, and Charter Schools in Post-Katrina New Orleans. *Qualitative Inquiry, 21*(3), 288–299.

Driskill, Q.-L. (2010). Doubleweaving Two-Spirit Critiques: Building Alliances between Native and Queer Studies. *Journal of Lesbian and Gay Studies, 16*(1–2), 69–92.

Du Bois, W. E. B. (1935/1998). *Black Reconstruction in America.* New York: The Free Press.

Du Bois, W. E. B. (1940/1986). *Dusk of Dawn.* New York: Library of America.

Dumas, M. J., & Ross, k. m. (2016). "Be Real Black for Me": Imagining BlackCrit in Education. *Urban Education, 51*(4), 415–442.

Duménil, G., & Lévy, D. (2005). The Neoliberal (Counter-)Revolution. In A. Saad-Filho & D. Johnston (Eds.), *Neoliberalism: A Critical Reader* (pp. 9–19). Ann Arbor, MI: Pluto Press.

Dussel, E. (1985). *Philosophy of Liberation* (A. Martinez & C. Morkovsky, Trans.). Eugene, OR: Wipf & Stock Publishers.

Dussel, E. (1998). Beyond Eurocentrism: The World-System and the Limits of Modernity. In F. Jameson & M. Miyoshi (Eds.), *The Cultures of Globalization* (pp. 3–31). Durham, NC: Duke University Press.

Dussel, E. (2003). *Beyond Philosophy: Ethics, History, Marxism, and Liberation Theology.* Lanham, MD: Rowman & Littlefield.

Dussel, E. (2008). *Twenty Theses on Politics* (G. Ciccariello-Maher, Trans.). Durham, NC: Duke University Press.

Dussel, E. (2013). *Ethics of Liberation: In the Age of Globalization and Exclusion* (E. Mendieta, C. P. Bustillo, Y. Angulo, & N. Maldonado-Torres, Trans.). Durham, NC: Duke University Press.

Dussel, E. (2018). Siete Hipótesis para una Estética de la Liberación. *Revista Praxis, 77*(77), 1–37.

Edu-Factory Collective (2009). *Toward a Global Autonomous University: Cognitive Labor, the Production of Knowledge, and Exodus from the Education Factory.* New York: Autonomedia.

Elbih, R. (2018). *Dialectics of 9/11 and the War on Terror: Educational Responses.* New York: Peter Lang.

Escobar, A. (2008). *Territories of Difference: Place, Movements, Life, Redes.* Durham, NC: Duke University Press.

Esteva, G., Stuchul, D. L., & Suri Prakash, M. (2005). From a Pedagogy for Liberation to Liberation From Pedagogy. In C. A. Bowers & F. Apffel-Marglin (Eds.), *Rethinking Freire: Globalization and the Environmental Crisis* (pp. 13–30). Mahwah, NJ: Lawrence Erlbaum Associates.

Evans, T. (2012). *Occupy Education: Living and Learning Sustainability.* New York: Peter Lang.

Evans-Winters, V., & Piert, J. (2014). The Skin We Speak: Locating Black Women in Critical Pedagogy. In P. W. Orelus & R. Brock (Eds.), *Interrogating Critical Pedagogy: The Voices of Educators of Color in the Movement* (pp. 30–45). New York: Routledge.

Fanon, F. (1963). *The Wretched of the Earth* (C. Farrington, Trans.). New York: Grove Press.

Fanon, F. (1967a). *Black Skin, White Masks* (C. L. Markmann, Trans.). New York: Grove Press.

Fanon, F. (1967b). *Toward the African Revolution* (H. Chevalier, Trans.). New York: Grove Press.

Farenthold, D., Hamburger, T., & Helderman, R. S. (2015). The Inside Story of How Bill Clinton Built a $2 Billion Global Foundation May Undermine Hillary's Chances. *The Independent*, June 3. Retrieved from http://www.independent.co.uk/news/world/americas/the-inside-story-of-how-bill-clinton-built-a-2bn-global-foundation-may-undermine-hilarys-chances-10295702.html.

Federici, S. (2004). *Caliban and the Witch: Women, the Body and Primitive Accumulation.* New York: Autonomedia.

Fisher, M. (2009). *Capitalist Realism: Is There No Alternative?* Winchester, United Kingdom: Zero Books.

Flores, A. R., Langton, L., Meyer, I. H., & Romero, A. P. (2020). *Victimization and Traits of Sexual and Gender Minorities in the U.S.* Los Angeles, CA: Williams Institute, UCLA School of Law.

Ford, D. R. (2017). Studying Like a Communist: Affect, the Party, and the Educational Limits to Capitalism. *Educational Philosophy and Theory, 49*(5), 452–461.

Foucault, M. (2008). *The Birth of Biopolitics: Lectures at the Collège de France, 1978–1979* (G. Burchell, Trans.). New York: Picador.

Fraser, N., & Jaeggi, R. (2018). *Capitalism: A Conversation in Critical Theory.* Cambridge: Polity.

Fregoso Bailón, R. O. (2015). Sobre una Trans-Colonialidad para la Construcción de la Pedagogía Crítica Descolonial: El Caso de la Propuesta Curricular de la Educación Bolivariana. *Contextualizaciones Latinoamericanas, 7*(13), 1–8.

Freire, P. (1974). *Education for Critical Consciousness* (M. B. Ramos, Trans.). New York: Continuum.

Freire, P. (1978). *Pedagogy in Process: The Letters to Guinea-Buissau.* New York: Seabury Press.

Freire, P. (1994). *Pedagogy of Hope* (R. R. Barr, Trans.). New York: Continuum.

Freire, P. (1996). *Pedagogy of the Oppressed* (M. B. Ramos, Trans.). New York: Continuum.

Freire, P. (1998). *Pedagogy of Freedom: Ethics, Democracy, and Civic Courage* (P. Clarke, Trans.). Lanham, MD: Rowman & Littlefield.

Freire, P. (2005). *Teachers as Cultural Workers: Letters to Those Who Dare Teach* (D. Macedo, D. Koike, & A. Oliveira, Trans.). Boulder, CO: Westview Press.

Friedman, M. (2002). *Capitalism and Freedom.* Chicago, IL: University of Chicago Press.

Fromm, E. (1964). *The Heart of Man.* New York: Harper & Row.

Galeano, E. (1973). *Open Veins of Latin America: Five Centuries of the Pillage of a Continent.* New York: Monthly Review Press.

Gandin, L. A. (2007). The Construction of the Citizen School Project as an Alternative to Neoliberal Educational Policies. *Policy Futures in Education, 5*(2), 179–193.

García, J., & De Lissovoy, N. (2013). Doing School Time: The Hidden Curriculum Goes to Prison. *Journal for Critical Education Policy Studies, 11*(4), 49–68.

Gilmore, R. W. (2007). *Golden Gulag: Prisons, Surplus, Crisis, and Opposition in Globalizing California.* Berkeley, CA: University of California Press.

Giroux, H. A. (1988). *Schooling and the Struggle for Public Life: Critical Pedagogy in the Modern Age.* Minneapolis, MN: University of Minnesota Press.

Giroux, H. A. (1992). *Border Crossings: Cultural Workers and the Politics of Education.* New York: Routledge.

Giroux, H. A. (2001). *Theory and Resistance in Education.* Westport, CT: Bergin & Garvey.

Giroux, H. A. (2015). Public Intellectuals Against the Neoliberal University. In N. K. Denzin & M. D. Giardina (Eds.), *Qualitative Inquiry—Past, Present, and Future: A Critical Reader* (pp. 194–219). New York: Routledge.

Goeman, M. R. (2014). Disrupting a Settler-Colonial Grammar of Place: The Visual Memoir of Hulleah Tsinhnahjinnie. In A. Simpson & A. Smith (Eds.), *Theorizing Native Studies* (pp. 235–265). Durham, NC: Duke University Press.

Goldberg, D. T. (2009). *The Threat of Race: Reflections on Racial Neoliberalism*. Malden, MA: Wiley-Blackwell.

Goldman Sachs (2016). *10,000 Women*. Retrieved from http://www.goldmansachs.com/citizenship/10000women/index.html.

Goodyear-Kaʻōpua, N. (2019). Indigenous Oceanic Futures: Challenging Settler Colonialisms and Militarization. In L. T. Smith, E. Tuck, & W. K. Yang (Eds.), *Indigenous and Decolonizing Studies in Education: Mapping the Long View* (pp. 82–102). New York: Routledge.

Grady, S., Bielick, S., & Aud, S. (2010). *Trends in the Use of School Choice: 1993 to 2007*. National Center for Education Statistics, NCES, 2010–004.

Grande, S. (2004). *Red Pedagogy: Native American Social and Political Thought*. Lanham, MD: Rowman & Littlefield.

Grande, S. (2013). Accumulation of the Primitive: The Limits of Liberalism and the Politics of Occupy Wall Street. *Settler Colonial Studies, 3*(3–4), 369–380.

Griffith, H. (2016). Anti-Depressants: WHO Concern over Use by Children. *BBC NEWS*. Retrieved from http://www.bbc.com/news/health-35756602.

Haider, A. (2018). *Mistaken Identity: Race and Class in the Age of Trump*. London: Verso.

Harding, S. (1993). Rethinking Standpoint Epistemology: What Is "Strong Objectivity"? In L. Alcoff & E. Potter (Eds.), *Feminist Epistemologies* (pp. 49–82). New York: Routledge.

Hardt, M., & Negri, A. (2000). *Empire*. Cambridge, MA: Harvard University Press.

Hardt, M., & Negri, A. (2004). *Multitude: War and Democracy in the Age of Empire*. New York: Penguin Press.

Hardt, M., & Negri, A. (2009). *Commonwealth*. Cambridge, MA: Harvard University Press.

Hart, R., Casserly, M., Uzzell, R., Palacios, M., Corcoran, A., & Spurgeon, L. (2015). *Student Testing in America's Great City Schools: An Inventory and Preliminary Analysis*. Council of the Great City Schools, October. Retrieved from http://www.cgcs.org/cms/lib/dc00001581/centricity/domain/87/testing%20report.pdf.

Hartman, S. V. (1997). *Scenes of Subjection: Terror, Slavery, and Self-Making in Nineteenth-Century America*. Oxford: Oxford University Press.

Harvey, D. (2003). *The New Imperialism*. Oxford: Oxford University Press.

Harvey, D. (2006). *The Limits to Capital*. London: Verso.

Harvey, D. (2014). Afterthoughts on Piketty's. *Capital*, May 17. Retrieved from http://davidharvey.org/2014/05/afterthoughts-pikettys-capital/.

Hayek, F. A. (1960/2011). *The Constitution of Liberty*. Chicago: University of Chicago Press.

Heiman, D., & Yanes, M. (2018). Centering the Fourth Pillar in Times of TWBE Gentrification: "Spanish, Love, Content, Not in That Order." *International Multilingual Research Journal, 12*(3), 173–187.

hooks, b. (1994). *Teaching to Transgress: Education as the Practice of Freedom*. New York: Routledge.

hooks, b. (2000). *Feminist Theory: From Margin to Center*. Cambridge, MA: South End Press.

hooks, b. (2003). *Teaching Community: A Pedagogy of Hope*. New York: Routledge.

Horkheimer, M., & Adorno, T. W. (2002). *Dialectic of Enlightenment* (E. Jephcott, Trans.). Stanford, CA: Stanford University Press.

Hursh, D. (2007). Assessing No Child Left Behind and the Rise of Neoliberal Education Policies. *American Educational Research Journal, 44*(3), 493–518.

Hursh, D. (2015). *The End of Public Schools: The Corporate Reform Agenda to Privatize Education*. New York: Routledge.

Illich, I. (1970). *Deschooling Society*. New York: Harper & Row.

James, C. L. R. (1963). *The Black Jacobins: Toussaint l'Ouverture and the San Domingo Revolution*. New York: Random House.

Jameson, F. (1991). *Postmodernism, or, the Cultural Logic of Late Capitalism*. Durham, NC: Duke University Press.

Jennings, M. E., & Lynn, M. (2005). The House That Race Built: Critical Pedagogy, African-American Education, and Re-Conceptualization of a Critical Race Pedagogy. *Educational Foundations, 19*(3–4), 15–32.

Johnson, T. (2020). When Black People Are in Pain, White People Just Join Book Clubs. *Washington Post*, June 11.

Jones, E. (2020, Fall). John Carpenter, Apocalyptic Filmmaker. *Jacobin*(39), 101–105.

Justice, D. H. (2016). A Better World Becoming: Placing Critical Indigenous Studies. In A. Moreton-Robinson (Ed.), *Critical Indigenous Studies: Engagements in First World Locations* (pp. 19–32). Tucson, AZ: University of Arizona Press.

Kahn, R. (2009). Towards Ecopedagogy: Weaving a Broad-Based Pedagogy of Liberation for Animals, Nature, and the Oppressed People of the Earth. In A. Darder, M. Baltodano, & R. D. Torres (Eds.), *The Critical Pedagogy Reader* (pp. 522–540). New York: Routledge.

Kelley, R. D. G. (1993). "We Are Not What We Seem": Rethinking Black Working-Class Opposition in the Jim Crow South. *Journal of American History, 80*(1), 75–112.

Kelley, R. D. G. (2002). *Freedom Dreams: The Black Radical Imagination*. Boston: Beacon Press.

Kelley, R. D. G. (Speaker) (2020). Racial Capitalism and Crisis. *Socialism 2020*. Retrieved from https://socialismconference.org/.

Kovel, J. (2002). *The Enemy of Nature: The End of Capitalism or the End of the World?* New York: Zed Books.

Krugman, P. (2021). This Putsch Was Decades in the Making. *New York Times*, January 11. Retrieved from https://www.nytimes.com/2021/01/11/opinion/republicans-democracy.html?searchResultPosition=7.

Lacan, J. (1977). The Function and Field of Speech and Language in Psychoanalysis (A. Sheridan, Trans.). *Ecrits: A Selection* (pp. 30–113). New York: W. W. Norton & Company.

Lacan, J. (1978). *The Four Fundamental Concepts of Psycho-Analysis* (A. Sheridan, Trans.). New York: W. W. Norton & Company.

Laclau, E. (2005). *On Populist Reason*. London: Verso.

Layne, N. (2020). Unequal Education: Pandemic Widens Race, Class Gaps in U.S. Schools. *Reuters*, September 29. Retrieved from https://www.reuters.com/article/us -health-coronavirus-pennsylvania-educa/unequal-education-pandemic-widens-race -class-gaps-in-u-s-schools-idUSKBN26K1WE.

Lemke, T. (2001). "The Birth of Bio-Politics": Michel Foucault's Lecture at the Collège de France on Neo-Liberal Governmentality. *Economy and Society, 30*(2), 190–207.

Leonardo, Z. (2007). The War on Schools: NCLB, Nation Creation and the Educational Construction of Whiteness. *Race, Ethnicity and Education, 10*(3), 261–278.

Leonardo, Z. (2009). *Race, Whiteness, and Education*. New York: Routledge.

Lewis, T. (2012). Exopedagogy: On Pirates, Shorelines, and the Educational Commonwealth. *Educational Philosophy and Theory, 44*(8), 845–861.

Lewis, T., & Valk, S. (2020). Educational Realism: Defining Exopedagogy as the Choreography of Swarm Intelligence. *Educational Philosophy and Theory*.

Lipman, P. (2011). *The New Political Economy of Urban Education: Neoliberalism, Race, and the Right to the City*. New York: Routledge.

Looney, A., & Yannelis, C. (2018). *Borrowers with Large Balances: Rising Student Debt and Falling Repayment Rates*. Washington, DC: Brookings Institution.

Lordon, F. (2015). *Why Piketty Isn't Marx. Le Monde Diplomatique*, May. Retrieved from https://mondediplo.com/2015/05/12Piketty.

Love, B. L. (2019). *We Want to Do More Than Survive: Abolitionist Teaching and the Pursuit of Educational Freedom*. Boston, MA: Beacon Press.

Love, B. L. (2020). Teachers, We Cannot Go Back to the Way Things Were. *Education Week*, April 29.

Lugones, M. (2008). The Coloniality of Gender. *Worlds & Knowledges Otherwise, 2*(2), 1–17.

Lukács, G. (1923/1971). *History and Class Consciousness* (R. Livingstone, Trans.). Cambridge, MA: MIT Press.

Luxemburg, R. (2004a). The Historical Conditions of Accumulation, from *The Accumulation of Capital*. In P. Hudis & K. B. Anderson (Eds.), *The Rosa Luxemburg Reader* (pp. 32–70). New York: Monthly Review Press.

Luxemburg, R. (2004b). The Mass Strike, the Political Party, and the Trade Unions. In P. Hudis & K. B. Anderson (Eds.), *The Rosa Luxemburg Reader* (pp. 168–199). New York: Monthly Review Press.

Luxemburg, R. (2004c). The Russian Revolution. In P. Hudis & K. B. Anderson (Eds.), *The Rosa Luxemburg Reader* (pp. 281–310). New York: Monthly Review Press.

Madkins, T. (2020). *Resources for Understanding and Supporting #BlackLivesMatter*. Retrieved from https://studentsatthecenterhub.org/resource/resources-for -understanding-and-supporting-blacklives-matter/.

Maldonado-Torres, N. (2007). On the Coloniality of Being. *Cultural Studies, 21*(2), 240–270.

Maldonado-Torres, N. (2008). *Against War: Views from the Underside of Modernity.* Durham, NC: Duke University Press.

Mallory, T. (2020). *The Most Powerful Speech of a Generation.* Retrieved from https://www.google.com/search?q=tamika+mallory+speech&rlz=1C5CHFA _enUS891US891&oq=tamika+mallory+speech+&aqs=chrome..69i57j0l4j0i22i30l2 .3500j0j7&sourceid=chrome&ie=UTF-8.

Marcos (1995). *Shadows of Tender Fury: The Letters and Communiqués of Subcomandante Marcos and the Zapatista Army of National Liberation* (F. Bardacke & L. López, Trans.). New York: Monthly Review Press.

Marcuse, H. (1955). *Eros and Civilization: A Philosophical Inquiry into Freud.* Boston, MA: Beacon Press.

Marcuse, H. (1964/1991). *One-Dimensional Man.* Boston, MA: Beacon Press.

Martí, J. (1891/2002). *Selected Writings* (E. Allen, Trans.). New York: Penguin.

Marx, K. (1964). *The Economic and Philosophic Manuscripts of 1844* (M. Milligan, Trans.). New York: International Publishers.

Marx, K. (1973). *Grundrisse* (M. Nicolaus, Trans.). London: Penguin Books.

Marx, K. (1867/1976). *Capital* ((B. Fowkes, Trans. Vol. I). London: Penguin Books.

Mbembe, A. (2001). *On the Postcolony.* Berkeley, CA: University of California Press.

Mbembe, A. (2003). Necropolitics. *Public Culture, 15*(1), 11–40.

McCarthy, C. (1998). *The Uses of Culture: Education and the Limits of Ethnic Affiliation.* New York: Routledge.

McLaren, P. (2003). Critical Pedagogy and Class Struggle in the Age of Neoliberal Globalization: Notes from History's Underside. *Democracy and Nature, 9*(1), 65–90.

McLaren, P. (2007). *Life in Schools: An Introduction to Critical Pedagogy in the Foundations of Education* (5th ed.). Boston, MA: Allyn and Bacon.

McNaughtan, J., García, H., & Nehls, K. (2017). Understanding the Growth of Contingent Faculty. *New Directions for Institutional Research, 176*(176), 9–26.

Means, A. (2011). Jacques Rancière, Education, and the Art of Citizenship. *Review of Education, Pedagogy, and Cultural Studies, 33*(1), 28–47.

Means, A. J. (2013). *Schooling in the Age of Austerity: Urban Education and the Struggle for Democratic Life.* New York: Palgrave Macmillan.

Means, A. J. (2018). *Learning to Save the Future: Rethinking Education and Work in an Era of Digital Capitalism.* New York: Routledge.

Melossi, D. (2008). *Controlling Crime, Controlling Society: Thinking about Crime in Europe and America.* Cambridge: Polity.

Menchú, R. (1984). *I, Rigoberta Menchu: An Indian Woman in Guatemala.* London: Verso.

Meyer, H.-D., & Zhou, K. (2017). Autonomy or Oligarchy? The Changing Effects of University Endowments in Winner-Take-All Markets. *Higher Education, 73*(6), 833–851.

Mignolo, W. (Speaker) (2020). The Politics of Decolonial Investigations. *Theory from the Margins*, November 18. Retrieved from http://theoryfromthemargins.com/archives -wdm.html.

Mignolo, W. D. (2011). *The Darker Side of Western Modernity: Global Futures, Decolonial Options.* Durham, NC: Duke University Press.

Mills, C. W. (1997). *The Racial Contract.* Ithaca, NY: Cornell University Press.

Mohanty, C. T. (2003). *Feminism Without Borders: Decolonizing Theory, Practicing Solidarity.* Durham, NC: Duke University Press.

Morales, M. C., & Bejarano, C. (2009). Transnational Sexual and Gendered Violence: An Application of Border Sexual Conquest at a Mexico–US Border. *Global Networks, 9*(3), 420–439.

Mordechay, K., & Orfield, G. (2017). Demographic Transformation in a Policy Vacuum: The Changing Face of U.S. Metropolitan Society and Challenges for Public Schools. *Educational Forum, 81*(2), 193–203.

Morimoto, S. A., & Friedland, L. A. (2013). Cultivating Success: Youth Achievement, Capital and Civic Engagement in the Contemporary United States. *Sociological Perspectives, 56*(4), 523–546.

Moses, M. S., & Chang, M. J. (2006). Toward a Deeper Understanding of the Diversity Rationale. *Educational Researcher, 35*(1), 6–11.

Nakata, N. M., Nakata, V., Keech, S., & Bolt, R. (2012). Decolonial Goals and Pedagogies for Indigenous Studies. *Decolonization: Indigeneity. Education and Society, 1*(1), 120–140.

National Inquiry into Missing and Murdered Indigenous Women and Girls (2020). *Reclaiming Power and Place.* Retrieved from http://www.mmiwg-ffada.ca/.

National Institute of Mental Health (2016). *Statistics: Anxiety Disorder in Children.* Retrieved from https://www.nimh.nih.gov/health/statistics/prevalence/any-anxiety -disorder-among-children.shtml.

Negri, A. (1999). *Insurgencies: Constituent Power and the Modern State* (M. Boscagli, Trans.). Minneapolis, MN: University of Minnesota Press.

Negri, A. (2003). The Constitution of Time (M. Mandarini, Trans.). *Time for Revolution.* New York: Continuum.

New York Times (2020). *Tracking the Coronavirus at U.S. Colleges and Universities,* December. Retrieved from https://www.nytimes.com/interactive/2020/us/covid -college-cases-tracker.html.

Nxumalo, F. (2015). Forest Stories: Restorying Encounters with "Natural" Places in Early Childhood Education. In Pacini-Ketchabaw & A. Taylor (Eds.), *Unsettling the Colonial Places and Spaces of Early Childhood Education* (pp. 21–42). New York: Routledge.

O'Flynn, G., & Petersen, E. B. (2007). The "Good Life" and the "Rich Portfolio": Young Women, Schooling and Neoliberal Subjectification. *British Journal of Sociology of Education, 28*(4), 459–472.

Olssen, M., & Peters, M. A. (2005). Neoliberalism, Higher Education and the Knowledge Economy: From the Free Market to Knowledge Capitalism. *Journal of Education Policy, 20*(3), 313–345.

Paraskeva, J. M. (2011). *Conflicts in Curriculum Theory: Challenging Hegemonic Epistemologies.* New York: Palgrave Macmillan.

Passavant, P. A. (2014). Neoliberalism and Violent Appearances. In J. R. Di Leo & U. Mehan (Eds.), *Capital at the Brink: Overcoming the Destructive Legacies of Neoliberalism* (pp. 30–71). Ann Arbor, MI: Open Humanities Press.

Peck, J., Theodore, N., & Brenner, N. (2009). Neoliberal Urbanism: Models, Moments, Mutations. *SAIS Review, 29*(1), 49–66.

Pereira, I. (2020). La Réception de Paulo Freire Face au Néoconservatisme en France. *Eccos—Revista Científica, 52*(52), 1–14.

Peters, M. (2001). Education, Enterprise Culture and the Entrepreneurial Self: A Foucauldian Perspective. *Journal of Educational Enquiry, 2*(2), 58–71.

Petras, J., & Veltmeyer, H. (2002). *Globalization Unmasked: Imperialism in the 21st Century*. London: Zed Books.

Picower, B. (2009). The Unexamined Whiteness of Teaching: How White Teachers Maintain and Enact Dominant Racial Ideologies. *Race, Ethnicity and Education, 12*(2), 197–215.

Pierce, C. (2013). Educational Life and Death: Reassessing Marcuse's Critical Theory of Education in the Neoliberal Age. *Radical Philosophy Review, 16*(2), 603–624.

Piketty, T. (2014). *Capital in the Twenty-First Century* (A. Goldhammer, Trans.). Cambridge, MA: Harvard University Press.

Quijano, A. (2008). Coloniality of Power, Eurocentrism, and Latin America. In M. Moraña, E. Dussel, & C. A. Jáuregui (Eds.), *Coloniality at Large: Latin America and the Postcolonial Debate* (pp. 181–224). Durham, NC: Duke University Press.

Rancière, J. (1991). *The Ignorant Schoolmaster: Five Lessons in Intellectual Emancipation* (K. Ross, Trans.). Stanford, CA: Stanford University Press.

Rancière, J. (2010). *Dissensus: On Politics and Aesthetics* (S. Corcoran, Trans.). London: Continuum.

Read, J. (2009). A Genealogy of Homo-Economicus: Neoliberalism and the Production of Subjectivity. *Foucault Studies, 6*, 25–36.

Reckhow, S., & Tompkins-Strange, M. (2015). "Singing from the Same Hymnbook" at Gates and Broad. In F. M. Hess & J. R. Henig (Eds.), *The New Education Philanthropy: Politics, Policy, and Reform* (pp. 55–77). Cambridge, MA: Harvard Education Press.

Rizvi, F., & Lingard, B. (2010). *Globalizing Education Policy*. New York: Routledge.

Robinson, C. J. (2000). *Black Marxism: The Making of the Black Radical Tradition*. Chapel Hill, NC: The University of North Carolina Press.

Rodney, W. (1972/2011). *How Europe Underdeveloped Africa*. Baltimore, MD: Black Classic Press.

Rogoff, B. (1990). *Apprenticeship in Thinking: Cognitive Development in Social Context*. Oxford: Oxford University Press.

Rogoff, B. (2001). Becoming a Cooperative Parent in a Parent Co-Operative. In B. Rogoff, C. G. Turkanis, & L. Bartlett (Eds.), *Learning Together: Children and Adults in a School Community* (pp. 145–155). Oxford: Oxford University Press.

Rose, N. (1999). *Governing the Soul*. London: Free Association Books.

Russakoff, D. (2015). *The Prize: Who's in Charge of America's Schools?* Boston, MA: Houghton Mifflin Harcourt.

Ryan, S., von der Embse, N., Pendergast, L., Saeki, E., Segool, N., & Schwing, S. (2017). Leaving the Teaching Profession: The Role of Teacher Stress and Educational Accountability Policies on Turnover Intent. *Teaching and Teacher Education, 66*(1), 1–11.

Saltman, K. J. (2007). *Capitalizing on Disaster: Taking and Breaking Public Schools.* Boulder, CO: Paradigm Publishers.

Saltman, K. J. (2012). *The Failure of Corporate School Reform.* Boulder, CO: Paradigm Publishers.

Saltman, K. J. (2014). The Austerity School: Grit, Character, and the Privatization of Public Education. *Symploke, 22*(1–2), 41–57.

Sánchez, P. (2007). Urban Immigrant Students: How Transnationalism Shapes Their World Learning. *The Urban Review, 39*(5), 489–517.

Santos, B. d. S. (2014). *Epistemologies of the South: Justice Against Epistemicide.* New York: Routledge.

Santos, B. d. S., Nunes, J. A., & Meneses, M. P. (2007). Opening up the Canon of Knowledge and Recognition of Difference. In B. d. S. Santos (Ed.), *Another Knowledge Is Possible: Beyond Northern Epistemologies* (pp. xix–lxii). London: Verso.

Scott, J. (2009). The Politics of Venture Philanthropy in Charter School Policy and Advocacy. *Educational Policy, 23*(1), 106–136.

Simons, M., & Masschelein, J. (2008). The Governmentalization of Learning and the Assemblage of a Learning Apparatus. *Educational Theory, 58*(4), 391–415.

Simpson, L. B. (2017). *As We Have Always Done: Indigenous Freedom through Radical Resistance.* Minneapolis, MN: University of Minnesota Press.

Slater, G. B. (2015). Education as Recovery: Neoliberalism, School Reform, and the Politics of Crisis. *Journal of Education Policy, 30*(1), 1–20.

Slater, G. B., & Griggs, C. B. (2015). Standardization and Subjection: An Autonomist Critique of Neoliberal School Reform. *Review of Education, Pedagogy, and Cultural Studies, 37*(5), 438–459.

Smith, L. T. (1999). *Decolonizing Methodologies: Research and Indigenous Peoples.* London and Dunedin: Zed Books/University of Otago Press.

Souto-Manning, M. (2010). *Freire, Teaching, and Learning: Culture Circles Across Contexts.* New York: Peter Lang.

Srivastava, P., & Oh, S.-A. (2010). Private Foundations, Philanthropy, and Partnership in Education and Development: Mapping the Terrain. *International Journal of Educational Development, 30*(5), 460–471.

Standing, G. (2011). *The Precariat: The New Dangerous Class.* London: Bloomsbury.

Stovall, D. (2015). Mayoral Control: Reform, Whiteness, and Critical Race Analysis of Neoliberal Educational Policy. In B. Picower & E. Mayorga (Eds.), *What's Race Got to Do with It? How Current School Reform Policy Maintains Racial and Economic Inequality* (pp. 45–58). New York: Peter Lang.

Stovall, D. (2018). Are We Ready for 'School' Abolition?: Thoughts and Practices of Radical Imaginary in Education. *Taboo: The Journal of Culture and Education*, *17*(1), 51–61.

Streeck, W. (2016). *How Will Capitalism End? Essays on a Failing System*. London: Verso.

Styres, S. (2019). Literacies of Land: Decolonizing Narratives, Storying, and Literature. In L. T. Smith, E. Tuck, & W. K. Yang (Eds.), *Indigenous and Decolonizing Studies in Education: Mapping the Long View* (pp. 24–37). New York: Routledge.

Sudbury, J. (2002). Celling Black Bodies: Black Women in the Global Prison Industrial Complex. *Feminist Review*, *70*(1), 57–74.

Tarkovsky, A. *(Director)*, & Demidova, A. (Producer) (1979). *Stalker* [Motion picture]. Soviet Union: Mosfilm.

Taylor, K.-Y. (2020). Of Course There Are Protests. The State Is Failing Black People. *New York Times*, May 29.

Third Continental Summit of Indigenous Nations and Pueblos of Abya Yala (2011). In G. Grandin, D. T. Levenson, & E. Oglesby (Eds.), *The Guatemala Reader: History, Culture, Politics* (541–544). Durham, NC: Duke University Press.

Trans Murdering Monitoring Update (2019). *Trans Day of Remembrance 2019*. Retrieved from https://transrespect.org/en/tmm-update-tdor-2019/.

Tuck, E., & Yang, W. K. (2012). Decolonization Is Not a Metaphor. *Decolonization: Indigeneity. Education and Society*, *1*(1), 1–40.

Urrieta Jr., L. (2013). Familia and Comunidad-Based Saberes: Learning in an Indigenous Heritage Community. *Anthropology and Education Quarterly*, *44*(3), 320–335.

Urrieta Jr., L. (2015). Learning by Observing and Pitching in and the Connections to Native and Indigenous Knowledge Systems. *Advances in Child Development and Behavior*, *49*, 357–379.

Urrieta Jr., L. (2017). Identity, Violence, and Authenticity: Challenging Static Conceptions of Indigeneity. *Latino Studies*, *15*(2), 254–261.

Vally, S., & Motala, E. (2017). Education, Training and Work under Neoliberalism in South Africa: Toward Alternatives. *Education As Change*, *21*(3), 1–20.

Van Oort, M. (2015). Making the Neoliberal Precariat: Two Faces of Job Searching in Minneapolis. *Ethnography*, *16*(1), 74–94.

Vassallo, S. (2013). Critical Pedagogy and Neoliberalism: Concerns with Teaching Self-Regulated Learning. *Studies in Philosophy and Education*, *32*(6), 563–580.

Vizenor, G. (1994). *Manifest Manners: Narratives on Postindian Survivance*. Lincoln, NE: University of Nebraska Press.

Vogel, A. (2006). Who's Making Global Civil Society: Philanthropy and US Empire in World Society. *British Journal of Sociology*, *57*(4), 635–655.

Wacquant, L. (2009). *Punishing the Poor: The Neoliberal Government of Social Insecurity*. Durham, NC: Duke University Press.

Wallis, C. (2006). The Multitasking Generation. *Time*, March 27.

Walsh, C. E. (2015). Decolonial Pedagogies Walking and Asking. Notes to Paulo Freire from AbyaYala. *International Journal of Lifelong Education*, 34(1), 9–21.

Weis, L., & Cipollone, K. (2013). "Class Work": Producing Privilege and Social Mobility in Elite US Secondary Schools. *British Journal of Sociology of Education*, 34(5–6), 701–722.

West, C. (2009). *Keeping Faith: Philosophy and Race in America*. New York: Routledge.

West, C. (2016). Goodbye American Neoliberalism. A New Era Is Here. *The Guardian*, November 17. Retrieved from https://www.theguardian.com/commentisfree/2016/nov/17/american-neoliberalism-cornel-west-2016-election.

Wilderson, F. B., III (2010). *Red, White & Black: Cinema and the Structure of U.S. Antagonisms*. Durham, NC: Duke University Press.

Wolfe, P. (2006). Settler Colonialism and the Elimination of the Native. *Journal of Genocide Research*, 8(4), 387–409.

World Meteorological Organization (2020). *United in Science, 2020*. Retrieved from https://public.wmo.int/en/resources/united_in_science.

Wynter, S. (2003). Unsettling the Coloniality of Being/Power/Truth/Freedom: Towards the Human, After Man, Its Overrepresentation—An Argument. *The New Centennial Review*, 3(3), 257–337.

Wynter, S. (2006). On How We Mistook the Map for the Territory, and Re-Imprisoned Ourselves in Our Unbearable Wrongness of Being, of *Désètre*: Black Studies Toward the Human Project. In L. R. Gordon & J. A. Gordon (Eds.), *Not Only the Master's Tools: African-American Studies in Theory and Practice* (pp. 107–169). Boulder, CO: Paradigm Publishers.

Zavala, M., & Golden, N. A. (2016). Prefiguring Alternative Worlds: Organic Critical Literacies and Socio-Cultural Revolutions. *Knowledge Cultures*, 4(6), 207–227.

Žižek, S. (1999). *The Ticklish Subject: The Absent Centre of Political Ontology*. London: Verso.

Žižek, S. (2008a). *The Sublime Object of Ideology*. London: Verso.

Žižek, S. (2008b). *Violence*. New York: Picador.

Index

www.ingramcontent.com/pod-product-compliance
Lightning Source LLC
Chambersburg PA
CBHW050442280326
41932CB00013BA/2207